THE HAPPY FAMILY

THE HUMAN MIND
by Karl Menninger, M.D.

RECONSTRUCTING BEHAVIOR IN YOUTH
by William Healy, M.D., *August F. Bronner*, PH.D.,
Edith M. H. Baylor and J. Prentice Murphy

THE HUMAN BODY
by Logan Clendening

These are Borzoi Books, published by
ALFRED A. KNOPF

JOHN LEVY, M.D., C.M.

A N D

RUTH MUNROE, Ph.D.

THE HAPPY FAMILY

1945

ALFRED A KNOPF

NEW YORK

PUBLISHED OCTOBER 24, 1938

REPRINTED FOUR TIMES

SIXTH PRINTING, JANUARY 1945

Published simultaneously in Canada by THE RYERSON PRESS

MANUFACTURED IN THE UNITED STATES OF AMERICA

To Timothy William, Abby Frances,
and, we hope, their many happy
children.

The case material used in this book refers to no actual person. Each case is a composite of the broad experience of the authors.

CONTENTS

THE HAPPY FAMILY

CHAPTER I

HOW FAMILIES BEGIN

" No, daddy, when I grow up I'm going to be a plain lady like mother."

Thus did my handsome four-year-old daughter reject my proposal that she train for the Follies chorus.

" I'm going to have five little children," she continued.

" That's lovely," I replied appreciatively. " And who is going to be the father of your babies? "

" Why, you, daddy."

This is the way families begin. Every little girl shares my daughter's ambition to establish a home of her own, and almost every girl in her twenties sees the fulfilment of this ambition. People do not marry because it is their social duty to perpetuate the institution of the family, or because the preacher and Mrs. Grundy both recommend matrimony, or even because they fall in love with each other. They marry because they lived in a family as children and still cannot get over the feeling that being in a family is the only proper, indeed the only possible, way to live.

First impressions are strong impressions. Adults cannot help reliving in some fashion the kind of life they knew in childhood. The warmth and intimacy of the family group become synonymous with life itself. Even if the warmth seems suffocating at times and the intimacy contentious, we are so bred up to them that we cannot exist in any other atmosphere any more than the proverbial fish out of water. My daughter does not reject the Follies out of a reasoned conviction that the joys of maternity are superior to the joys of the footlights. She simply doesn't know any better, since her experience to date has been confined to family life. Nor does she have an incestuous passion for daddy which leads her to choose him as the father of her children. I must admit reluctantly that her choice is due largely to the fact that I am first in the field and have to date very little competition. She thinks of life in terms of the family, and the family in terms of her own parents. Her affections, her expectations of happiness and pain, are being moulded constantly by the little group into which she happened to be born. By the time her worldly knowledge has progressed far enough to make her critical about the family, it will be too late for her to change her basic feelings. Whether she likes it or not, her emotional bias toward family living will be so strong that she cannot overcome it.

Idealists, troubled by the obvious deficiencies of the marriages they see around them, are for ever devising new systems guaranteed to run with an oiled precision. Free love, companionate marriage, easy divorce, state care of children — these projects and many others like them are designed to solve the problems of people seeking to live happily together. Logically almost any one of these schemes is superior to the curious institution we call holy matrimony. Institutions which have grown haphazard out of the necessities of succeeding generations never make sense if you look at them rationally. Unfortunately logic is not very effective in ordering people's lives. Psychologically these Utopian systems of marriage make a fundamental blunder. They ignore the point we have just been making: that marriage begins in infancy. People who have learned about family loves and hates and rivalry and devotion in their parents' home carry the lessons into their own homes. The most perfect system fails if it does not meet the expectations formed in childhood. We make ourselves wretched very frequently by adhering to foolish outworn ideas about marriage, but I fear we should be even more miserable without them. My little daughter in her twenties will still want a family, and her family will somehow or other continue the emotional atmosphere of her present home.

Nevertheless there comes a time when the orderly sequence of development from one generation to the next is sharply interrupted. The little girl who planned cheerfully for a family of five becomes a slightly gangling young lady who turns up her nose at all boys. She's not going to tie herself down with children. If she can't manage to be a nurse or an author or an explorer, she'll get a job in Woolworth's. So many parents come to me in alarm about the behaviour of their teen-age children, boys and girls alike, that I would like to chat at some length about the meaning of this adolescent revolt.

Their children, parents complain, have suddenly become impossible. Affectionate, dutiful daughters treat their homes "like a hotel." They sleep there and occasionally "grab a meal," but their real life is lived elsewhere. They fly into a fury when mother mildly suggests helping with the dishes. Johnny's conversation is almost exclusively of the "gimme" variety. His resentment knows no bounds if he cannot have the family car, or a dress suit. Parents I see are about equally divided between those who worry because their daughters won't look at a boy and those who are distracted because their girls stay out till all hours with the crowd doing heaven knows what. Listening to these lurid tales about the young, one gets the impression that the whole institution of the family is going on the rocks for want of a new generation to carry on.

It is usually possible to give full reassurance to these anxious parents. While the adolescent revolt is so common as to be almost universal, the family has maintained itself for a very long time. As a matter of fact, the revolt is an essential preliminary to the business of getting married. I should be more concerned about those children who remain wholly docile and affectionate during this period. Growing up means growing away from the old family in preparation for founding a new one. The child who remains safely cradled in the parental home becomes the man who never establishes a home of his own. Or who, if he happens to marry, is for ever trying to force his new life into the mould of the old — to make his wife exactly like his mother, and his children exactly like himself. Since his wife is after all not his mother, he is perpetually dissatisfied, while she, poor woman, is frustrated at every turn.

A new marriage must not be hampered by old loyalties and attitudes. The adolescent has to shift gears from the low speed of childhood to the high speed of parenthood. All his life he has been dependent and protected. As a father he must do the protecting. His childish devotion to his parents must change to a mature affection, very much less intense in quality. His absorbing emotional relationships must be focused on his contemporaries. Gears very often grind badly during a shift, but they are rarely stripped. The unpleasant noise we hear from our teen-age children is just the grinding of the gear shift — cacophonous, but useful.

The adolescent revolt is healthy preparation for the serious task of finding a mate. None the less, parents and children alike find it difficult to bear. Let us consider the parents' side first. They cannot be expected to preserve an Olympian calm while their youngsters engage in sprightly adventures which can easily lead to serious trouble. Parents are used to taking care of their children, and the habit of protection persists after the same type of care is no longer possible. The mother who held little Tommy's hand crossing Fifth Avenue to the park just a short time ago, cannot help being at least a back-seat driver when

Tommy whizzes past the red lights in his new sport road-ster. Habits are made of durable stuff. It takes more than Tommy's first pair of long pants to change his parents' attitude toward him. Tom may appear to himself and his schoolfellows practically grey-haired, but his parents still see him in rompers. They have looked after him for years, and they continue to look after him even when their care has become an insult to his manhood. They have obtained a fair measure of obedience and respect in the past. The impertinence and ingratitude of the adolescent come therefore as a painful shock. Young people are apt to ascribe most of their difficulties with their parents to this cause — " they can't realize that we're grown up."

Parents have more to overcome during this period, how-ever, than habits of protection. Parents, especially moth-ers, *need* dependent children. They have built their life around them and cannot help feeling like an empty shell when the children have grown away from their home ties. Almost always rearing a young brood means curtailing other interests. Mothers with little children are too busy to keep up with outside affairs, hobbies, or even close friendships. Moreover, they are so intent upon their chil-dren, so emotionally absorbed in them, that these ex-traneous matters seem unimportant. I used to commute with a group of women who illustrated this point very nicely. They were highly trained and highly intellectual college teachers, but many of them had young children of their own. During the relaxed moments on the train the forthcoming election, the tense European situation, or the latest college gossip did indeed receive some attention. But if you listened in on the most animated and bright-eyed discussions you found that these so-called blue-stockings talked about Jimmy's feeding problem, or the cute thing little Betty did last night. The really important conversation was in no way different from that of the little knot of suburban mothers down the aisle, going to town for a day's shopping.

Small children need a great deal of attention and a great deal of emotion. They get it, too, one way or another, from every mother I know. Older children have no use for this emotion. Indeed, they suffer from it, since they are trying desperately to get on their own feet. But you cannot turn a parent's love for children on and off like a faucet. When it is dammed up, the backwaters choke the parents, and the children still get wet from the overflow. My friends the college teachers are going to find their discussions of the European situation pretty thin gruel after the rich diet to which they have accustomed themselves during the childhood of their youngsters. Perhaps their professional interests and hobbies will help if they are firmly connected with the main stream of their emotional life. At best, though, they are in for a bad time, like all parents. No mother ever delivered a child at adolescence with less pain than at the hour of birth. It is impossible to give up without pain a creature which has matured as part of ourselves.

Perhaps the hardest thing parents have to face during this period of adolescent revolt is the way their children refuse help and discipline which they obviously need. If Tommy drives so recklessly his mother is sure he'll get killed. If Mary carries on with the boys at her present pace she'll get into trouble and ruin her whole life. You can't let Johnny tie himself up for life with a fast girl like Charlotte. He'll be wretched later on.

Very often — not always, but very often — parents are quite right. Tommy may get killed, and Mary is spoiling for trouble. But almost always there seems to be very little parents can do about it. Their old techniques for handling their children have become distressingly ineffective. Discipline during the period of the revolt is anathema to the young girl or boy — discipline from parents. Mary's sorority sisters may tell her to behave herself or else — and get her to behave. But if mother tries the same methods she meets a storm of protest and frequently finds herself outwitted into the bargain. The mother of one Mary I know sent her to her first football game with a chaperon. The chaperon, it was learned later, went quietly to bed at ten and didn't even wake up when Mary came in at five slightly the worse for a few highballs. Reasoning is rarely successful because neither party can stay reasonable long. Calm analysis of Mary's behaviour soon degenerates into a series of high-pitched recriminations and self-justifications on both sides. Mary complains that you " just can't talk to mother," and mother confidentially tells you the same thing about Mary. Appeals to Mary's affection and sense of fair play in an effort to elicit obedience are perhaps the most ill-advised of all, since Mary is quite properly trying to outgrow her affection and naturally resents the fact that she is still in many ways dependent on her parents.

No, parents during the adolescent revolt just have to "take it." I do not mean that they should relax all attempts to control their children. On the contrary we shall soon see that their guardianship is still of major importance psychologically. Continued effort to guide these obstreperous youngsters in the way the individual parent feels to be best is, I think, essential to their best development. But the apparent results, for the time being, are sure to be disappointing. Disputes, accusations, rebellious and sulky withdrawals follow upon any course of action in the majority of homes.

I wish I could offer a pain-dispelling drug to mothers during this second birth, this delivery of children into the adult world. Or that I could at least, like a good obstetrician, tell the mother exactly what to do every step of the way. More than one woman has said to me grimly: "I'm at my wits' end. Whatever I do for Mary, it seems to be wrong." Exactly! Mary is rebelling against mother, not against anything special mother is doing. (We'll soon talk about Mary's side of it.) It does follow, then, that whatever mother does is wrong — or right, since no other plan of guidance works any better. That is why a set of psychological rules of conduct would not help. The real problem of the adolescent revolt is this: a particular kind of love relationship — namely, that of mother and dependent child — is in process of dissolution. Mother and child are frankly suffering, the mother even more than the child because it is harder for her to find substitutes for her loss.

The help I can offer, as a psychiatrist, to these mothers is an understanding of the problem, and assurance that all parents of adolescent children suffer alike. Mothers are bound to be worried about the escapades of their rebellious offspring. But they do not have to feel the added torment of a sense of guilt, and they do not have to feel that the children turn against them because of their own short-comings. " I've tried so hard to be a good mother," they wail, " and just look at the result." The result is as natural as the dropping of leaves in autumn. Indeed, as we shall see, the more Johnny has loved his mother, the more neces-sary it is for him to fight against her for a time until he has freed himself for a new love. His childhood love was good, his new love will be successful, and the fight is the necessary bridge between them. Johnny *wants* a fight. He *needs* a fight. So let him have it. Heartache and worry and vexation come to all parents during the adolescent revolt. It is not their fault, and there is nothing much they can do about it except continue to be the kind of parent they have always been. They just have to " take it."

Johnny has a difficult time during this period too. He gets into plenty of scrapes, and he does have a good deal to put up with from parents who cannot help giving him more care than he wants. But his main problem is that half of him *likes* to be protected and loved, while the other half is trying to be independent. He is not really rebelling so much against mother as against his own love for his mother. Growing up is a fearsome task. It is safer and pleasanter to remain a little boy, coddled by parents who love him and tell him what to do. The adventurous part of him that wants to grow up and do things is in constant war against this timorous self that wants familiar affection and security. Civil warfare is bitter warfare. The adolescent revolt is a fight against oneself. The conflict would not be half so violent if it were a simple struggle between children and parents. Its virulence comes from the revolt of the maturing self against the baby self. Parents are dragged into the strife because they are all mixed up in young folks' minds with the baby self.

Young people cannot admit, even to themselves, that they do not wholly want freedom, that they are — to be blunt — scared of it. They cannot admit that in part they do not want to grow up. So they pretend that their parents are over-anxious and won't give them freedom. This guile is unconscious. They do not know that they are putting off their own feelings on their parents. They genuinely believe that they are whole-hearted in their desire for independence and are only held down by dominating adults.[1] I have often observed that parents are frequently less dominating than their children think. Florrie's mother brought her to me because she would have nothing to do with men. At her first visit Florrie told me with tears in her eyes that she could never marry — her parents wouldn't allow it. She was an only child and so dear to them that they couldn't give her up. At first sight

---

[1] Psychiatrists call this little game of self-deception the mechanism of projection. It is very common at all ages.

Florrie's story was quite plausible. Parents often do reproach their children for behaviour which they themselves unconsciously encourage. (More of this tendency later.) Careful study of this family revealed, however, that Florrie's parents were no more selfish and absorbing in their love than the rest of us. They had, perhaps, cherished their only daughter a little more protectively than was good for her. But the protection was not holding Florrie back as much as her own fear of leaving them. Florrie was afraid to grow up and assume the responsibilities of wifehood. Unwilling to face her own timidity frankly, she had managed to fool herself into believing that she was not allowed to go out into the world. Florrie herself *wanted* dominating parents.

Parents and educators, impressed by the voluble reproaches of their charges and also by modern theories of freedom in child-training, frequently grant a high degree of independence during adolescence. The results show that Florrie is not alone in her rejection of freedom. Many students in our " progressive " colleges clamour for marks, examinations, and all the paraphernalia of discipline which in conservative colleges cause rebellion. Looking back on a wasted semester, they say: " Why didn't you *make* me work ? " forgetting that they selected the college because it sponsored student initiative, and also that they had vigorously resisted any efforts of the college to enforce its academic regulations. Parents suffer the same censure. A college freshman writing a paper on " How I was Brought Up " concluded with this remarkable sentence: " My parents have given me everything except punishment." She was quite innocent of any attempt at humour or irony. She regretted that she had not been forced to behave properly. When young girls discuss with me the scrapes their friends get into, their most frequent comment is this: " Their parents shouldn't have *allowed* them to get into such a mess."

When we understand the adolescent revolt as a revolt against the baby self as well as against parents, we can sympathize with these reactionary youngsters. Too great leniency in adolescence increases anxiety. If a boy has the independence he wants without fighting for it, he comes perilously close to realizing that he doesn't really want it. Love and protection that you struggle against are nevertheless love and protection — and very comforting at times. Going away to college, starting out in the business world, deciding on a career, learning about sex and choosing a wife — these are the tasks of adolescence. At no other time of life do people have to make so many decisions of far-reaching importance. It is natural that young people should want to work out these choices independently and establish themselves as adults. But it is also natural that they should frequently feel frightened and dismayed. When things go wrong they are glad enough to " pass the buck " to parents — to be forced to make certain choices without the painful necessity of making up their minds, and to be relieved of responsibility for mistakes. If they can obtain real help without sacrificing their feeling of independence they can handle their dilemma with a minimum of discomfort.

The adolescent revolt accomplishes just this sleight-of-hand. Since the young person is apparently fighting tooth and nail for freedom, he can preserve his own feeling of independence and growing maturity. At the same time he receives from his parents the support he needs — and wants in an under-cover way. As his real independence grows, he becomes less noisy but more decisive in his demands for freedom. Meantime parents have become accustomed to the loss of their babies and usually are ready to grant full adult status. In this wise the painful struggle of the parent to renounce his protective attitude is really very helpful to the child. The boy gains security while he fights free of his own need for parental love. It is much easier for the child to liberate himself than to be forcibly emancipated by an over-progressive parent.

Falling out of love with parents is, then, the first step toward falling in love with a mate and beginning a new family. Of course we never fall out of love with our parents entirely, never quite reach that man-to-man affection which is our goal. The adolescent revolt is not completely over by the time serious courtship begins. Frankly, it is never entirely put down, nor does it start with a sudden coup d'état at the age of fourteen, as I have perhaps suggested. The toddler has sporadic moments of rebellion, and the baby self still carries on its underground campaign when old age returns us to the toddler stage. None of us gets entirely free from his childhood way of loving. We still crave the all-encompassing warmth and protection of our earliest years. We still cover our own fear of a cold world with a blustering independence. But the most dramatic years of revolt are those of adolescence. We say that the American Revolution lasted from 1775 to 1783, though everyone knows that serious tension existed between England and America for many years before and many years after. The war period brought hostile feelings into the open. Just so the adolescent revolt permits parents and children to recognize their antagonisms. Everyone knows too that America remained dependent on England, culturally and economically, long after she declared herself a free state. The two countries are still interdependent and at times show both the exaggerated affection and the bitterness of a dissolved mother-child relationship. But America after 1783 was outwardly free to conduct her affairs with other nations as she would. So the adolescent, while still subtly influenced by his relationship with his parents, proceeds to fall in love on his own, to pick a mate and guide his new family as best he may.

How do young people pick a life partner? We have developed a curious mythology about the process of falling in love. It runs something like this. " Love is the most beautiful thing in the world. Mary Jane, and you too, Jim, keep your hearts pure. Don't cheapen yourselves by playing around with Tom, Dick, and Harry. After a while Mr. Right or the not impossible She will come along. You will be engaged for a year. Then, after such a *pretty* wedding, you will settle down in a little house with chequered curtains at the window and live happily ever after." See the *Ladies' Home Journal,* the *Saturday Evening Post,* and any popular " romance " for variations on this theme. Mary Jane, rarely Jim, may have a few moments of uncertainty at the beginning of the story, for there has to be a story, but she soon realizes that Jim is the man she " really " loves.

It is too bad that such a pretty story is not quite true. Or is it too bad? Most of us find the story rather dull after a while, and turn to a good detective yarn which keeps us guessing a little longer. The true story of courtship and marriage is much more exciting. Philo Vance himself couldn't work out the ending from the clews most of us have about people. It is also more original. Each couple makes up a unique plot, weaving together joys and sorrows, disappointments and satisfactions, hopes and cynicisms into a novel as crowded as *Anthony Adverse.* A realistic account of the most humdrum engagement would make the best offering of the *Saturday Evening Post* sound like something about Peter and Peggy in my son's first reader. Any life-sized Mary Jane is a thousand times more interesting than the cute paper doll of the magazines.

The very richness of the material drawn from life makes it impossible to outline a neat sequence of steps like those of the magazine story, guaranteed to lead to successful courtship. I said in the beginning that marriage starts in infancy. The child prepares for marriage during every minute of his waking hours, and perhaps alsc in his dreams. You cannot pick half a dozen episodes out of this welter of experience, tell a young man how to act realistically on these few occasions, and expect him to meet his marital problems triumphantly. The length of the engagement, for instance, is frequently of some importance in getting a marriage off to a good start. But a year's engagement may be far too long for one couple, not long enough for a second, and just right for a third, depending on the kind of preparation the couple has had from babyhood onward. Almost any courtship procedures lead to successful — that is, *satisfying* — marriage for some people, while the very same procedures end in prompt disaster for others. There are no magic rules of conduct to guide young folks to the altar.

The magazine story does suggest some important elements which go into the making of a marriage — the state of the lover's " heart " — that is, his emotional development — his relationship to earlier loves, his choice of a particular mate, and his expectation of living happily ever after. I want to talk about these four points, criticizing the simple magazine version and trying to tell what really happens. Our inquiry will take us back to those childhood experiences which mould the attitudes every individual brings to marriage. It will also lead us to a consideration of the conventions and social ideals to which all of us, willy-nilly, are subject. A frank description of the many ways people learn to be wives and husbands will not lead to a formula for perfect marriage. It will, I hope, help us to understand and value the marriages we have.

First the admonition: " Keep your hearts pure." A heart can be pure if it's dead — or if it is so wrapped up in cotton wool that no air can get to it. In which case more often than not it gets mouldy. Hearts are alive. They need exercise like anything else. People have to learn marital love by practice on other forms, just as they have to play Czerny exercises before they can play Beethoven. The first lesson in the course on learning to love a husband is love for parents. John B. Watson was right in worrying about those children who never go beyond loving their parents, but when he considers any sort of parental love dangerous he throws out the baby with the bath. The child who has not learned tenderness and regard from his ties to parents may never learn them from anybody else.

Newborn infants are the last word in selfishness. They seek pleasure and comfort for themselves first, last, and always. Altruism is not an instinct. It has to be taught, just like the multiplication table. Babies find the love of their parents both pleasurable and reassuring. Eventually they learn to love in return — partly because they discover that expressions of affection on their part tend to increase the tender ministrations of their elders and partly because all of us develop a liking for anything that gives us pleasure. In time the sources of the impulse to love become very much obscured, so that most older children and adults appear capable of disinterested affection. This account of the development of the ability to love is distressingly sketchy, but it will serve to show the importance of nursery cuddling as preparation for marriage. If parents should ever succeed in treating their offspring with the completely impersonal " objectivity " recommended by some psychologists, they would create a species of monster, adult in appearance, but emotionally as self-centred as an infant. Fortunately, so long as parents are themselves human, there is no danger of any serious application of objectivity in the rearing of children. Not even the antiseptic Dionne nursery is free from natural affection for its small occupants — or, I suspect, from occasional equally natural feelings of annoyance when they go on a rampage.

These feelings of annoyance are always part of a parent's attitude toward his child. I'm going to talk about parents and children at length in Chapter vii, but I do not want to give the impression here that an atmosphere of undiluted love is necessary or even desirable for a child's development. No mother is capable of such love, and if through some miracle she were a paragon of unselfish devotion, the child would suffer. He would be unprepared for the highly variegated emotions of everyone else he encountered. Moreover, it is helpful for the child to realize that his own wicked feelings are not unique, that parents get cross too. The adult who is obviously not perfect but manages to handle his feelings well enough for practical purposes sets a better example to the young than one who maintains a virtuous demeanour at all times.

We needn't be afraid of loving our children, then, or of being cross with them. We can congratulate ourselves when they love us in return and get thoroughly annoyed with us on occasion. They are learning the emotional responsiveness they will need in marriage. School years and especially adolescence will wean them away from us, as we have seen. " Fixations " — the over-strong attachments between parent and child which have received so much publicity in recent years — are not prevented by efforts to conceal either love or vexation. In exaggerated form these stultifying bonds are fortunately rare. In a mild form they are common, as are reactions to a sense of being unloved. We can't help influencing our children. We are not perfect. Neither will our children be perfect. If it were not too undignified for a serious book my comment would be very brief: so what?

For parents do teach their children more than love in the abstract. They teach them love (and hate) for a particular kind of person — namely, themselves. Children never quite get over this bias, even those who develop most normally. Hamilton, in his study of the married life of one hundred couples, found that when the marriage was successful the wife usually somewhat resembled the mother. This resemblance between mother and wife does not, of course, mean complete identification. The wife remains herself, but she is the same general kind of human being the boy learned early to love and revere.

If the boy has remained too closely bound up with his mother he may be afraid of a woman who is like her. He is not allowed to love his mother as a wife, of course, and this prohibition covers any woman like her. On the other hand he cannot really love any other kind of woman. Picking a mate is hard for people whose emotional development has taken this form. As a matter of fact most adolescents go through a phase of this kind. They are still too close to their parents to choose a partner like them. Many young girls have been worried because the only men who "thrilled" them were men they couldn't respect, and they never felt "that way" about the boys they liked best. The much publicized tendency of young men to fall in love with actresses may be based partly on their need to find someone as different from their mothers as possible for a time.

Every kind of relationship with parents has its own specific effect on courtship and marriage. The boy who has disliked his mother, for instance, will pick a wife as different from her as possible. Any trait his sweetheart shows which unconsciously reminds him of his mother will throw him into an unreasonable fury. A man I know actually broke off his engagement because the young lady had the waiter replace a tough steak when he took her out to dinner. His mother, whom he detested, had been fussy about her food and occasionally made unpleasant scenes in restaurants. He had forgotten all about this behaviour on the part of his mother, whom he had not seen for many years, and told himself that a woman who would be inconsiderate to a waiter would be unkind to a husband.

Education for love begins at mother's knee, then, with the nurse, the maid, the chauffeur, sisters, cousins, and aunts for assistant teachers. Very early the child registers in a larger school — the neighbourhood. The young child's playmates do their part in preparing him for marriage. If I stick conscientiously to the number of pages allotted to this chapter, I shall not have time to go into the way games of marbles or cops and robbers teach prospective husbands the fundamentals of a good give-and-take relationship with their wives. But I must mention early sex experimentation which has a more direct bearing on later love life. The Age of Innocence is a pretty picture, about as realistic as Arthur Rackham's fairies. Any adult who has won the confidence of a group of youngsters or who looks back honestly at his own childhood is well aware of the giggling interest in unmentionables of all varieties. Interest commonly goes on from looking to touching and other kinds of frank sex play. Usually no one is any the worse for these games. In fact they are a necessary part of emotional training. The young lady who reaches marriage without any awareness of her own body has a hard time learning to enjoy it. Sexual feeling which has been systematically cut back for twenty years does not suddenly burst into flower during the honeymoon. We might liken this childish play to the apple blossoms which precede the fruit of autumn. If we pick off the blossoms there is no fruit. And if the blossoms get wormy the fruit will be imperfect.

Wormy blossoms are all too common in our society. Adults are apt to maintain a stony silence on the subject of sex, or else to be violently disapproving. Children, therefore, turn to one another for this aspect of their training. It is carried on surreptitiously. The feelings of guilt and dirtiness attached to sex at this period often persist into marriage. Instead of expressing fully the tender love of married couples sex too frequently destroys it by introducing a sense of smuttiness learned in childhood. A college professor I know was unable to have intercourse with her husband for the first six months of married life because she was always reminded of a four letter Anglo-Saxon word whenever her husband approached her.

After this early period of experimentation sex frequently recedes into the background for a time. Many children continue some form of frank sex play right through their school years, but the majority give it a rest from the age of about seven until puberty. During this period they become more acutely aware of themselves and their own kind. Boys play with boys, and girls with girls. They come together only to fight. The violence of the fight is sure testimony that sex feeling is not dead. My ten-year-old son can't stand girls. He and his friends spend most of their time plotting against them! A lone little girl visited us this summer at a time when my boy had one of his school chums with him. From the moment she arrived the boys thought of nobody else. They put pepper in her sheets and nutmeg on her toothbrush; they apple-pied her bed, read her letters, moved the hands of her clock, and hid her purse. They informed her every few minutes that she was a sap, a dumbbell, and an old stuck-up. The brook flowed unheeded through the dam they had carefully constructed before her arrival. Their shack of packing boxes was deserted. The puppies laid sticks at their feet in vain. All their energies and attention were devoted to the young lady whose presence they so violently deplored!

This very common negative phase is also part of emotional development. It is love in reverse. The boys are confirming their difference from girls, their boyishness. For once parents are pretty well out of the picture. The battle is waged against girls — and the girlishness within the boy's own breast. Just as the adolescent revolt is directed against the baby self with which parents are confused, so the anti-girl campaign also contains the bitterness of a civil war. Boys at this age are mortally afraid of doing anything which might by the farthest stretch of imagination be considered womanish. Dick refused pointblank to wear his favourite shoes because someone remarked that they were *girls'* style. " Sissy " is of course the final insult, only to be wiped out with blood. Touchiness like this always means insecurity. The man who has fully attained masculinity washes the dishes and changes diapers with equanimity. Woman's work is beneath his dignity only when his dignity is so tremulous that it needs defence. Aggressively masculine men are usually men who have not quite outgrown their boyish need to prove themselves.

With adolescence the child graduates from Czerny finger exercises and plays real pieces — simplified selections from Chopin and Mozart. He is still not ready for the full symphony of marriage, but he begins to experiment with the realities of adult love. Sex again rears its head, often quite undisguised, but by no means necessarily ugly. Maturing sex glands are largely responsible for this awakening. Menstruation is dramatic testimony for the girl that her body has grown up. The boy experiences nocturnal emissions and more specific sex desires. Secondary sex characteristics — breasts, hips, hair, the changing voice, and the beard proclaim to the world the physiological ripening of the adolescent. Intrinsically, these changes are no more alarming or portentous than the eruption of the permanent teeth in childhood. Margaret Mead, the anthropologist, tells us [2] that in Samoa, where youthful sex activity is taken with casual good nature, the storm and stress we associate with adolescence is entirely absent. No mystery is made of sex in any of its forms. Children know all about coitus and birth from first-hand observation. As their own bodies mature and genital impulses develop, custom grants them a number of years for free sexual adventuring. Eventually a marriage is arranged, following which monogamy is the rule. The Samoan household is large, blood relatives to the number of forty or fifty living under the same roof. Any mature woman in the group acts as mother to any child when occasion arises, even to the extent of nursing an infant who happens to cry when its mother is away. Under these circumstances close ties between parent and child do not develop. Since it has no function, the adolescent revolt is conspicuously absent. Coming of age is a very smooth, uneventful process.

[2] In *Coming of Age in Samoa* (New York: William Morrow & Company; 1928).

I am not suggesting that our young people imitate the Samoans. I wish merely to emphasize the point that the physiological changes of adolescence are not in themselves trouble-breeders. Growing into manhood or womanhood is not a disease even though the process may cause as much alarm and distress as a bad case of whooping cough. Adolescent physical changes are healthy, normal signs of growing up, in no way responsible for the " temperament " characteristic of this period of life in our society. The emotional problems of the teens cannot be explained away by a vague reference to puberty, glands, or what have you. They come from the effort to break away from parents, from the strain of choosing and starting a career, from the sudden demands of a more exacting life at college or in business, and — our major concern here — from the attitude our society takes toward beginning sex activity.

We are not casual about sex, like the Samoans. In our country the child who is just becoming a man or a woman is a highly romantic figure. Any art gallery has dozens of lovely representations of the young girl or boy. Anthologies of verse teem with apostrophes to divine youth. Adonis, the perennial adolescent, is celebrated and adored by everyone. The Greeks honestly connected his worship with fertility rites, but we have carefully expurgated our version of the Adonis legend. Our ideal youth is beautiful, but dewy-eyed and chaste. He bears small resemblance to our real youth, who, more often than not, is a pimply specimen wretchedly ashamed of the intimations of fertility his body thrusts upon him. " Keep your hearts pure." What is a serious-minded New York or Kansas City boy to do with his uncontrollable nocturnal emissions, with his unmentionable dreams, with the unseemly thoughts which come to him when a girl's skirts fly up in the wind, and with a very natural interest in burlesque shows?

I am reminded of the pathetic Brian in Huxley's *Eyeless in Gaza,* who fled the girl he loved because he found her kisses enjoyable. I am reminded of an unmarried middle-aged friend of mine who told me that at fourteen she and another girl drank a quart of vinegar in the hope that it would stunt the growth of their breasts. Of a very thrifty college professor who suffered from a lack of spending money and an overwhelming feeling of guilt about masturbation during his undergraduate days. He made a bargain with himself to burn up a five-dollar bill "the next time he did it." It cost him fifteen dollars to learn that sex drives are incorruptible. Even money cannot bribe them into submission. Another young girl took her mother's frenzied warnings about sex so to heart that for a whole year she contrived never to sit next to a boy or walk beside one on the street. She was afraid she might get pregnant. Since she attended a coeducational school you may imagine what ingenuity and effort went into this achievement. In this collection of clinical notes belongs the boy who visited a house of prostitution on a dare from his schoolmates. He fled after one kiss, but still felt himself so sullied by the adventure that he could never again talk to a pure young girl. One becomes a little bitter about pretty ideals which cause misery like this for perfectly nice youngsters.

Purity is not the only ideal we give our children these days. Indeed, purity is slightly outmoded in many quarters. A variant of the magazine story of sex has become very popular. You find it in more sophisticated literature and in crusading texts on sex education and marriage. Sex in this version of the story is an overwhelmingly beautiful and thrilling experience, while frigidity (the modern word for chastity) is a disease — almost a sin. Even in the movies, even in the magazines, the first embrace is pictured as rich beyond compare. Clark Gable and Dr. Marie Stopes have combined to build up a romantic ideal of physical love for the adolescent. Eventually, with or without the sanction of an " engagement," Mary Jane and Jim try it out for themselves. Neither realizes that the glamorous Gable has had years of practice in the art of kissing, that even sex *feeling* needs training just as connoisseurship in wines depends upon long experience in tasting. The first embrace, whether it follows upon the formal presentation of a ring in the best parlour or takes place in the rumble seat of a car after a wild party, is very often plain dull, almost certainly not comparable to the build-up it has received in the movies and True Love magazines. A young teacher in a girls' college tells me that her students in confidential mood occasionally say: " Do *you* feel dizzy and faint when you're kissed? Because I don't. There must be something the matter with me." When the girl goes beyond kissing and actually sleeps with her boy friend, the experience is often more painful. The act usually costs her a great deal in sense of sin and fear of discovery. It is carried out under most unfavourable conditions — guilty secrecy, discomfort, ineptitude on the part of both youngsters. And the reward is nothing. Sex is not even fun, let alone the thrill of a lifetime. Sometimes this unsatisfactory experience has the effect of turning the girl against sex for a long time, even permanently. " It's a much overrated pastime," one disillusioned young lady confided to me. " Why should I get married and put up with it all the time? " Another girl was not so categorical in her rejection of marriage. Before accepting her engagement she made an explicit stipulation: " Not more than three times a year."

More often, perhaps, the girl takes out her disappointment on herself. She continues to believe in the Gable-Stopes version of love, but feels herself to be that nasty creature, a frigid woman, a woman without normal sex feeling. Too often her partner covers his own disappointment by blaming her. Or she may point out to him that he is no sheik. I have seen young girls drift from one affair to another, never enjoying themselves, but unable to accept what they consider defeat — their inability to feel the devastating glory of passion. Each failure confirms their feeling of inadequacy and makes a satisfying embrace more difficult even under good conditions.

It is my experience that " nervousness " arises less often from the woman's lack of satisfaction in the sex embrace (orgasm), as the textbooks say, than from worry over this lack. (There is more about the details of physical love in the fourth chapter.)

The point I am making now is simply this: romantic notions about sex make for trouble. It doesn't matter very much whether we teach our children to be ashamed of physical relationships or to glorify sex. In either case the discrepancy between what they feel and what they think they *ought* to feel causes a sense of sinfulness, cynicism, and self-distrust.

The true story of adolescent physical love is less readily told, chiefly because its major characteristic is variability. Sex feelings do need expression, but since no two youngsters feel quite the same way, you cannot draw up a chart for normal sex outlets. People differ even in their bodily needs. For some, specific sex desires develop quickly, while others may go through life without being aware that they have a body. Neither type is abnormal. Neither should be forced by notions of what they *should* feel into either celibacy or promiscuity. We do not feel queer if we are not expert tennis-players or passionately fond of bodily exercise. We do not get excited about differences in the colour of hair, food tastes, or other organic idiosyncrasies. There is no more reason to expect everyone to have the same amount and quality of sex feeling than to be " standard " in any other respect. Some people like to kiss and cuddle. Others find these preliminaries a boring prelude to what they call the " real " thing. Even purity is a natural state for a few people and there are probably also a few individuals who really need frequent sexual experience from an early age.

The trouble is that a great many people are either pure or promiscuous not because of bodily need, but because of the kind of education they have received. It is rarely possible to disentangle genuine bodily needs from the attitudes learned during childhood and adolescence, just as it is hard to tell whether onions disagree with you because your stomach is peculiar or because you picked up a notion about them somewhere. Notions are important. You can get sick from onions you have knowingly eaten even if your wife has been serving them to you in disguised form for years.

The youngster who has been sheltered from all sex experience and taught to consider it " taboo " cannot suddenly free himself from his " inhibitions " under the influence of more liberal companions. Even the most innocent kiss may assume the aspect of a hideous transgression for these young people and cause genuine distress. I had in my office a pretty little Italian girl who had recently developed a curious habit — a tic. Every few minutes she would draw her under lip between her teeth. The lip, extending for half an inch down her chin, had become an unsightly red. Tessa was also very depressed. Her mother said that Tessa had acted queer ever since she had been allowed to attend her first dance at school. Her mother hadn't wanted her to go in the first place — she herself had never gone out as a young girl. But the teacher telephoned specially to urge her to let Tessa attend like the other girls. Tessa's story to me, confided with tears, was that one of the boys had danced her into the coat-room, where he had soundly kissed her. And Tessa liked it! Her lip-biting habit was unconsciously developed as a punishment for her mouth, which had sinned. She had told no one about this episode; indeed, there was no one to tell, since she had no close girl friends in the American school, and she fancied that her mother would turn her into the street if she knew.

Tessa's story is unusual, of course, both for the violence of her reaction to the little escapade and the extreme shelter of her home. Few American girls are so naïve.[3] But the moral — no more sex than you have been educated up to — holds for all of us. It is not possible to lay down any general rules for the direction of adolescent sex life. A single kiss may be more harmful for one girl or boy than a dozen full-blown affairs for another. We may be sorry that Tessa's education for sex was so limited. But we must accept Tessa as she is and help her find a sex life which will be satisfying to *her*, not to some abstract ideal. Most people today would feel that she should be given a concentrated cram course in sex to bring her up to the kind of reactions we have come to consider " normal " for her age group. Too often Tessa flunks even after the cram. With

---

[3] They are more naïve frequently than we realize. A rather prim young lady electrified a college class on " the Family " by announcing that to her certain conviction no girl over sixteen was a virgin. In the course of an illuminating group discussion of this point it came out that the young lady understood by virgin " one who has never been kissed."

her background, and perhaps her physical make-up too, she *cannot* be as free in her behaviour as many other girls. Our tutoring is apt to leave her not only with her deep sense of guilt about sex intact, but also with the feeling that she is queer and that she is missing something terribly important. Wouldn't it be better to help Tessa enjoy whatever form of sex activity she likes, given the kind of girl she is?

Steam-roller methods are nowhere more objectionable than in dealing with the sex problems of adolescence. Each girl or boy requires sensitive understanding and un-prejudiced assistance. The dean of a well-known school realized this necessity. Ordinarily very conservative in her opinions and advice, she rose vigorously to the defence of one youngster caught in a highly compromising situation. " She's just a healthy little animal," the dean said. " In a few years she'll be a fine wife and mother. I won't let her be punished now."

Adolescents usually turn to their contemporaries for help with their sex problems. On the whole they are good doctors for one another. Any youngster who has reasonably close friendships will learn for himself that he is not a uniquely horrible monster whether he likes to kiss when he thinks he shouldn't or doesn't like it when he thinks he should. A rehash of the prom in the girls' dormitory is usually very comforting and helpful. Mary Jane finds that Peg and Dotty and Eleanor, like herself, are neither absolutely pure in heart nor yet as passionate as Mae West. They learn to correct the magazine stories in terms of reality. According to their temperament they still feel slightly guilt-ridden or slightly cynical about a society which pretends to so much more virtue than it possesses. But they get along and manage to live fairly decent lives like the rest of us. Only the young who are too isolated to compare notes with friends, or who are too uncompromising in the ideals fostered by our mythology of love, really come a bad cropper. The psychiatrist would, of course, want to understand why these youngsters are solitary and uncompromising in the first place. Serious sex maladjustment in adolescence always has a history. The most perfect sex education conceivable would help perhaps, but by no means cure such people.

The only danger in this dormitory discussion of sex lies in the fact that the whole group may have swallowed some old wives' tale about sex too completely. They may reinforce each other in a fear of pregnancy, syphilis, sin, or what not. Straightforward objective talks by well-informed adults are an excellent corrective to these powerful legends. They also serve the purpose of loosening tongues so that the students tell each other more frankly how they really feel. Larger groups get into the discussions, demonstrating to each girl a variability which she is likely to miss if she only talks to two or three intimates. It helps perhaps to read in a book that there are individual differences in sex feeling. But if you find that Marian Bowers feels just the way you do, and Millicent is like Peg — well, you're a lot more comfortable.

Advising adolescents about their sex life is, then, a

highly personal and individualized problem. You cannot recommend the same behaviour for all of them indiscriminately. I rather hope that my own daughter will pet or neck or whatever the proper term may be, preferably with boys she knows well and likes, and only with her contemporaries. Love-making of this type is healthy preparation for marriage. I hope that she will not have intercourse or end up merely a technical virgin. Quite aside from any moral implications, such a step is risky, as I have indicated above. If she does have a complete relationship, though, I most earnestly hope that she will know what she is about, that she will not go into an affair because she happens to be tight, or thinks it's " the thing," or wants to prove that she can carry it off. These are my hopes. They are based on my observation of the kind of behaviour least likely to cause trouble in our particular social group. But she may order her life quite differently and be none the worse for it. If she is neither afraid of sex nor bamboozled by its glamour I shall be very content.

Much of the so-called sex life of adolescents has nothing to do with sex. By that cryptic statement I mean that bodily needs are not so important in determining many forms of sexual behaviour as are the needs of the social personality. " Popularity," for instance, has an enormous prestige value among young people. The girl who collects male scalps assiduously at every prom is by no means a nymphomaniac. Collecting stamps would be just as satisfying for many of these young coquettes if stamps were prized as highly by their associates. Many girls who " pet " indiscriminately do not like it very much themselves. They tell me they have to do it to get dates. I know a girl who dazzled her roommates by lurid tales of her numerous affairs — all quite fictitious. Sometimes of course these tales really have a sexual value to the inventor. Often enough, if the group happens to be impressed by sexual adventures, their psychological value is no different from that of any tale of prowess. A Southern girl said to me: " You know, I'm afraid to go home this summer. The marrying bug is around and I might get married just because everyone else is." Boys especially are prone to be led into sex experience just to prove themselves one of the gang.

So much for the first point I wanted to discuss: the state of the lover's emotional development. He cannot be " pure," but I have not been able to recommend a specific amount or quality of experience. Life laughs at recommendations. I have tried to show how people differ in their sexual needs to start with and how all their experiences from infancy to adult years further emphasize their individuality. No single rule of conduct, whether purity or freedom or a happy medium, can be expected to fit such diverse needs. Rules of conduct, as I have said, cause most of the trouble. In trying to be St. Catherine or Mae West a girl loses much of the fun of being Mary Jane, aged seventeen, with a love life all her own.

Our next points for discussion are attitudes toward earlier loves and the choice of a particular mate. I am going to discuss them together because the distinction between Tom, Dick, and Harry and the ultimate Mr. Right is not as clear as our magazine story would have us believe. One of the most frequent questions I get from the young is: "How can you tell when you're really in love?" They have all sorts of theories. One girl said: "I know love should come like a bang on the head, and I've never felt that way about Chuck. I've known him ever since we were kids. We always have a swell time. I like to have him kiss me and all that too. But I want my marriage to be perfect and it can't be unless I feel just devastated, can it?" Chuck and Marian now have a ten-months-old baby. They are happy and look with pity on their friends who are "still in a stew." Kitty, on the other hand, complained because she was too devastated. She thought it must be "just infatuation" because she used to feel that way about Bill, and even about Carl and Fred.

Unhappily, true love does not announce itself with a rash, red eyes, and white spots in the mouth like measles. Indeed, there is, I fear, no such thing as True Love, capital T, capital L. People do develop feelings for each other which can be the basis of lifelong happiness, but the feelings are not the same for everyone. Marian is not the kind of woman who has a grand passion. For her love is compounded largely of companionship and affection. Her loyalty and tenderness grow with association. In my sentimental old age I expect to attend her golden wedding and from my wheel-chair admire the happy brood of children and grandchildren clustered about her. And I shall have a small sense of proprietorship in this family, because I helped release Marian from a lifelong search for a bang on the head which she never would have received.

Kitty's head, on the other hand, is already somewhat bruised from too many bangs. Love for her contains much more excitement than for Marian, much more passion, much more poetry — and much less stability. Very often her whole conception of love is limited to the thrill of its initial stages. Pride of conquest and the uncertainty of a new relationship give a pleasurable fillip to love. For a time, too, she can see herself through the man's eyes as a glamorous beauty. The less confidence she has in herself, deep down, the more she needs the extravagant homage of a new suitor. She feels grand, and, naturally enough, considers the man who occasions this heightened self-appreciation the great love of her life. The exploration of a new personality is also exciting; it leads to the discovery of unsuspected kinships of interests and ideas.

Unhappily most of these delights are born of novelty. As the man's devotion flags or becomes a commonplace the glamorous princess turns again to plain Kitty. There are jangling differences in interests to be discovered as well as kinships. Uncertainty is lost or becomes a torment. Hoping against hope that the telephone will ring is exciting for a while, but it gets nerve-racking in the course of time. And nobody stays at a high pitch of thrill if it rings every night at seven thirty for months. At this point Kitty feels herself painfully disillusioned. She loved an ideal, not the real man, she tells herself. Her misery or ennui continues until another admirer crops up, to repeat the same theme in a new voice.

Most young girls — and with some variation young men — have a good deal in common with Kitty. Their feelings in the opening measures of each affair correspond closely to the descriptions of love they have read in the magazines. They are of an age to want True Love and recognize its features in every new romance.

Some people never get beyond this pleasing phase of courtship. Their idea of love stops permanently at the falling-in-love and being-loved stage. Their love is like a fire of pine boughs — crackling, colourful brilliance one moment and dull ashes the next. It must be constantly renewed by fresh boughs. Fortunately most young people go further — else our divorce rate would be even higher than it is. They may use pine boughs to start the fire, but they soon throw on a solid birch log. True love, they find, is not this scintillating emotion, but a complicated relationship with another person, built deep into the personalities of both partners. Love is what lovers make it. You cannot accept or reject your feeling for your sweetheart by comparing it with a standard model. One man will find his most satisfying love in a woman who mothers him a bit. Another will fulfil himself in protecting a weaker nature. Still another will work out a comradely, almost brotherly relationship with his wife — to mention only some of the most obvious types of marital bliss. But whether the pattern is that of an apache and his woman or

Albert and Victoria, the marriage is founded on true love if it proves a durable combination of the needs of two natures.

At what point in their development do young people throw the birch log on the fire of pine boughs? How do they really find their Mr. Right? One year they are full of doubts and hesitations and the next they are safely married, usually with a fairly solid conviction that their choice is a good one. I say fairly solid because doubts do recur in the best-regulated engagements. One girl said: "Mostly I think I'm the luckiest girl alive, but sometimes I can't understand how I came to pick up such an awful drip."

Many theories are current as to how to pick a husband. " I don't dare marry Jack — we're too much alike." " I can't marry Jim. We love each other, but we've absolutely *no* interests in common." " Marvin is swell, but he's really tight about money. I think differences about money ruin more marriages than anything else." " Tom always has to be the boss, and I'm the kind of girl who can't stand that attitude." " I think Johnny would interfere with my career. He says he won't, but I can tell he really likes a woman who darns socks and can boil an egg exactly three and one half minutes." " Harry is immature. I'm sure he'd be unstable as a husband, and besides he's tied to his mother's apron-strings."

I believe that these character analyses are usually ir-relevant, both in choosing a mate and in getting along with him afterwards. Nine times out of ten such critical com-ments mask a deep reluctance to marry — not Jack or Jim or Marvin, but anyone at all. In courtship, as later in marriage, differences about money, interests, values, temperament, are used as weapons in a more subterranean warfare. In part this warfare is directed against the partner in marriage — more of that in the next chapters. But in part, like the adolescent revolt and the anti-girl campaign, it is civil warfare. Wanting marriage, young people are also afraid of it. They find it easier to pick faults in a suitor than to realize that they dare not accept the responsibilities of marriage and do not want to give so much of themselves to another person. My proof of this diagnosis of the elaborate and destructive character analyses made by the young is the sudden shift in emphasis once they have made peace with themselves and are emotionally ready for marriage. The same arguments formerly used against marriage now become cogent reasons for getting a licence right away. " It's a good thing we see eye to eye " — if Jack is too much like the young lady. " Common interests keep you too much together, so you stagnate " — if he's too different.

The choice of a mate — once the person in question truly wants one — is comparatively easy. And it doesn't matter so much just what kind of a man he is. If both parties are emotionally educated for marriage almost any pair can make a go of it.[4] Some few people seem to fall in love exclusively with one person or one type of person, just as some few people seem to be born with a desire to

---

[4] When the prospective mate is strikingly different, in walk of life, race, or personality, character analysis is useful — analysis of yourself. Have you enough flexibility to handle a drastic change in your general way of living?

paint, play the piano, or collect snakes. But most of us make out with the work that happens to come our way and the partner that, half fortuitously, we pick out of the hat. We do a good job too, often coming to believe in time that we were cut out from the beginning to be a buttonhole-manufacturer or a school-teacher, and the husband of our particular Mary Jane. In point of fact we probably would have done just as well manufacturing bobby-pins or being a public accountant. If we'd happened to lose ourselves with Betty Ann that very significant time on the mountain we might have married her instead of Mary Jane and been none the worse for it.

When Mary Jane and Jim get ready for marriage, then, they find a mate. A great deal too much pother has been made over just *whom* to marry. *When* to marry, in terms of your own development, is much more important. Readiness for marriage is our last point for discussion. " You settle down in a little house with chequered curtains at the window and live happily ever after." What expectations do young people bring to marriage?

I have found among the young people I know an almost terrifying desire for a " perfect " marriage, and an equally terrifying desire to tear it up and start over if imperfections develop. Many have indeed proposed experimental marriages, temporarily childless, to prove compatibility before settling down to a life of union. The vision of the perfect marriage entertained by these youngsters is for the most part so conventionalized and so stereotyped as to be grotesque. It has no body to it, no shadings of grief and quarrels, no individual expression. Against this prettified æsthetic standard they measure their flesh-and-blood marriages and find them wanting. These inconsistent modern youngsters have a lively regard for realism in art and literature. They hang Hogarth on the walls, yet they plan their marriage in the style of Reynolds. They read Walt Whitman and seek in their wives a heroine out of Tennyson, or her modern equivalent. Cynical about everything else, they are desperately intent upon making their wedded life ideal. And they want all the old love, devotion, and fidelity, plus comradeship and complete self-expression. They examine themselves like hypochondriacs to make sure marriage is giving them everything they expect and that it is stifling no part of their personality. The natural shortcomings of any human relationships, the sacrifice of potentialities that comes with any way of life take on exaggerated importance. Realism in marriage seems to them failure. They lay the blame on themselves or their partners instead of upon the naïve and excessive demands they make upon marriage.

Now, marriage can be almost anything. I have already suggested in several places that the quality of love depends upon the lovers. In the next chapters I want to talk about many kinds of marital relationships which can be very satisfying to both members. Every variety of marriage, if it is to be successful and enduring, has one requirement, however; two people shall be ready to sink themselves in the creation of a new unit bigger than either of them. The creation must be important to them. They must accept their relationship as the permanent framework of their lives. Readiness for marriage means that we can with entire honesty repeat the words: " to love, honour, and cherish, for better or for worse, till death do us part." Acceptance of the relationships is the big thing — not careful adjustment of money and interests and in-laws. A man and woman who are sure of their marriage, of each other, can fight openly about the other problems and work through to some sort of solution. The experimental approach is fine in the laboratory. In marriage it has a signpost: " To Reno."

CHAPTER II

SETTLING DOWN TO MARRIAGE

NINE tenths of the human misery in this world is sheer nonsense. Hunger and cold, sickness and death — these are the ills which flesh is heir to. We share them with our brothers the foxes and our sisters the birds. Nowhere, however, does man show his superiority over his four-footed friends more clearly than in his ability to devise new troubles peculiar to himself alone. His ingenuity has expended itself in reducing natural evils to a minimum on the one hand and multiplying spiritual hazards on the other. Our primitive ancestors lived precariously and uncomfortably at the mercy of the elements. Yet it is quite possible that the Neanderthal woman suffered less from the lack of any coat at all than certain ladies of my acquaintance do from wearing muskrat instead of mink. And that she found the probable frank brutality of her mate far less trying than her descendants find the polite " mental cruelty " of their spouses. The success of modern marriage does not depend on the satisfaction of crea-

ture needs, but on the fulfilment of a thousand complicated expectations and desires whose connection with any
basic biological need is both remote and elaborately disguised.

Man is the least practical and rational of the animals.
The moose and the elk shift their feeding grounds with
shifts in vegetation. The wolf follows the moose. But
there are 9,849 doctors struggling to make a living in New
York City while areas in Kansas are almost without medical attendance. The market of any country is obviously
supported by its populace, most of whom are wage-earners.
Yet employers with one hand reduce wages and with the
other try frantically to stimulate the market by high-pres-
sure advertising. Depressions are caused by " over-produc-
tion " while millions of people live below the subsistence
level. The nations fought a war to end war. Victors and
vanquished alike went bankrupt in the process. Nevertheless twenty years later they are spending three times as
much on armaments as they did in 1913. Mr. Jones painfully divorces one woman in order to marry her spit and
image. Mrs. Brown falls in love with Mr. Brown because
of his boyish charm and leaves him because of his irre-
sponsibility. Hazel marries Arthur just to spite Bill and
finally discovers that Arthur was the one she wanted all
along.

Perhaps the quaintest notion man has invented is his
belief in his own rationality. We always have a reason for
anything we do. Listen to anyone who has just succeeded
in making an egregious ass of himself. Not that you have

any option — he'll talk your arm off explaining just what perfectly natural misconceptions caused him to make the blunder. He will prove to the hilt that, given his understanding of the situation, he followed the only reasonable course of action. The real reasons for his behaviour may seem so obvious to you that you assume he is merely trying to " save his face " with his audience. The chances are, though, that he is far more convincing to himself than to you. Suppose our friend has fallen for a confidence man who rushed him into an obvious fake by flourishing big names and assuring him that he was the kind of shrewd business man who nails opportunities promptly. You know he has been a sucker for appeals to snobbishness and vanity against all common sense, but have you ever known a man who could admit such a thing frankly and simply to himself? He really believes he was taken in by the flimsy " facts " the confidence man gave him.

Marriage is often a sort of confidence game. When we are taken in we think we were misled by falsification of facts — we didn't know our husbands would turn out unfaithful and financially irresponsible or that our wives were slatterns, given to bossiness and irritability; that our interests would be divergent and our ideals incompatible. Or if the marriage is successful we say it is because we were canny in our choice of a mate and have handled the problems of daily living very cleverly. Sometimes almost any outsider can see that our difficulties and our complacencies are alike ill-founded. Everyone but Millicent knew that Willard was a playboy and that she married him out of snobbishness and vanity, whatever she may say or believe. More often the impulses which lead us to marry and to conduct our marriages as we do are less obvious to interested observers and more completely hidden from ourselves. The " facts " seem more important. In every marriage, however, the real determinants of success or failure lie much deeper than the reasons we give ourselves.

This distinction between what psychiatrists call " unconscious " factors and the superficial problems of marriage is so important that I am going to devote several pages to its clarification. We are not primarily rational beings. We act in accordance with deep biological and psychological impulses. Some of these impulses are part of our physical heritage. Others come from our early emotional experiences, as we saw in the last chapter. We do not understand these impulses clearly. Often we are unaware of their existence. Therefore much of our behaviour is quite unreasoning and unreasonable, out of key both with the demands of the situation in which we find ourselves and with our notion of the way we ought to act. Such discrepancies are intolerable to us. Above all things we must think ourselves sane — that is, " rational." So we tack a sensible interpretation on to our behaviour and believe firmly that this interpretation explains *why* we acted as we did.

The behaviour of people under the influence of posthypnotic suggestion is a dramatic illustration of our tendency to supply reasons for our actions, however whimsical they may be. The procedure I am about to describe is a stock psychological experiment which has been repeated hundreds of times. Under deep hypnosis the conscious mind is asleep. The subject of the hypnosis accepts uncritically any suggestion offered him. He will chew shoe leather under the impression that it is a succulent piece of filet mignon. At the behest of the hypnotist he will transform himself into a child, a dog — anything that appeals to the whimsy of his audience. He will experience any emotion from fear of a mythical earthquake to amorous passion for a rag doll. On awakening from the trance he remembers nothing that has occurred. Now, it is possible to suggest, while the subject is still in the trance, that he will perform some particular act after he comes out of the hypnosis. The act will be duly performed, but the subject, not remembering *why* he is doing it, invents reasons of his own for his behaviour. For instance, suppose the hypnotist impresses upon the unconscious subject the idea that in half an hour he must open his umbrella and walk down the street. It is a clear winter's day and there is no real occasion for the man to leave the house. The subject is then brought out of hypnosis. He chats comfortably with his friends, feels and behaves in a perfectly ordinary manner. After half an hour he becomes uneasy, then suddenly decides that he must go out — better get some more cigarettes. He looks at the cloudless sky, remarks rather self-consciously that it might rain — you never can tell — hunts up his umbrella and goes down the street. This is post-hypnotic suggestion.

The interesting thing about this experiment is the inability of the subject to say frankly: " I want to put up my umbrella and walk down the street. I don't know why, but I feel like it and I'm going to do it." We have to have a reason for everything we do and we believe fanatically in our reasons. No mind is so lost that it does not seem reasonable to itself. The rational machinery is usually very clear, even when the person is actually insane. Early in my medical days I listened to a woman who had recently persuaded herself that she was Jesus Christ. Her eyes glowed with transcendent beauty as she talked of her long spiritual growth and her final awareness of her glorious mission. She was so convincing that for a moment I found myself actually wondering whether she might not be in truth an incarnation of the Saviour and I of clay too crass to understand.

Post-hypnotic suggestion and the rationality of the insane are, of course, extreme examples of the universal human tendency to attach reasons to every act, however impulsive. I have described them in detail because they show so clearly the difference between the real cause of our actions and the explanation we supply for them. Our hypnotized friend went out with his umbrella solely because his unconscious self, obedient to a powerful suggestion, insisted upon it. He thought he went out because he needed cigarettes.

In less obvious form this tendency to act in accord with some unrecognized impulse and hastily attach a sensible interpretation underlies all human behaviour. Let us take a less colourful example. Mr. X is presented to Mr. Y for the first time and dislikes him instantly. Since Mr. Y has committed no more serious crime than to remark pleasantly upon the weather, Mr. X might well be taxed with a certain whimsy in his reaction. He will tell you, however, that he never trusts men who are well groomed and smooth in manner. Beastly fop, that's what he is. You examine Mr Y attentively without discerning any particular foppishness. Seems a nice chap, in fact. You observe further that Mr. X is behaving like a petulant and belligerent little boy, and that, too, is unusual for him. It is all very puzzling. You wonder vaguely about the " chemical " attractions and antipathies you read about somewhere and dismiss the matter. What you do not know and what Mr. X has forgotten is that Uncle Edward had curly, sandy hair and odd, grey eyes, very like this chap. You do not know, nor does Mr. X remember very clearly, that Uncle Edward was the bête noire of his childhood — superciliously teasing and troublesome. Mr. X doesn't know it, but he dislikes Mr. Y because he is reminded of his uncle. If he knew, of course, he would realize that Mr. Y is like his uncle only in possessing sandy hair and grey eyes and would promptly recover from his antipathy. Since he does not recognize this similarity, he must find other reasons for his strong distaste and discovers that poor Mr. Y is unbearably foppish.

Recently I found myself very much attracted to an inconspicuous young lady sitting across the aisle in the subway and set myself to discover why she seemed so appealing. She was not a type that I usually admire. She was, I noted, dumpy in figure, pasty in complexion, dressed without spirit or imagination. Yet she caused me quite a flutter. Suddenly it occurred to me that her coat, a somewhat unusual black and white plaid, was like one worn by a girl I had courted years ago in college. With this discovery my interest in my fellow passenger evaporated.

It is not often possible to trace so easily the source of these reactions to people. Some little mannerism, an inflection of the voice, the gait, almost anything, may serve to set off some association not the less potent in its effects because unrecognized. When you know the person well, the task is still further complicated. Reactions to the things the person has actually done are all mixed up with reactions to the person of whom he unwittingly reminds you.

Situations also call forth this dual response — a response to the present and to the unrecognized past. A business executive I know handles people with admirable poise and assurance so long as he is sitting at his own desk. He is also at ease during luncheon conferences or at meetings where the staff sits together around a table. Quite another mood appears, however, when he comes to the private office of another executive and takes the chair beside the desk. He loses countenance at once, becomes too ingratiating or too truculent, is uncertain of himself, apologetic and blustering at once. This regrettable collapse occurs even when he happens to go to one of his subordinates. His associates have come to wonder a little at his informality since of late years he always stands, sits on the desk or the window-sill, any place except the obvious convenient chair next to the desk. He says frankly that he dislikes the second-fiddle position. When I heard of this little quirk I hazarded the guess that he had once put in uncomfortable months in some sort of soliciting position — perhaps as an insurance agent. It was sheer luck that I hit the nail precisely on the head. His first job was selling insurance. Sensitive and dominating at the same time, he had found the requirements of his job intolerable, sought the first opportunity for release, and soon forgotten the whole venture in a successful advertising career. Yet not quite forgotten. The miseries and resentments of those months renewed their being whenever he found himself in the familiar chair next to the prospect's desk.

The real causes for our emotions are not always simply forgotten. We manage to substitute our own interpretation of our behaviour if we don't like the real reason for it. Suppose our friend Mr. X disliked Mr. Y because of jealousy. Suppose Mr. Y is more successful and more popular than Mr. X. If Mr. X has any natural human competitiveness he will be somewhat annoyed at Mr. Y. And if he has any natural human pride in himself he will not be able to say frankly: "I don't like him because he's a more successful man than I." It's not good form to dislike people because they're too perfect, though most of us do unless we can find some engaging flaw to feel superior or protective about. Mr. X wouldn't dream of such a thing, so he emphasizes or, if need be, invents a fault which will make his antipathy acceptible. Mr. X is not a hypocrite. He has no idea that he is capable of what he would consider a nasty subterfuge. But he is, and so are you and I. A very large proportion of the reactions of every one of us is determined by impulses we don't know anything about — either because we don't see the connection between the present situation and some past emotion, or because we don't like the looks of the impulse we really feel. At the same time every activity is accompanied by a perfectly sensible explanation which usually fools us, if not our neighbours, very effectively.

Another reason for censoring our impulses is that they are often self-contradictory. It is common to love and hate a person at the same time, to wish him both success and failure, to feel superior and envious simultaneously. These conflicting attitudes do not make sense, so we cut one of them out of consciousness. A woman I know believes that her husband should maintain his masculine friendships, both for his own enjoyment and as a matter of business expediency. She sees to it that he pays his dues at several clubs, that he arranges for golf, tennis, and squash at frequent intervals. But she is also a little sorry for herself because she lives in the suburbs and is pretty well tied down to her house and baby. Moreover, she is extremely fond of her husband. She likes to have him around. Now, it often happens that she " forgets " about his club nights. She invites guests to the house so that he finds it awkward to leave. She is apt to get a violent headache on Sunday morning. Although she urges him to go right ahead with his golf regardless of her sufferings, somehow her husband always stays at home. Occasionally she drops into his office for a surprise at five o'clock. Curiously enough, the day she comes turns out to be his afternoon for squash.

In short, though young Mrs. Wilson is generous in her wish to have her husband enjoy himself and sensible about his business contacts, she is also a bit resentful because he has more freedom than she, a bit jealous of his friends, a bit lonely. Her impulses toward helping her husband go out and keeping him at home are both genuine, both natural and sufficiently praiseworthy. They are incompatible, however. No woman in her senses would deliberately get her husband to pay high club dues out of a meagre salary and deliberately keep him from using the club. Mrs. Wilson solves her dilemma by consciously arranging for her husband's masculine pursuits and unconsciously — " accidentally " — managing to keep him home pretty often.

Plainly this subterfuge does not really solve the problem, as Mrs. Wilson would admit with chagrin if she realized how effectively her " mistakes " were blocking her conscious purpose. Mrs. Wilson's conflicts are not very important. She and her husband remain a devoted and happy couple. When the contradictory impulses reach deeper into the personality the marriage is more seriously endangered. You find many wives who want their husbands to be able men and good providers and simultaneously dependent little boys. Neither desire is in itself incompatible with an excellent marital relationship, but the combination is impossible. Whenever the husband does show signs of strength the wife, with a deft criticism, turns

him into a little boy. She is then indignant because he is
flabby and inconsequential. Everything he does gives her
pain. To the extent of her ability she defeats all his attempts at establishing his own character. Consciously, of
course, she is for ever urging him on to achievement. She
would be dismayed to learn that she is also thwarting any
gestures he makes toward independent success.

Later on we shall study marriages like this in detail.
I have sketched them here merely to illustrate further the
importance of what psychiatrists call " unconscious motivation " in marriage. We cannot understand marriage if
we confine our study to the obvious felicities and quarrels
of any wedded pair. You remember that we found in the
adolescent revolt against parents an unconscious revolt
against the baby self; in the antagonism between boys and
girls unrecognized sexual impulses and an effort to establish their differences from each other; in the critical
attitude of young ladies toward their suitors an unacknowledged reluctance to marry. The relationship between husband and wife, so intimate in every respect, is
even more heavily loaded with a substratum of disguised
impulses. The least important part of any marriage is the
part you see. I hope that this brief discussion of sub-
surface attitudes will help us understand more fully the
problems and satisfactions of marriage which we are going to take up in the following chapters.

After this long didactic parenthesis let us return to Mary
Jane and Jim. We left them as they were about to settle

down in a cute little house with chequered curtains at the window. Three years later we peek in at them.

Mary Jane, in a crisp house dress kept spotless and un-faded by Lux, has laid out breakfast — everything Beech-nut but the eggs. Jim Junior is busily eating up his cereal for the fun of finding the Micky Mouse at the bottom of the dish thoughtfully supplied by the makers of Cream of Wheat. Jim Senior, spruce in an Arrow collar and forti-fied by a perfect night's rest under the auspices of the Simmons Bedding Company, is about to make his way to the office to earn the thirty-five dollars a week which are somehow to pay for the hundred-dollar radio, the Monel metal kitchen, the dapper little car, and the self-satisfied look that comes to those who have provided munificently for retirement at fifty-five. This intimate view of Ameri-can home life is familiar to us all through the kindness of advertising mediums of every variety and haunting ubiq-uity. We are fortunate because without their aid we should never see such a pretty picture.

Let us peek in again without the rosy spectacles supplied by the nationally advertised brands. Mary Jane's frock for mornings at home looks a little frayed and faded. Her apron has definitely seen neither Lux nor a harsh washing soap for several days. She scrapes dispiritedly at the break-fast plates, slightly repulsive with congealed egg yolk and slimy cold bacon grease. For the fourteenth time she ex-horts Junior to stop dawdling and eat his cereal. She is not, at the moment, enjoying her marriage very much. Why should she? Washing dishes day in and day out is not the same thing as canoeing in the moonlight with your heart's beloved. Neither, to be sure, is taking dictation from a pudgy boss who mumbles his words through a fat cigar and always speaks either too fast or too slow. Mary Jane is not thinking of dictation, however. She is remembering five o'clock with Jim waiting at the corner, of dinner with dancing, of going to the movies, or a concert, or the theatre, or just a long ferry-boat ride. Of the difficult good-night kiss and the ecstatic knowledge that soon she would have Jim all the time for always. She is thinking rather wryly of how entrancing, how full of promise, this battered dishpan looked when it first emerged from pink tissue paper at the shower the girls gave her. She may even think, a little cynically, as she surveys the grey grease-pocked surface of her dishwater, of the foaming pans of eternally virgin suds she expected from her perusal of the advertisements. Well, she's married now. She has her own house, her own dishpan, her husband, and her baby. All the time and for always. She doesn't even go to the movies any more because there's no one to stay with Junior. She speaks so crossly to the child now that his tears fall into the objectionable cereal. Why on earth won't Jim let her get Mrs. Oldacre in to stay evenings? He'll be earning more soon; Mr. Bayswater practically told him he would be put in charge of the branch office as soon as old Fuzzy retired. Five dollars a week savings — much good that does anyway. Mary Jane's thoughts about her husband become quite definitely uncharitable. " If he only had the least understanding of the kind of life I have, but all he notices is Junior's shoes are scuffed out and he wouldn't even try that Bavarian cream I fixed yesterday. It's all very well for him to think Jimmy Junior's cute when he sneaks out of bed — he doesn't have him all day and all night and nothing but Jimmy Junior."

Thus Mary Jane at nine o'clock of a Monday morning. At three p.m. the sight of Junior tugging a large packing box about the yard suddenly makes her heart turn over with delight and pride. What a duck he is! She smiles all to herself with pleasure at the sunlight falling through the peach curtains on the blues and browns of her living-room furniture. That recipe for apple pan dowdy — she'll try that for supper. Jim will be home in two hours and a half, home for a whole lovely evening. And Monday is Philadelphia orchestra night on the radio. For no reason at all life is abruptly good, very good.

Jim, meantime, is having his own problems, big and little. Mary Jane is a frequent pain in the neck to him. He likes his eggs with the whites firm and the yolks runny. Mary Jane gets them wrong every time — sometimes leathery, sometimes slimy. Why does she have to be so cranky with Junior, and why can't she keep him quiet mornings? She should know a man needs all the rest he can get. He has to give his best to the job — marriage is too expensive to loaf or to be too tired. Mary doesn't understand that at all. He gave up his big chance in the Texas branch just for her, didn't he; but does she appreciate it? And yet Jim, too, has his hours of excitement and delight, of deep satisfaction in his wife and his son and his home and himself in the role of paterfamilias.

This view of marriage, more accurate than the version thrust upon us by the advertisers, is still only the top layer, the part you see, the common-sense interpretation of satisfactions and discords which have their roots much deeper in the personalities of Mary Jane and Jim. Their problems, one might feel, arise from their economic difficulties. Mary Jane needs more help with the housework, more opportunity for fun. Jim needs more security in his job. Since we have created these two young people out of our fertile imaginations, we can easily step up their income. Let us give Jim at once the full confidence of his boss and the job of branch manager at ten thousand dollars a year. The new maid cooks his eggs to a turn. The nurse keeps Junior as quiet as a well-ordered Electrolux. Mary Jane can go to the movies — or to the bridge club she has recently joined — as often as she pleases. Have their problems vanished? Well, look at the people you know who make ten thousand a year. The ones *I* know are given to saying wistfully: " Remember that little house we had in Forest Hills when we were first married? You know, we've never been as happy as we were then, just the three of us, even if we did have to pawn the typewriter some months till your salary cheque came in."

We must, I fear, abandon Mary Jane and Jim without probing into the deeper reasons for their joys and discontents. They are " typical " youngsters made up out of whole cloth to illustrate a few common surface aspects of marriage. I am not enough of a novelist to equip them with the highly individual characterization necessary to a full understanding of their marriage. Hereafter I will humbly resort to real people whose deeper attitudes I know from first-hand study. From real people we can learn something of the factors which turn superficial problems like those we have given Mary Jane and Jim into a source of serious tension, or which keep them at the level of petty annoyances without influence on the stability of the marriage.

While I cannot, in fairness to the couples who have taught me so much, describe the actual situations of which they have told me, their experiences form the basis of the stories of married life appearing in the following chapters. The stories are accurate in spirit, though wholly fictitious in detail.

Thousands of women are bored with housework at times, irritable with their children, and are dubs at cooking eggs, while their husbands fret about savings. The crux of this situation *seems* to be lack of money, but we found that increased income did not solve the problem. We could introduce other variations into marriage. We could send our typical Mary Jane out to work, or keep her at home with six babies instead of one. We could make Jim a travelling salesman or a college professor who worked at home most of the time. Whatever the setting of their marriage, they would always find occasions for delightful intimacy and for rousing quarrels. The balance between intimacy and vexations does not depend on the setting, but on the particular kind of people Mary Jane and Jim happen to be. The difficulties of their daily life can bring them closer together or alienate them. Prosperity can foster harmony between them or actually drive them apart. Look over the married people you know with these questions in mind. Are the happiest couples the ones who have few problems to face — economic, social, health, children, what you will? Or, conversely, are the ones who have suffered most bound together with special tenderness? I think you will find examples of both possibilities — and as many more as you care to think up. In short, the real problems don't matter so much in the long run. What matters is how Mary Jane and Jim take them. Something deep in the character of man and wife determines the success or failure of their marriage, not the circumstances of their daily lives. For this reason advice about how to control circumstances (in-laws, the budget, the children, etc.) does not touch the real relationship existing between two very special people, and therefore has no effect upon their marriage. Our task in this book becomes then exceedingly difficult. We cannot give general advice about how to make a budget and whether to live with the old folks and how many children to have. We are forced to consider those very intangible, elusive factors in marriage — attitudes, expectations, desires, and fears, many of which are quite unconscious. Not only are these attitudes exceedingly complex; they are also highly individual. No two marriages work the same way because no two people have the same expectations from marriage.

I think we can best study the attitudes underlying the marital relationship by considering a series of situations which are frequently held responsible for disharmony and divorce. The series will not be complete. Anything at all can be used to break up a marriage. I remember a woman, a Bryn Mawr graduate, who told me that her husband was often drunk and sometimes abusive, that he had struck her on two occasions and was consistently mean to their child, that he contributed almost nothing to the support of the family. She seemed to be able to make allowances for these sins. The one thing she could not forgive was his practice of wearing his underwear to bed! She was not ironic. This plebeian habit was a more devastating threat to her respect for him and her self-respect as his wife than all his other vices. I hope that a discussion of the more common problems may serve to make clear the way marriage is moulded by the attitudes, the basic character trends, of two people, the intangible, unavowed impulses of the individuals involved.

The first " problem " I want to take up is the disillusionment of marriage — the kind of reaction Mary Jane was having when we looked in on her Monday morning. Now, marriage is, in actual fact, just a way of living. We don't expect life to be all sunshine and roses, or even beer and skittles. But somehow we do expect marriage to be that way. People who are accustomed to bickering with everyone else are shocked when they find that they bicker with their wives. Women who have found everything somewhat disappointing are surprised and pained when marriage proves itself no exception. Most of the complaints about the institution of holy matrimony arise not because it is worse than the rest of life, but because it is not incomparably better.

There are reasons for this almost universal feeling of disillusionment about marriage. One is that we are taught to expect too much from it. I've already talked a bit about these exaggerated and stereotyped expectations. But even if we have become profoundly cynical about marriage in general, we are apt to be disillusioned about our own, because most of us marry when we are in love, or rather when we are in the falling-in-love stage described in the last chapter. The sexual excitement, the uncertainties and novelties of the new relationship, actually lift us out of ourselves for a time. With the best will in the world we cannot during the falling-in-love stage show ourselves to our beloved as we really are, nor see her in her everyday personality. We are quite genuinely not our everyday selves at this period. We are more intense, more vital than usual. Moreover we see ourselves through the eyes of our beloved. Unconsciously we match our feeling about ourselves with the glorified impression she has formed of us.

This excited state of mind cannot endure the protracted association of marriage. The thrilling sexual tension which normally keeps engaged couples in a state of fervid and delighted expectation abates with frequent, satisfying intercourse. The element of uncertainty is dissipated — and there is no doubt that a goal we have not yet won is more intriguing than one which is wholly ours. We are deliciously stimulated by the desire for an object not yet obtained, but almost within our grasp. Sooner or later, when the flamboyant anticipations of betrothal give way to the sober satisfactions of marriage, we lapse back into our ordinary selves. Fortunately. We can only surpass ourselves during emotional crises without seriously depleting our reserves. We can run from a bear very fast indeed, but if we made that speed habitual we would soon collapse entirely. Walking is the most practicable gait for common use, and marriage too must be paced at the rate of our usual temperament. This inevitable change of pace is what we call disillusionment. Our disillusionment does not proceed wholly, or perhaps even primarily, from the unromantic facts we learn about our partner in the course of daily observation. It comes largely from our bored recognition of the same old self within our own breast. Our own new-found charm and prowess and glamour evaporate when we can no longer read them in a worshipping gaze, when we are no longer stimulated by the desire for conquest.

Woe unto him or her who cannot understand and accept this " disillusionment " of marriage. I have already spoken of those girls who maintain their glamour by a constant succession of suitors. The quest for glamour does not cease just because a marriage ceremony has accompanied one of their affairs. These women (and men) are at the mercy of any new admirer. Frequent trips to Reno, a series of extra-marital affairs, or a perpetual sense of frustration — or all three — are a poor substitute for a solid marriage geared to the needs of the everyday personality.

The psychiatrist who studies men and women like these glamour-chasers usually finds at the core a profound feeling of inferiority and dislike of the self. Deeply uncertain about themselves, they find their own value only in the eager devotion of another person, in the uncritical exaggerated devotion of a new passion. Occasionally one will say frankly: " When I'm in love I can do anything, and when I'm not I'm just nothing at all." More often, however, they give you the case history of each marriage, showing how they were misled into believing the chap was far better than he turned out to be. As we saw in the case of Mary Jane and Jim, there always seem to be sound external reasons for the problems of marriage. It is never impossible for the deluded lovers to produce perfectly plausible excuses for failures which they claim have nothing to do with a far-fetched psychiatric interpretation. Nevertheless the basic pattern of intense passion, gradual " disillusionment," ennui, misery, and suddenly a new great love worthy of any sacrifice repeats itself too monotonously to be quite accidental. There are usually other signs of the presence of this basic sense of inferiority: sensitivity to criticism, over-dependence on the opinion of others, a blustering or frankly timid demeanour, a need to be preeminent in something however trivial, avoidance of situations likely to show one at a disadvantage. The final proof of the correctness of the psychiatric diagnosis lies in the sudden domesticity which develops after the person has learned through treatment how to accept himself as a valid personality in his own right.

One illustration: Emily Bowen was a pretty girl, but her sister had the kind of beauty which launched a thousand ships. The sister married when Emily was nineteen, and went to live in California. Until that time Emily lost all her beaux to the reigning belle with depressing regularity. Living in the same house with Helen of Troy was more competition than any merely pretty young miss could stand. Emily put a good face on it. She admired her sister to the point of adoration and joked about leading lambs to the slaughter whenever she brought home a boy friend of her own. Everyone commented on her beautiful character, so lacking in jealousy, and whispered that Emily wasn't the type to care for boys. Indeed, Emily studied nursing with intensity and planned to devote her life to her parents and to the care of the sick. Only three months after her sister's marriage, however, Emily suddenly married a doctor newly arrived at the local hospital. Fifteen years her senior, he appeared quite carried away by her youthful prettiness. Emily discovered in herself an unsuspected talent for loving. She was deliriously happy. Unfortunately the doctor was very busy. He was also older than the young married set into which Emily's school friends had grown. Really a stuffy sort of person when you came to live with him. Emily took to going out alone. Partly from convenience, partly from malice, partly from goodwill, people began pairing her with Harry Stevens, one of the few spare men in Charlottesville. One night, driving home in the summer night after dancing and a few highballs at the country club, Harry discovered that he was in love with Emily. It took only a couple of weeks for Emily to find out that she had made a ghastly mistake in marrying the doctor and that Harry was her predestined mate. Her mate he became in due process of law, after certain unpleasant preliminaries had been got through. After a few months it became apparent that while Harry was certainly more romantic than the doctor, he was by no means so good a provider. Emily complained about an income which was not only meagre but spasmodic. Harry was not appreciative of the unadorned stew she served up to him night after night. He neglected to bring home a cornflower to match her eyes or fluffy slippers for her dear little feet. They bickered about money, about Harry's personal untidiness, about his growing tendency to drop in at cocktail parties alone on his way home. Emily told all her friends that she had given up everything for Harry and that he had turned out to be a selfish brute.

We can omit the details of Emily's love for Stanley and Harold and Malcolm and Maurice, stalwart youths all, becoming perhaps a little less stalwart as Emily's prettiness declined. There is always some kind of man about to make love to the woman who wants love. Emily was not a conscious flirt. She never chased men, though occasionally one of them would be disconcerted by finding a routine flirtation transformed before his eyes to a grand passion. Nor did Emily marry or even sleep with all of these admirers. As she grew older she was more and more given to acts of noble renunciation. Three times at least she gave up the great love of her life out of pity for her current husband.[1]

The early hopeless competition with her sister was disastrous for Emily. Her situation was difficult at best and was not improved by her refusal to look at it squarely. She had every reason to hate her sister, who, however innocently, stole from Emily the masculine appreciation she would otherwise have received. But she did not hate her sister. Instead she hated herself. She grew up with the conviction, not wholly conscious, that she was dull, uninteresting, unattractive, and unlovable. Only the most hectic protestations of devotion and admiration could give her reassurance against this profound feeling of her own inadequacy. She loved the doctor, Harry, and the rest, not for themselves, but for the heightened self-appreciation they gave her. Naturally she could not tolerate the " disillusionment " of marriage. Ordinary affection and loyalty were not strong enough to keep at bay her distress about herself. Her numerous affairs meant to her not love but relief from feeling unvalued and unvaluable. The reasons she gave herself for the failure of her marriages were not the real reasons. Take, for example, her feeling that her first husband, the doctor, was too old and too busy to give her an adequate love relationship.

[1] I have deliberately left out of Emily's story a number of complicating factors for the sake of brevity and in order to lay bare the basic pattern of her relationship with men. Emily is a simple woman, as women go, but she is a more complex person than I have indicated. For purposes of clarity, however, I have dissected out one phase of her personality — and will continue to do so with most of the people who find their place in these pages.

Other women have married busy, older men. They have not enjoyed being neglected either, but they could put up with it because the marriage as a whole represented a fundamentally satisfying partnership. Probably they never thought of their husbands' preoccupation with their work as " neglect," but only as a vexatious fact — an annoying but necessary part of their way of life. In every marriage problems have these two facets: the real difficulty and the psychological meaning of that difficulty for the people involved — the *fact* of a busy husband and the interpretation of intolerable neglect. Of these two facets the latter is far more important. Suppose that Emily's doctor had decided to neglect his practice instead of his wife and had put himself at her disposal every evening. Emily would quickly have discovered a new grievance. He didn't notice her clothes, he forgot their anniversary, he acted bored with her friends, he seemed interested in another girl. Her own feeling of insecurity made her read neglect in any normal behaviour. Until she understands herself, the most perfect husband cannot create a " real " situation which will satisfy her. And when she does understand herself, she can tolerate and love a husband who is far from perfect.

Resentment against men is a frequent, perhaps constant accompaniment of this type of behaviour on the part of women who feel defeated like Emily. Sometimes the resentment is hidden. Emily was a mild, unprotesting person, so the resentment she quite naturally felt toward men for preferring her sister never came to the surface. With some women it forms a dominant and often perfectly conscious motive for revenge. The girl who has been jilted or somehow let down by a man (sometimes her father) will be compelled to prove her charm to herself and others by making men love her, time after time after time. As soon as her conquest is assured, she loses interest in the victim. Men show this type of sexual vanity quite as frequently as women. Almost always it can be traced back to the need to demonstrate beyond all shadow of doubt that the man is a powerful fellow and the woman devastatingly attractive. The man or woman who *knows* he or she is all right doesn't have to prove it. Unfortunately no actual conquest can allay these fears because they lie deeply buried at the core of the personality. Any number of victories fails to satisfy a boundless appetite for appreciation. Victory must follow victory to the point of exhaustion.

None of us is so smugly self-satisfied that we do not crave the reassurance of conquest. Every woman enjoys having men in love with her and every man is comfortably flattered when a girl falls for him. For most of us these gratifications are side lines. We put other values first — the warm loyalty of our marriage, our fondness for the children, our interest in a job, our companionship with friends. Mrs. Happily Married Brown may come home in a pleasant glow from a party where that handsome guest of the Joneses showed unmistakable signs of interest in her. But it would never occur to her to walk out on Mr. Brown and the children in order to maintain the glow or fan it to flame. That's just what Emily and people like her would do. The glow is so tremendously important to Emily, her husband and children so incidental to her deepest needs, that her marriage is threatened every time such a situation arises.

The person who must have glamour, who cannot take the disillusionment of settling down, is not ready for marriage. Divorce and a new deal will not help. Only a genuine acceptance of himself as he is, or at the very least a recognition of the irrelevance of his personal problem to the marriage situation, will bring stability into his married life.

Sage older women sometimes advise brides to keep the honeymoon shining by remaining not quite accessible to their husbands, by hiding even in matrimonial intimacy the machinery of their femininity,[2] by making themselves permanently costly, fragile, exquisite, and remotely desirable. If a husband never discovers that his wife is as human as himself, if he is always afraid of losing her to another man, if he is kept busy providing her with luxuries, then he will continue faithful and devoted. Men appreciate only what they pay for. They want only what they cannot have or what they fear will be taken from them.

I personally dislike this view of marriage intensely. It recommends a relationship based on conscious dishonesty.

---

[2] I remember a story-book wife who rose stealthily at dawn every morning to put on a fresh nightgown so that her husband should never guess that she crumpled it at night like an ordinary human. As I recall the story, the husband eventually left his superlatively dainty lady for a rather dowdy librarian who could talk with him companionably.

It deliberately fosters insecurity. The unfortunate husband is supposed to pass his life on the run in a constant state of anxiety and adoration. He must always live somewhat above himself emotionally, never be lulled into the comfort of feeling himself accepted for good or ill by his life's partner. The wife leads an equally strenuous existence. She is forbidden to relax into comfortable humanity. The siren role is very exacting. She comes to demand appreciation for her efforts. Like a prima donna who has failed to get a flattering number of curtain calls, she is apt to be resentful and hurt whenever her act doesn't come off, whenever her husband is too tired or bored to play up to her glamorous wiles.

My own distaste for this type of marriage is not important. More significant is the fact that in practice it doesn't work. A permanent, satisfying marriage must be an honest marriage. Both partners must be permitted to be themselves in full security and ease. The husband who is always kept on tiptoe will eventually tire of the awkward position. He will very likely drop to his heels in the company of a woman who allows a more comfortable gait. Or if he is the male counterpart of Emily and really prefers being on his toes (because he has a sore heel, as it were), he will hunt out a new lady who holds him up more easily. The most conscientiously glamorous wife cannot compete with a handsome rival in sheer romance. The other woman always has the advantage of novelty and usually that of youth and freedom from responsibility as well.

No, the wife who wants to hold her husband must be

primarily a wife and not a mistress. A remote mysterious angel is intriguing for a few weeks, but an awkward life companion.

Must we then give up all idea of romance after the honeymoon and settle down to unrelieved concentration on the more lasting values of marriage? Must the stable wife see her husband only as a satisfactory, though some-what crotchety, partner in the business of life? Must she be constantly and exclusively aware of his annoying habit of dropping his clothes on the bedroom floor, of the inti-mations of a pot belly in his figure, of his sturdy worth as a responsible member of the community? Is it necessary for her to see herself with monotonous honesty as a woman of not more than average prettiness, lacking in brilliance as a hostess, at times inexcusably irritable with the children, a shabby enough little figure compared with Marlene Die-trich or even the gracious ladies of the ads?

Maybe there are some sober folks who can subsist on a diet of sensible regard for each other, the same people perhaps who plan their activities so carefully that they never have to take a taxi to keep an appointment on time or stay up late to finish a report or worry about turning up in a dress suit when they should have realized the party would be informal. Most of us are not so even in our mood. Five days out of the week we plug along without thinking or feeling very much about our job or our marriage, or anything — just doing whatever has to be done the best we can. The sixth day we're fed to the teeth, bored and irritable with everything. And the seventh day we're as keen on the job as any youngster and as much in love with our wives as the day we got engaged. I don't mean, of course, that we set aside Tuesday for irritability and Friday for romance. But there are days or moments when the old mood of glamour and delight takes posses- sion of us again, enriched by the associations of marriage perhaps, but still lifting us out of our humdrum selves. These moods don't make a marriage, but they are a lovely and valid part of the most stable and healthily " disillu- sioned " relationship. Life is much more fun when you can take your wife out dancing and feel that she really is the most charming creature you ever saw and you're a pretty interesting fellow yourself and love is wonderful. Or whatever your formula for romance is. The fact that she looks a little blowsy when she gets you a Bromo-Seltzer next morning is irrelevant, unless you still have the child- ish longing to live above yourself twenty-four hours a day every day. Glamour in marriage cannot be continuous, but it needn't be absent. The morning after does not destroy the reality and value of the night before.

Of course, it takes two to make romance, and the mood of two people doesn't always overlap. My wife complains that every time she orders oysters and champagne and puts on her best dinner dress just for the two of us I call up and say I am detained at the office by an emergency. I have noticed myself that when I come home early with flowers for the loveliest girl I know, I find her bawling out the kids like a fishwife and apologetic about stew for supper. Both of us in turn feel let down and sore. When we plan to go to the theatre Saturday night alone it's just as bad. The baby runs a fever and my wife insists upon calling up during every intermission to make sure she's all right. Or a patient gets in a jam and I do the calling up and maybe miss the last act entirely.

But " every time " is an exaggeration. Often enough I do fall into the mood of my wife's little dinner, and the theatre party does turn out well, or just an ordinary late Sunday breakfast with the kids at Sunday school will suddenly turn into one of those leisurely honeymoon affairs. Even the failures have their merit. After I get over being cross about the reception my flowers got, I remember the champagne I gave up to take care of a patient and feel warm again. These ups and downs are part of marriage. A true disillusionment will recognize the moments of rapture and the moments of disappointment and the strong undercurrent of partnership in the run-of-the-mine emotions of daily life.

There is also the question of glamour outside of marriage. An old song runs:

> If in your heart one corner lies
> That has no room for me
> You do not love me as I deem
> True love should ever be . . .
> You do not love me, no!
> Bid me good-bye and go.

To this exacting young lady I reply: " Bushwah." No man is so deeply in love with his wife that he loses his eye for a pair of pretty legs wherever he finds them — unless he's the sort of man who never notices his wife's legs either. A lady with a worried air said to me: "Whenever I'm feeling particularly keen about my husband I start behaving like a schoolgirl with other men, kissing in the moonlight and that sort of nonsense. I fall for sweet nothings like a ton of bricks. Does that mean I don't really love my husband?"

Not at all. Happily married people are by no means impervious to the romantic attractions of outsiders. Indeed, I sometimes think that the woman who has developed strong sex feeling in the arms of her husband is somewhat more susceptible to other men than the woman to whom sex has proved a disappointment. Moreover, however attractive a husband may be, he is *ipso facto* not a new story, and we have already described the contribution sheer novelty makes to a love relationship. If we were picking reading matter for a winter in Little America we would take with us the Bible and Shakspeare and the Iliad. We recognize and enjoy their permanent value. Here at home the most highbrow literati are not above chuckling over an ephemeral paragraph in the *New Yorker*. Flirtations are ephemeral, but many married folk find them amusing and seem to be none the worse for them.

When the marriage is really stable, however, these extra-marital adventures are not compulsive. We can take them or leave them with small disappointment. We can be pleasantly thrilled about the other woman without for a moment considering throwing over our marriage for her or even changing our affection for our wife. Or — if it seems best — we can give up the whole thing the way we give up a trip to Europe that runs counter to the plans of the family. The renunciation may be disagreeable, but it is not " noble " like Emily's because we do not fool ourselves into believing that we are giving up a great love.

The first step, then, toward permanent and satisfying marriage is disillusionment, the willingness to accept oneself and one's partner on the level of everyday living, to take the worse along with the better.

꙳

CHAPTER III

THE OTHER WOMAN

Disillusionment, willingness to accept marriage for better and for worse as the framework of our daily lives, is only the first step toward a satisfying union. Many couples feel that they have long ago renounced all impossible romanticism. Their expectations in marriage have become humble indeed. They are ready enough to take the worse along with the better, but they say ruefully that they really would like a little better along with the worse. Marriage for them has degenerated into a constant and painful struggle, unrelieved by tenderness, loyalty, or passion. Looking at their problems realistically only makes them seem more disheartening because they appear to proceed inevitably from the necessary circumstances of daily living or from a fundamental " incompatibility " of character.

The Browns live with Mrs. Brown's people because they cannot afford a home of their own. Mr. Brown so resents his wife's divided loyalties that their marriage is embittered by constant quarrels. Mrs. Jones solves the financial problem by working herself, but her husband is jealous of her success and feels himself woefully neglected. Mrs. Jones herself is exhausted and irritable most of the time from the strain of carrying two sets of responsibilities, her home and her business. The Smiths hurt each other because they have no children, and Mrs. Dudley leaves her husband because they cannot agree on methods of handling their three boys. The Lewises are mismated sexually. Infidelity breaks up the Parker home. The root of the difficulty between the Fosters seems to be a difference in temperament. Mrs. Foster likes to entertain lavishly and gad about while her husband prefers sitting cosily at home with the newspaper.

All these problems — and a thousand others like them — are problems of ordinary living. The most sensible, unromantic couples often have to face them. Should they accept marriage based upon continual struggle as the " framework of their daily lives "? Are there not practical situations so difficult that a harmonious union becomes impossible; temperaments so hopelessly incompatible that no basis remains for friendly co-operation in living together? Often divorce seems to be the only resource for people who simply make each other miserable.

Now, no doubt some marriages cannot and should not be maintained. Financial worry, an over-dose of in-laws, childlessness, and the like put a severe strain on a union which might otherwise prove reasonably comfortable. Yet many couples are drawn closer together by poverty and adversity. Incompatibility of temperament would seem to be a more basic problem. It may happen that one or both partners are not ready for any sort of integrated life with another person, much less to withstand with his partner the slings and arrows of outrageous fortune. Indeed, when we think back on the long and intricate emotional preparation for marriage described in the first chapter it seems miraculous that any of us emerges with enough flexibility and warmth to make a success of so intimate a relationship. None of us has in fact outgrown childish attitudes completely, and a few of us hold on to early phases of our emotional development so tenaciously that we cannot accept the mature give and take of marriage. The child who has learned a thoroughgoing distrust of love in his relationship with his mother does not easily relax in the affection of his wife, even though she may give him a greater measure of devotion than is common. I do not mean that his childish attitude persists unchanged throughout the years. A youngster who expects rebuffs is always confirmed in his expectations. His belligerent behaviour may bring him more than his share of enmity, or he may see hostility even in friendly acts. Thus his original distrust is intensified and elaborated as he grows older. The marriage of such a person is apt to be stormy and may become intolerable, whatever the actual circumstances of his lot in life. He complains that his wife does not love him, deceives him, or neglects him, but a second marriage will usually prove just as disappointing. He carries his feeling of neglect with him. He is not ready for marriage.

There are some people who are ready for marriage, but only to a specially and carefully selected partner. They are compatible only with certain other personalities. Two "decent human beings," both reasonably mature, find themselves at odds with each other whereas they get along well with other people. The combination in marriage is not easily workable. A man who hates to be bossed bitterly resents the mothering attitude of his wife, but there are many other men who crave just the protecting love she has to give. An artistic soul may be irritated to the point of murder by a practically-minded spouse who would make another type of man an admirably sensible wife.

Utterly hopeless situations of incompatibility or of sheer unreadiness for marriage do occur. It is my experience, however, that they are rare. Many couples come to me on the verge of separation, usually after a long period of quarrels and dissatisfaction. They tell me a story of the kind I have outlined and ask my advice as to whether or not they should take the final step of divorce. Now, advice is a commodity which I use very sparingly. I usually urge these people to talk out their problems with me and see for themselves what they are really about. Sometimes they come to me half a dozen times — sometimes for several months. When they are finally clear about their own attitudes, they decide the question of divorce for themselves. Thus far every couple has had no hesitation about continuing marriage. Thus far. Perhaps tomorrow I shall encounter the hopelessly mismated pair who find their way out in divorce. I hold no brief against divorce as such. But if the experience of psychiatrists dealing with marital maladjustment means anything at all, it means that most of our divorces are a needless waste of human happiness.

In the following chapters we are to examine many of the problem areas of marriage in detail and try to discover the means of salvaging potentially happy unions from failure. According to the law of many countries and states sexual disharmony in the form of adultery is the only marital problem sufficiently serious to warrant dissolution of the marriage bond. Out of respect for legal precedent we will begin our discussion of trouble-breeding areas with a consideration of sex. This chapter will be duly restricted to the legally proper cause of divorce: infidelity. In the next chapter we will take up the question of sex adjustment between man and wife. Most people, even though they protest against the naïve single-mindedness of the law, feel that sexual compatibility is after all a fundamental requirement for successful marriage. Physical attraction between a man and a woman, they say, is not enough to ensure a stable, satisfying union perhaps, but failure in sexual relations is a threat of the first magnitude to happiness in other aspects of married life. Some earnest thinkers go so far as to recommend that young people make sure of their sexual suitability for each other by conscientious experimentation before marriage. Such premarital freedom is, however, conceived as a guarantee against infidelity after marriage. The most liberal minds frown upon infringement of monogamy. Unfaithfulness is scarcely less tolerated by popular feeling than by legal decree. It is generally considered a perfectly adequate reason for breaking up a marriage. The wife or husband of an erring spouse is regularly the "injured" party. She (or he) is expected to take a strong stand of aggrieved indignation or melancholy though noble forgiveness. If she decides upon divorce her friends understand and approve her action.

It is my professional experience, however, that sexual maladjustment, including infidelity, is seldom a primary cause of marital discord. Let me cite the experience of the Caswells. Louise Caswell dropped in to visit one of her friends unexpectedly and found her own husband in familiar possession of the bedroom. She went home, packed up the wayward man's things, sent them to his club, called on her lawyer, and instituted divorce proceedings. A week later she called on her doctor to get a sleeping-powder. The kindly physician persuaded her to try psychiatry instead of bromides and so it happened that she talked over her problem with me. Now, the interesting thing about her talks with me is this: Mrs. Caswell was divorcing her husband because he betrayed her under very humiliating circumstances. Yet the question of her husband's infidelity was scarcely mentioned after the first quarter of an hour. This transgression was actually so insignificant a factor in their disturbed relationship that she herself quickly lost sight of it. Indeed, her occasional references to it showed more than a trace of triumph and pleasure. She was in a way glad to have a definite acceptable grievance, to be put incontrovertibly in the right. She enjoyed feeling so righteous in her indignation. Behind the scenes this marriage had been for years embittered by a subterranean struggle for supremacy between man and wife. Both of them were sensitive and ambitious — a not unusual combination of traits. They needed each other badly, but had at the same time developed a competitive relationship. Each one was trying in little ways, not wholly conscious, to get ahead of the other, to be more admired and respected by the world. Naturally each resented the competitiveness of the other. The details of the struggle between these two nice people are irrelevant. Later on I will describe similar conflicts in detail. The point at issue is the part the husband's infidelity played in the situation. Mr. Caswell had begun the flirtation chiefly to annoy his wife, as it were. He had continued it partly because the girl's infatuation gave him relief at least for the moment from the effort to prove himself superior to his wife, and partly because he was still enjoying this indirect attack on his wife. The whole episode was no more important psychologically to either of them than a hundred little sallies and quarrels which had preceded it. The husband's " affair " and the wife's method of handling it were just a bigger and better fight between them. Legally and socially it provided " grounds for divorce " and assumed the proportions of a major catastrophe.

This story has a happy ending. Taking stock of their relationship during this period of violent disruption had a sobering effect on the Caswells. They came together again with a greater feeling of their need for each other and greater understanding of the impulses which led them to fight each other. As a matter of fact they went home, made a baby, and lived happily ever after. Not wholly without friction of course, but with a firm reliance on the fundamental cohesion of their marriage.

It is clear that infidelity was not the primary cause of the suit for divorce even though neither Mr. nor Mrs. Caswell had ever thought of divorce before. Their marriage was already going on the rocks. Both of them used the " other woman " as a weapon in their battle against each other. A big bombing aeroplane may demolish the last defences of a city and lay it open to destruction, but the bomber is not the cause of the attack, or even in itself responsible for the success of the campaign. The war in the Caswell household, like most wars, was caused by rivalry between the two interested parties, rivalry based on the desire of both to have first place in the sun. Steady bombardment with smaller guns, sniping at vulnerable points, minor offensives and counter-offensives had been going on for years. Mr. Caswell's affair was merely another attack, somewhat more vigorous than the others. Mrs. Caswell's drastic reply (sending his clothes to the club and beginning divorce proceedings) was her strong counter-attack. Both of them were trying to punish the other and demonstrate their own superiority just as they had scores of times before.

Mrs. Caswell might actually have put through her divorce if she had not taken time out to talk over her marriage with a psychiatrist. Or she might not.

Psychologically nothing desperate had happened, nothing different in kind from all that had gone before. Mrs.

Caswell still loved her husband, needed him, and hated him. Socially her discovery of the infidelity was a major catastrophe. Her friends, her family, even her servants and tradespeople would encourage her feeling of indignation and push her toward divorce. Tolerating known faithlessness is itself a social and moral offence. It takes a great deal of personal courage and strong convictions to resist public opinion of this nature. Mrs. Caswell's convictions were not strong. Her love for her husband was already confused by her rivalry with him. Nor was she very courageous. A large part of her struggle with her husband was due to her feeling of insecurity, her need to be approved of and admired superlatively by society, as well as by her husband. Social pressure would probably have tipped the precarious balance of this marriage toward divorce.

Mrs. Caswell's own reaction to her husband's behaviour was strongly influenced by the attitude of our society toward infidelity. Like all of us she had been taught from childhood that the emotions appropriate to this situation are jealousy, indignation, and hurt of a very special kind. Whenever she read a book or went to the movies, she was reminded that sexual betrayal is the worst possible affront to marriage. She was told subtly and continually that if she were normal she would feel jealous and mortally insulted. Quite naturally, therefore, Mrs. Caswell developed the proper emotions when she found out about her husband's infidelity. She was angry and hurt and jealous and felt that " this was the end." She acted upon this conception of her reaction to the extent of seeing her lawyer.

Only in her talks with me she soon forgot all about these conventional emotions. She learned that her own native feelings for her husband were much more compelling than society's rules and regulations as to how a betrayed wife should feel. Other episodes, other aspects of her relationship with her husband, came to the fore. Mrs. Caswell was not really a jealous woman. Her recriminations against her husband centred in the idea that he had treated her like a brute, not the fact that he had slept with another woman. In other words, her jealousy was social, not sexual.

Nevertheless, the high valuation placed upon sexual fidelity by our society makes transgression in this field a particularly serious threat to marriage. Mrs. Caswell, because of direct social pressure and the attitudes she herself had developed from social propaganda, reacted with more violence to the discovery of unfaithfulness than to any other attack her husband might have made upon her. A marriage which still possessed many constructive aspects, which was perhaps as satisfying as any marriage could be for these two people, very nearly came to an end when they took up weapons from the sexual field to carry on their struggle with each other.

So much for the Caswells. They have taught us, I think, that adultery means more than sexual attraction to the "other woman" followed by jealousy on the part of the injured wife. These factors, commonly considered all-important, may be relatively insignificant. Many men withstand varying degrees of sexual attraction to other women

out of loyalty to their wives or to their own ideals of marriage. Many women know that their husbands are unfaithful or given to milder forms of philandering, but
do not send them packing. They usually (not always)
feel jealous and hurt, but their feelings do not swamp
the marriage. Rather common in our culture is the wife
who enjoys the full respect and strong affection of her
husband, but who sees him turn to the Follies chorus
for light-hearted sexual amusement. She knows that none
of the little ladies of the evening threatens her marriage.
Her husband's taste for them may seem to her very distressing, but if his relationship to her is firmly established
and satisfying to both, she will not upset the apple-cart in
her indignation. A great many men, graduates of the
gutter school of sex education mentioned in our first chapter, associate physical enjoyment with vulgarity. It may
be impossible for them to bring their wives to the level
of their conception of amusing sexuality because of their
idealistic picture of marriage. Or the wife herself may be
offended when her husband expresses this taste for smuttiness in his approach to her. It is very natural that the husband should, under these circumstances, seek another more
suitable outlet for his " lower " impulses, or at least should
in imagination follow out his childish notion of sex as a
delightful but surreptitious and not nice activity. These
attitudes are unfortunate, but they need not wreck a marriage. Until sex education is put on an entirely different
footing, they are bound to occur. Probably, indeed, what
we call human nature would have to be modified funda-

mentally before they could be eliminated entirely. People do find a special value in the forbidden — women no less than men. We shall see in the next chapter how this taste for vulgarity and cruelty can be woven into a happy sex relationship between husband and wife.

I have given only one or two examples of the special meaning extramarital affairs may have for a couple. There are almost as many meanings as there are couples in the world. Infidelity may be an attack upon the wife, a refuge from her, an attempt to prove one's manliness, a revolt against childish taboos, a method of working out impulses arising from early experiences, an act of revenge either upon the other woman, the wife, or women in general, the gratification of a physical urge uninhibited by moral scruples — almost anything. It may take the form of frank adultery, promiscuous " necking," flirtatiousness, or merely frequent daydreaming about the desirability of other women. The *fact* of infidelity is relatively unimportant to the stability of marriage. What matters to the relationship is its *meaning,* the motive behind the man's defection and the interpretation both of them put upon his act. The slightest flirtation may be a major calamity for some couples, whereas others can tolerate a large amount of " playing around " without serious dismay.

I am frequently asked whether I believe in monogamy. As a husband I have to settle that question like anyone else in terms of my own ideals, my own personality and milieu, my own relationship with my wife. But as a psychiatrist I don't have to answer it. A code of behaviour in which one family finds its greatest happiness might break up another group of people overnight. My job is to help my patients work out the kind of marriage they want, not the kind I fancy for myself. Through me they can learn something of the real meaning monogamy or infidelity has for them. Usually the problem solves itself once it is clearly understood. The chap who has been proving his masculinity in the arms of numerous women no longer needs their reassurance after he has fully realized that he is a normal male after all. If he wants to continue his affairs, that is his business. My contribution ends when he is no longer driven into promiscuity by unconscious fear of impotence, but is in a position to make a sensible, workable choice himself. My contribution is exactly the same to the man who goes into a blind panic whenever a woman other than his wife smiles at him. It would be bad psychiatry for me to tell him either to sleep with the lady or to keep away from her — he is probably incapable of following either plan. My responsibility in treatment consists in helping him get rid of the panic that devastates his relationship to women. After treatment he may still elect monogamy, but he will not be forced into chastity by his terror of women or of his own unrecognized impulses toward them.

Speaking as a psychiatrist interested only in helping people find permanent satisfactions in marriage, I cannot in general recommend either sexual freedom or strict faithfulness as a general mode of conduct. I know many marriages where freedom seems to have acted as a disruptive force. I know others where the practice of monogamy built up such deep resentments against the partner in marriage that the union went to pieces. Mrs. Arkwright, after a few unpleasant scenes with her husband, gave up her accustomed charming flirtatiousness in favour of rigid decorum. Unfortunately she felt that she was making a very considerable sacrifice to her partner's silly whim, whereas Mr. Arkwright took her reformed behaviour merely as his due. The lady became more and more bored with the flatness of her social relations and increasingly aggrieved at her husband's unappreciative attitude. The marriage did not develop happily. A woman who renounces a really important love relationship for the sake of her husband or her ideal of wedlock can scarcely help making excessive demands on the marriage by way of compensation and naturally comes to resent unduly its inevitable shortcomings. Monogamy does not in itself solve the triangular or polygonal situations which occur and recur in most marriages. Neither does freedom. The most broad-minded husband or wife is likely to be profoundly upset when infidelity actually takes place.

A great many people in our hypocritical society attempt to reconcile monogamy with freedom by pretending to the former while actually enjoying the latter. In practice this solution appears to work as well and as badly as any other. It is based on the theory that what people don't know won't hurt them. Neither will they be able to retaliate. Many men, obviously, conceal their adventures because they are afraid of their wives and afraid of social condemnation.

Perhaps this motive of practical self-protection is never entirely absent, but it rarely operates alone. Faithless husbands and wives usually wish to spare their partners the pain of jealousy. The extramarital adventure frequently seems to its chief actor quite irrelevant to his marriage. He knows that it is transitory and unimportant, or at least wholly distinct from his family responsibilities. He feels perfectly capable of handling the situation himself without harm to anyone. He does not expect his wife to accept his transgression so calmly. She would naturally be unable to understand his point of view. She would suffer from a sense of betrayal, would be hurt and distressed out of all proportion to his real intention. Most of us have a tendency to believe that laws are for other people. We think ourselves well able to control the essentials of a situation without adherence to strict rule, whereas we are terrified when anyone we care for takes similar liberties. The erring husband maintains the rules of monogamy for the rest of the world while he orders his own life as he thinks best. He protects his wife from unnecessary pain by concealing his own freedom.

The husband usually feels, moreover, that his sexual conduct is his own affair. As a mature man he does not have to give an account of himself to his wife or to anyone else. Reticence about his love life is a mark of independence and self-sufficiency.

Sometimes this procedure works very well. I suspect, however, that it works well only in those marriages which are fundamentally sound anyway. A man who is genuinely fond of his wife, thoroughly responsible as a husband, and well integrated as a personality can handle hidden deviations from monogamy adequately. If the marriage is already disturbed, however, or if the man is himself very much upset by his behaviour, the results of concealment are often as unhappy as they are unexpected. To understand these results fully we must bear in mind what we have learned of the part unconscious motives play in our behaviour. We saw that faithlessness is sometimes an attack upon the wife — as it was for Mr. Caswell. Now, an attack is not successful if the victim knows nothing about it. The husband, therefore, must bring his infidelity to her attention. This whole process is, of course, unconscious. He is not aware, usually, that he is attacking his wife in the first place, and he is certainly trying to maintain secrecy. Nevertheless he manages " accidentally " to give himself away. Mrs. Caswell told me, for instance, that she had actually mentioned to her husband at breakfast her plan to visit her friend during the afternoon. He " forgot " this important bit of information entirely. A mere whim led him to leave his business and call upon the lady at that particular moment. This behaviour sounds very much like the experiment in posthypnotic suggestion, doesn't it? A powerful unconscious impulse led him to the meeting with his wife, although he told himself that he had been working too steadily and deserved a little relaxation with his friend. Certainly many apparently accidental discoveries of infidelity are actually brought about in this way by the husband, in spite of his careful efforts to avoid detection.

Unexpected discoveries of this nature are peculiarly devastating to a marriage. The wife has to endure not only her jealousy but the sense of having been lied to and betrayed. It is hard for her to regain confidence in the honesty of her relationship with her husband. Any doubts she may already have about him become focused and exaggerated by this experience.

Even when the secret is kept, the marriage frequently suffers from concealed infidelity. If the husband feels very guilty about his actions, another problem arises. People who feel guilty *want* punishment. Some religions recognize this basic human need by providing a system of voluntary penances for wrongdoing. Men who have committed a crime not infrequently give themselves up to justice even though they have successfully evaded the police and are in no danger of being apprehended. Punishment relieves guilt. If the unfortunate husband cannot confess his sexual transgression, he may misbehave in other ways in order to call down upon his head the condemnation he thinks he deserves. Buying the wife a fur coat is a common gesture — a sort of *fine* for a misdemeanour. The gesture is often made even when the wife suspects nothing and does not need to be placated. Gross lack of consideration is frequently a means of provoking an indignation which the wife should feel toward his faithlessness and cannot feel because she knows nothing about it.

These illustrations will serve to show the kind of tension which may develop in marriage when infidelity is concealed. They are merely illustrations. Different personalities have different problems and work them out in a variety of ways. Strain of some kind between husband and wife is none the less a frequent accompaniment of unfaithfulness even though it is carefully hidden from view.

Frankness about interest in other women, on the other hand, is attended by its own dangers. They do, indeed, appear so threatening that few couples are bold enough to try this method of handling the problem. Some say it is like sticking your head in the noose to tell your wife about her rivals. This criticism is valid. The emotions attached to infidelity are very intense. Even if a person is not naturally jealous, he has been taught from childhood that he should be. Even if he has intellectually repudiated society's viewpoint, he cannot easily rid himself of feelings so deeply ingrained. Most of us know young couples who have decided that monogamy is an absurd limitation. They enter upon experiments in freedom with the full knowledge and consent of their partner in marriage. More often than not the results are distressing. They are unable to preserve their fine logical detachment in the face of actual infidelity. Few of us can really be objective and rational about sex. Frankness does lay the marriage open to unexpectedly violent reactions of jealousy and indignation.

Other people say that it is cruel or babyish to "tell." It is true that some people confess in order to receive absolution. They are not strong enough to flaunt social taboos without the support of their wives. Other men take an obscure pleasure in tormenting their wives with jealousy. Jealousy is a proof of love — or at least it is so considered by many people. Men who are uncertain about the affection of their wives gain reassurance from their jealousy and at the same time punish them for lack of love. Flirtation based upon this motive is perhaps more common among wives than among husbands. Sometimes it is a perfectly conscious technique, but often the woman is quite unaware of the fact that she is trying to hurt her husband or stimulate his love by her accounts of amorous passages with other men.

Exponents of frankness about sex matters usually declare that honesty is all-important in marriage and that deceit is intolerable between two people who love each other. Emotional problems, however painful, should be worked out together. One woman told me that she lay awake in agony every time her husband spent the evening with another girl, but she still insisted on being informed of his activities. She could bear even less the idea that he might be with the girl when he said he was tied up with a business conference. So long as she had his confidence she felt that she also had his love and that her dignity as wife and companion was unimpaired. Study of this marriage showed that it was not as honest as the good lady believed. Her husband, without being wholly aware of his feelings, resented somewhat the close, dependent relationship she exacted. His frankness contained an element of punishment for his wife. Indeed, his interest in other women was based in part on an unwitting desire to hurt his wife and prove his independence. The wife herself, since she denied direct expression to her indignation about her husband's behaviour, was often unreasonably vexed by trivial actions. I do not mean that the problems of this couple would have been solved by greater reticence nor even by perfect monogamy. I mention their difficulties merely to show that verbal frankness does not necessarily mean an honest relationship.

Frankness may be the most satisfactory method of handling the problem of infidelity for some couples. It never solves the problem completely and sometimes appears to make matters worse. Neither frankness nor concealment can be recommended in principle as the method of choice. Married people will do better, I think, to follow the course of procedure that seems to them individually natural and right rather than to base their decision on elaborate theorizing.

This discussion of extramarital relationships may sound pretty gloomy. I am stating frankly that emotional entanglements of greater or less severity (not necessarily culminating in technical infidelity) are very apt to occur in the best-regulated of marriages, and that there is no ideal way of handling them. Monogamy and freedom, concealment and frankness, all lead to unhappy consequences. The discussion is gloomy, however, only if you demand of marriage a vapid perfection. Gliding slowly along smooth unfrequented city avenues in a closed limousine saves you the bumps and dangers of the open highway, but it's not much fun. If we want the flavour and richness of a real marriage in a real world we have to accept jolts and risks as part of our experience. There is no escape from the complicated joys and sorrows of marriage. We must accept the jangling, painful aspects of a relationship along with the harmonious intimacy. A good marriage is none the worse for periods of jealousy and resentment and struggle. The grave danger of most extramarital relationships, platonic or not, is that we take them too seriously. The motorist is so disturbed by occasional rough roads that he renounces his whole journey, so appalled by a bashed-in fender that he refuses to drive a car again.

I think that this rather discursive treatment of faithlessness in marriage yields several points of general helpfulness to married folk. One is a recognition of the frequency of the problem. The pain of divided love is easier to bear if we realize that we share it with a great many other people, that we are not singled out for special punishment because of our own inadequacies. Almost all men and women, regardless of the intensity of their love for each other, do have impulses toward infidelity. They are by no means granted physical expression in all or even in the majority of marriages. Indeed, very often the sexual basis of attraction to another person is very attenuated or wholly unconscious. While most of us have a romantic yearning for absolute single-heartedness in our mate, complete devotion is beyond human power. We would do well to prize the strong loyalty and affection and love which we have rather than torment ourselves and our partners with demands for the unattainable. A happy marriage accepts the fact that union between two people cannot be complete and contents itself with a firm, human attachment. Much of the poison of jealousy can be extracted by recognizing it as a natural, frequent, and relatively unimportant concomitant of marriage.

Another protection against the dangers of infidelity is to keep clear of society's steam-roller attitude. We don't have to whip ourselves into a lather of indignation about every deviation from pure monogamy just because we have been taught to believe that unfaithfulness is a sin and a betrayal. Too often nice people are stampeded into a divorce by an episode which really doesn't matter very terribly. They are devastated by emotions which they think they *should* feel, which they cultivate as *normal,* when their genuine reactions are much more tolerant and understanding or even indifferent. One is not more " normal " because one feels jealous or less " normal " because one doesn't. People differ in the degree of their emotional reactions to infidelity as they do in everything else. Some of us are profoundly disturbed by the slightest infringement of an exclusive love. Some of us are not affected at all by the wanderings of our spouses. Most of us fall between these extremes. We are upset to varying degrees, but usually not so deeply as we think. Let us take time to consult our own feelings in the matter and not allow our friends or the movies to impose upon us emotions which are not our own. Without pretending that we don't care at all, without adopting an attitude of impossible nobility compounded of forgiveness and understanding, we can usually absorb these shocks to our marriage just as we handle problems of a non-sexual character.

The third suggestion I have to make is that we examine into the meaning of the acts of faithlessness for our own marriage. We have seen that their significance almost always goes far beyond mere sexual urgency. Often analysis of their deeper function will relieve some of the strain on marriage. For instance, in periods of severe strain a man will frequently seek reassurance of his power by conquering women sexually. During the depression many men whose self-confidence was undermined by their vocational failure sought to re-establish it by sexual prowess. Since their wives were also suffering from curtailment of income — doing their own work, giving up many cherished activities — the poor women were apt to feel aggrieved even beyond the ordinary by their husbands' unfeeling behaviour. " The least he can do to show his appreciation of my sacrifice," they argued, " is to be loyal to me." Some felt that the disloyalty came because they no longer had leisure or money to make themselves sufficiently attractive, and were correspondingly humiliated and hurt. If these women realized that the sight of their sacrifices intensified their husbands' feeling of inadequacy, they would understand better the masculine need to regain mastery in some form or other. To be sure, these husbands *should* not seek to restore their self-respect in any such silly, childish fashion, but they *do,* since they are human beings instead of supermen. Their action does not mean to them a repudiation of their wives. It is not a major crime against their marriage and should not be so interpreted if the union is to survive the combined strain of depression and infidelity. Understanding of the significance of their husbands' behaviour makes the position of these wives much more endurable. They will be hurt in any case, but not intolerably. In addition to the hurt they will also have increased sympathy and lessened resentment.

Understanding the meaning of an episode of infidelity may also reveal danger spots which should be corrected if the marriage is to endure. Mr. Caswell's behaviour showed up clearly the competitive, hurtful aspects of his relationship to his wife. These two people needed to achieve a more complete acceptance of each other, of their partnership, to see their marriage more in terms of mutual support than as a battle for supremacy. Very often under the stimulus of a major threat like infidelity a couple can examine for themselves the areas of struggle in their relationship and arrive at a satisfying resolution of their conflicting attitudes. Sometimes these attitudes are too deeply buried for recognition. Or they may be so thoroughly incorporated in the personality of either partner or both that mere reflection and conscious effort cannot change them. The help of a psychiatrist may then be necessary to straighten out the situation.

Looking over this chapter, I find I have spoken as if the husband had a monopoly on extramarital affairs while the wife remains the "injured party." Of course, their roles are frequently reversed. Everything I have said applies to the betrayed husband as fully as to the lonely wife. In communities where the "double standard" is firmly held, the husband has a difficult time maintaining his emotional independence in the face of strong public censure of the erring wife, but our three recommendations still hold. He must take time to examine his relationship with his wife honestly and without prejudice or blind anger before smashing the marriage to bits.

I should like to state once more that I have omitted all discussion of the moral and social implications of infidelity, not because they are unimportant, but because they are outside the province of the psychiatrist. Each couple must decide these matters for itself. I have not provided a formula for avoiding or handling emotional entanglements. I do not take much stock in logical discourses on the sanctity of the home, the beauty of perfect monogamy, or the richness of varied emotional and sexual experiences. Perhaps, though, I do believe, even as a psychiatrist, in the sanctity of the home — that is, in fostering a workable, satisfying relationship between the man and woman who have taken each other in marriage. Such a relationship is not cut to a single pattern out of whole cloth, but must be specially designed for each couple out of the stuff both partners bring to the marriage. The design may feature monogamy or freedom or any variation you please, but it must *fit*. Ready-to-wear garments, however exquisite in themselves, almost always require alterations to suit the individual customer. You may choose monogamy as the general style of your garment, but don't be afraid to take in a few tucks where necessary.

CHAPTER IV

֍

SEXUAL SATISFACTION

SOONER or later — usually sooner — the people who come to my office in distress about their marriage tell me that their sex life is not going very well. Complaints and worries are brought forth in bewildering variety. One woman tells me that her husband expects her to give him sex too often. She is sure that frequent indulgence will be bad for his health as well as hers. Or she may feel that a man needs intercourse more than a woman and fears that if she refuses his advances she will injure him physically and lessen his love for her. And perhaps drive him to other women. Or she resents his demands as an attack upon her more spiritual nature. Another lady confides that her husband doesn't make love to her enough. Her sexual appetite is greater than his. Sometimes she censures herself for being coarse and unfeminine and sometimes reproaches her husband for being less manly than he should be. Some husbands tell me that their wives are never really interested, that they submit to intercourse with dignified acquiescence when they cannot manage to get out of it. " If only she would seduce me sometimes, or even show that she wanted me." Whereas other men object to the initiative shown by their wives. They want a soft, yielding woman. They are shocked and resentful when she makes advances herself, or even when she enjoys herself in a way which they consider " unwomanly." Some wives are scandalized by " indecent proposals " from their husbands, and others weep because they have been cruelly rebuffed by a puritanical man for acts which seemed to them natural and good. Some complain that their men are too brutal, others that they are too tender. One woman longs for a little romance and idealism in her sex life, while her sister craves from her man roughness and egoism. Women frequently find that their husbands reach a climax too soon, before they are ready for completion themselves. But others state that their orgasm comes quickly and they become fatigued and bored when the act is protracted as long as the husband wishes.

Every couple has its own story of sexual disharmony. The details are not important. The fact that some form of maladjustment in the sexual field occurs in almost every case of disturbed marital relationship is very striking.

Many people very naturally conclude that sexual maladjustment is a *cause* of marital discord, since examination of disturbed marriages so constantly reveals lack of harmony and pleasure in physical relations. Logicians have a word for such conclusions. They call them specimens of the *post hoc propter hoc* fallacy. Situation B always develops *after* Situation A. Therefore Situation A is the *cause* of Situation B. Now the appearance of snowstorms is regularly preceded by the dropping of leaves from the trees. Nevertheless we do not consider the fall of leaves responsible for snow. We know very well that the coming of winter produces both these effects. Just so it may be that some fundamental struggle between husband and wife brings about both sexual disharmony and the other evidences of discord which make them consider their marriage a failure. Actually the relationship between sexual incompatibility and the failure of a marriage is very intricate. I believe that close study of the problem will show us that it is both cause and effect, and also perhaps just an accompaniment, an expression of general lack of harmony. We will do well to give up the idea of finding the *cause* of marital difficulties in sex or in anything else. Instead let us simply look at the intimate relations of married couples, both happy and disturbed, and try to understand them. We will find, I think, that sexual maladjustment, like infidelity, has a different meaning for every marriage. There is no such thing as Ideal Sex Life in the abstract, but only sex life which is good and satisfying to the people who are living it. The same physical acts delightful to one couple can be frustrating and unpleasant to another.

I said that almost all dissatisfied spouses complained about the sexual activities of their mate. Now, in the course of treatment I have commonly observed a very interesting phenomenon. Usually the sexual behaviour of the spouse does not change, yet my patients stop complaining. They often tell me that their sex life is " now " very enjoyable, though the physical maladjustment frequently persists during treatment and occasionally afterwards. The difficulties which apparently caused sexual unhappiness are still present, but the distress has disappeared. This common circumstance suggests, does it not, that the attitude toward the sexual partnership is more important than the physiological details of the union?

We receive confirmation of this impression if we turn to people who consider themselves happily married. They too, if we get them to tell us in detail about their sex life, report anxieties and vexations and unsatisfied desires. As a rule they also report periods of successful intercourse — close, tender, amusing, or passionate hours which are deeply satisfying to both husband and wife. In fact a description of these hours usually comes first and we uncover the less perfect episodes only after the visitors settle down to a fairly exhaustive discussion of their sex relations. Their reticence about the less happy aspects of their sex life is not deceit. These episodes are apt to be forgotten or discounted as unimportant. Sometimes you even find a couple whose enjoyment of sex is very slight indeed, but who are nevertheless happily married and well able to handle the shortcomings of their sexual adjustment without pain.

The conclusion I draw from these findings is that sexual adjustment involves much more than a greater or lesser degree of physical satisfaction. If two people love each other, if their marriage as a whole is harmonious and satisfying, they can accept even major discrepancies in sexual tempo without becoming resentful and upset. They value the positive side of their sex relations and remain serene when less agreeable aspects show themselves. On the other hand a man and a woman who are in conflict with each other will use any difficulty in the sexual field to reinforce their grievances. An illustration:

Let us suppose that it is Sunday evening in the home of our old friends Mary Jane and Jim. Jim has had a restful and pleasant day with his family and friends. When he is left alone with his wife he turns to her with romantic tenderness — only to be put off with a somewhat irritated plea that she is dreadfully tired. And she is. Sunday, with the family home and friends dropping in and a big dinner to get, is very strenuous in a maidless household. This situation — or a comparable one — arises in every marriage. Two people cannot always be "in the mood for love" at the same time. Jim will sometimes have to give up having intercourse when he wants it, or Mary Jane will have to simulate a responsiveness which she does not feel. This maladjustment is a simple fact, an inevitable fact in any relationship. It is a disagreeable fact, too, however you look at it, quite out of key with the refulgent picture of shared passion we are taught to consider good sex adjustment. But the important part of this little story is what happens next, and that depends on the kind of marriage Mary Jane and Jim have built up already. If it is a good marriage, a realistic, understanding relationship between two mature people, Jim will kiss Mary Jane affectionately and go to bed and to sleep. He will be disappointed, sorry, perhaps a little over-stimulated physically, but his mood will soon dissipate itself. Or Mary Jane may accept his advances — more passively than usual perhaps, but with tenderness and love. She will be more tired than ever, but she too will fall asleep promptly. It will not occur to either of them that anything serious has happened or that their sex life is a Problem.

Now, if Jim is already fighting Mary Jane, if he feels that she does not care for him, if he must prove his power by winning her submission, this little discrepancy in mood becomes a devastating attack. Jim goes to bed sore and resentful. He lies awake for hours nursing his anger and his sexual need. He convinces himself that abstinence is bad for his nerves and his health. In the morning he is still annoyed. The next time such an episode occurs he is more ready than ever to see in it a major rebuff to his love and his manliness. His conflict with his wife comes to a focus in their sexual differences. In the course of time sexual incompatibility appears to be the *cause* of their discord. As a matter of fact it is a result or rather the chief expression of discord rooted much more deeply in their personalities.

Jim, in our second version of the story, is not very sensible. He should know better than to expect a complete dovetailing of passionate moods. No doubt he does if you argue the point with him. Logically he bears no grudge against his wife for being tired at times, and freely admits that he doesn't always respond to her advances. The trouble is that neither Jim nor anybody else is logical and sensible about sex. If he is already feeling insecure about himself and his marriage, he is badly hurt by episodes which another man would scarcely notice. Just as a man whose physical condition has been weakened by a chronic anæmia catches pneumonia from getting his feet wet.

Mary Jane and Jim have no actual sex problem. These little discrepancies in mood are universal. Suppose, however, we intensify the physical differences between them. Suppose we make Jim now a " highly sexed " individual who needs frequent intercourse, while Mary Jane has little interest in sex. Or the other way round. Surely one would expect real incompatibility like this to cause discord in the marriage. Jim may feel that his health suffers from too great abstinence. He may feel that his wife doesn't love him, that he is too gauche to give her the satisfaction she should have, or that she is deliberately holding him off from sheer malice. Or he may tell her that she is too cold and threaten to look elsewhere for a woman who appreciates him and gives him a good time. An idealistic Jim may feel that his desire is sinful or at the very least unworthy of his wife's spirituality. Mary Jane on her side may believe that her strength is being exhausted by forced intercourse. She may resent bitterly the " brutality " of her husband, or conversely nurse a growing sense of inadequacy on the basis of her own coldness. She may fear that her husband will be driven to infidelity and torment herself with the idea that other women succeed where she is a failure.

These unhealthy attitudes — or others like them — appear to proceed inevitably from a disturbed physical relationship and to lead to painful distortions of the whole marriage. Sexual incompatibility in these marriages does indeed seem to be the *cause* of unhappiness. The difference in degree of sexual drive is apparently a physiological fact, bound to produce suffering for both husband and wife.

The number of marriages suffering from sexual maladjustment due to a basic difference in physiological drive is greatly exaggerated. I have seen scores of cases of sexual incompatibility. Out of the lot not more than three or four have proved to be based primarily upon physiological differences. Indeed, to find three or four I have to include friends and acquaintances whom I have not studied psychiatrically. People do differ in their bodily need for sex and it may happen that two individuals at opposite extremes of sexual appetite are linked together in marriage. This combination can result in genuine hardship. I know one woman who says frankly that sex bores her. She sympathizes with her husband's needs, however, to the extent of actually supplying him with suitable ladies to fall in love with. Now, as a psychiatrist I suspect that there is more in her boredom and in her husband's great capacity than meets the eye, but let that pass. The marriage has maintained itself comfortably for twenty-three years and promises to slip into a calm old age. Obviously this solution of the problem is not available to everyone. Most people have both moral and emotional scruples against this objective acceptance of sexual differences. I know another woman who has been properly brought up to consider sexual desire indecent. She impresses me as having unusually strong, healthy biological drives herself, but she is married to a man to whom sex means very little. This lady suffers from frequent nightmares in which she is attacked by a man or by a ravening beast. She wakens, screaming, just in the nick of time. She appears rather restless and tense, complains at times of headaches and sleeplessness. If any psychologically-minded person pointed out that this lady needs more sex than she is getting I could not deny the possibility, though I have no direct evidence that it is so. But in my turn I should like to point out that she has been happily married for fifteen years. Occasional nightmares and headaches seem a small price to pay for a lifelong companionability based upon shared interests and mutually sustained ideals, even assuming that the headaches do proceed from chronically unsatisfied sex impulses. In other words, genuine sexual incompatibility of an extreme sort is rare. Even when it occurs, however, disaster does not inevitably follow. A good marriage can take this problem, like many others, in its stride.

Before I go on to describe the cases of incompatibility I see frequently in my office I should like to introduce a brief digression on this matter of health and sex. Many people feel that even partial abstinence is unwholesome. They take their sex in regular doses like a cathartic. If their wives are away or are un-co-operative they carry forward their wanderings from the strict path of monogamy under the white flag of physical hygiene. Now, I would not go so far as to say that there are not a few people with strong sexual impulses who suffer from long periods of abstinence. But I do know that the danger to health of complete celibacy, to say nothing of partial satisfaction, has been greatly exaggerated. As much harm has been done by prescribing "sex" indiscriminately to persons married and unmarried as by the most hide bound puritanism. Similarly there is little chance of "sapping your strength" by excessive indulgence in intercourse. I know only one rule to govern the amount of intercourse in marriage for the best maintenance of health: as much or as little as you and your partner enjoy. To compromise with your own wishes either in the direction of more sex than you quite want or less out of deference to your partner will not result in neurasthenia or any unpleasant consequences. Ninety-nine times out of one hundred the physical symptoms associated with a disordered sex life are due to worry about sex, not to any direct influence of sexual habits. Worry and guilt do lead to neurasthenia, insomnia, pallor, dark circles under the eyes, trembling of the hands, and so on. Sexual acts, whether they are peculiar in form, excessive in quantity, or rigidly repressed do not in themselves bring about any such results.

With this reassurance about the physical hygiene of sex, let us get back to the problem of incompatibility. I said that cases of extreme difference in sexual need between husband and wife, based upon their genuine physiological make-up, are rare, so rare in fact that I sometimes question their existence.[1] Minor divergencies of interest in sexual activity are, on the other hand, universal. We do not expect two people to eat exactly the same amount regardless of their body build and glandular constitution. Neither should we expect their sexual appetite to correspond exactly. Happily married couples cheerfully accept the fact that one is usually more eager for intercourse than the other. They work out some sort of compromise. They don't worry about either starvation or excess, do not feel thwarted or unloved or inadequate. Or rather these disturbing emotions remain at a moderate pitch and do no one any harm. Any man dislikes being turned down by a woman, even temporarily and by a sensible, sympathetic wife. He dislikes even more perhaps being wooed when he is not ready to respond. But if his marriage is going well he recovers quickly from these moods and does not himself take them too seriously.

When he is uncertain about himself and his wife, however, he magnifies the difficulty involved in a chronic difference in sexual tempo until it becomes a major tragedy. He reacts to a slight coldness on the part of his wife as if it were a serious offence. His attitude is not only painful in itself; it intensifies the differences between his wife and himself. His tenderness and love might bring her to a more vigorous physical response. His anger or hurt lessens

---

[1] The fact that a man believes himself to be highly sexed is no guarantee that his native physiological drives are unusually strong. Very often, as we have seen, the man who feels that he *must* have frequent intercourse is covertly afraid that his sexual forces are abnormally weak. His aggressive sexuality is a defence against an unconscious fear of impotence.

her pleasure in sex still further. The course of development taken by their physical relationship depends upon the personalities of husband and wife, but without trust and affection the situation grows steadily worse. The problem does not arise from the cooling of sexual ardour with familiarity, or from a real change in the physiological capacity of the married folk, but from the progressive deterioration of their attitude toward each other and themselves. An example will show more clearly how serious sexual incompatibility grows out of a minor physical maladjustment. It is, of course, merely an example. The story changes its form for every marriage.

Mr. and Mrs. Ellis were charming young people, idealists to the bone, bent upon making their marriage a huge success. They were both sensitive, rather shy youngsters, a little shaky in their self-esteem and at the same time inordinately ambitious in a polite, not easily recognizable manner. Neither had had very much experience with love before marriage. Being very up-to-date youngsters they pored conscientiously over a massive tome offering advice to newly-weds on the best conduct of their sex life. They wanted to make the most of their physical intimacy without inhibition or false modesty.

Unfortunately Mrs. Ellis failed in the first weeks of their marriage to obtain the " climax " so clearly and diagrammatically explained in the fat textbook. She found intercourse pleasant, to be sure, though she did wish her husband were not quite so eager and persistent in his enthusiasm. Also his technique was not so subtle as the book recommended.

Thus far the story of their sex life is banal to an extreme. Probably the majority of nice young married couples have the same experience. Well-brought-up young ladies who have conscientiously avoided all varieties of sex experience do not as a rule respond vividly in the early weeks or months of marriage. If they are comfortable in their own skins and fond of their husbands, stronger sex feeling usually develops as time goes on. Not always. Some women never do find physical relationships completely thrilling, either because they are " made that way " or because their early training in purity has become such an integral part of their personality that it cannot be discarded even in marriage.[2] This failure to reach the pinnacle of passion does not by any means necessarily ruin the marriage or even cause sexual disharmony. Husband and wife can readily accept a less intense kind of physical union provided they have trust in one another. Such a union can indeed be peculiarly satisfying and lovely. Their kind of sexual satisfaction may be the proper and right expression for these two personalities, regardless of the unkind re-

[2] Moral preachments in childhood " take " differently with different people. Very often they do not affect the person profoundly. Sometimes they bring rebellion later on so that the inhibited young girl becomes the unusually passionate matron. But at times they are so deeply accepted by the personality as to become second nature. *What* is taught is not nearly so important as *how*. A " pure " woman who is loved and accepted by her daughter will deeply influence the girl. Another woman may say and do exactly the same things, but if her relationship to her daughter is more superficial the effect on the girl's sex life will not be lasting.

marks of the textbooks about incomplete intercourse. A good sex act springs from love and confidence, not from a particular set of sensations.

Let us see what Mr. and Mrs. Ellis did with their problem, their slight and perfectly normal physical maladjustment, so called. Mrs. Ellis soon became acutely concerned about her " lack of satisfaction." She felt she was missing something — and she was not a girl to be content with second best. In all her undertakings anything less than tops was reckoned as complete failure. She felt defeated and anxious about her own capacities. This mood is naturally not conducive to the free, uninhibited sex feeling she most desired. In fact, it made passion impossible. As time went on she was also troubled by the idea that she was failing her husband. He longed for the complete fusion of their bodies and souls, which never took place. The book told him that a considerate man could never be satisfied without the full co-operative enjoyment of his partner and that a skilful man could bring his wife to the proper pitch of passion. Mr. Ellis tried very hard to set aside his own preferences in favour of caresses which he thought would stimulate his wife. He, too, became anxious and insecure about his own approach, felt himself unloved and a poor sexual partner.

Both these young people were generously blaming themselves for the situation. Less openly they blamed each other. Mrs. Ellis dreamed of a subtle, tender, and passionate insistence in the approaches of a man — and really her husband always seemed to do the wrong thing at the wrong moment. He was, she decided, gauche and insensitive. Mr. Ellis began to be impatient with his wife's lack of response. She was too cold, too self-conscious, too aloof. Each of them felt dimly the reproachful attitude of the other — and resented it. Even without definite reproach resentment develops in such situations. No one likes to feel inferior and we all turn against the person who, however innocently, makes us feel awkward and uncertain.

Within a year this young couple had developed a thoroughly unsatisfactory sex relationship. Mrs. Ellis no longer found intercourse even pleasant. She felt beaten and half paralysed after each attempt. Mr. Ellis lost his early boyish pleasure in the sex act. They considered their marriage a failure and further they ascribed the failure to their sexual maladjustment. Actually the same problems occurred in every phase of their relationship. For instance, Mrs. Ellis was irritated by her husband's habit of whistling vigorously well off key. She was a musician herself, acutely sensitive to discordant sounds, so that this irritation was not surprising. She said nothing, however, feeling that a good wife should not make a row about trifles. In time she convinced herself that the interminable whistling was another sign of Mr. Ellis's insensitiveness to her moods and that her continued annoyance was further proof that they did not really love each other. A hundred little grievances sprang up between them. Both felt sore and defeated because they were unable to make marriage the glowing companionship they had envisaged.

The trouble with the Ellises was this: They could not

forgive themselves or each other their inevitable shortcomings. They were not sure of each other and they did
not trust themselves. Their sexual problem merely illustrated this fundamental difficulty. It did not create discord, but gave expression to the doubts, misgivings, and
resentments which lay at the very roots of their relationship.

Mrs. Ellis responded very well to psychiatric treatment.
In the course of a few months she lost a great deal of her
anxiety about herself — and consequently of her need to
have everything perfect before she could enjoy it at all. She
came to find great pleasure in giving herself to her husband even though her physical reactions still fell short
of the ecstasy for which she had striven so frantically. Her
husband, feeling her lack of tension and her genuine enjoyment, relaxed in his turn. When I last heard from Mrs.
Ellis she was at times actually having the prescribed orgasm and was thoroughly content with the milder forms
of tenderness she experienced in the interim. As for the
whistling, she simply asked her husband to cut it out. She
no longer read into his noise implications of insensitiveness
and lack of love. She felt it as a straightforward annoyance. Her protest had no venom and caused no distress.
So with the other sources of friction. Open quarrels became somewhat more common in the Ellis household, but
the agonizing tension of their first year disappeared.

In telling the story of the Ellis marriage I have tried
to make clear how a moderate and perhaps temporary
difference in sex drive can be elaborated into serious mal-

adjustment by attitudes which proceed from the deep levels of the personality of both partners. Different attitudes would result in a different type of maladjustment. A calm, realistic acceptance of any physical incompatibility, on the other hand, limits its influence. Married couples need not fear that variations in the amount of intercourse will injure their health or lead to emotional instability and the breakdown of the marriage. Discord and nervous conditions do arise in the course of a poorly conducted sex life, but they are due to the emotional states people work up. They are not the direct physical or emotional consequence of too much or too little sex expression.

The *kind* of sexual activity they follow is also a source of worry to many people. Our society preaches that only one kind of sexual expression can be countenanced, the so-called " normal " intercourse between husband and wife. Any other type of activity is labelled shocking, disgusting, antisocial, and perverse. Moral and social condemnation (rigorous to the point of a jail sentence) is backed up by the threat of nervous disorders and insanity to those who practice variations on the standard form of sex. I am speaking now of homosexuality, of masturbation, of sadistic and masochistic behaviour,[3] of the use of unusual parts of the body or unusual objects to obtain or enhance sexual enjoyment.

Not many people in our society practice any one of these variations (with the exception of masturbation) ex-

[3] *Sadism*, enjoyment of hurting others. *Masochism*, enjoyment of being hurt.

clusively or in open, clearly recognizable form. I can state emphatically, however, that every one of us engages in all of them to some extent, consciously or unconsciously. Sex is by no means the simple genital act children read about in books beginning with the pollenization of flowers. It is a highly complex drive with ramifications into every part of the body and every aspect of the personality. The isolated facts of erection and emission in the male, of vaginal secretion and orgasm in the female, are merely details in an elaborate picture. I refer anyone interested in the physiological side of sex not to the books on Ideal Marriage, but to a modern text of neuro-anatomy. There he can see for himself how closely the nerves involved in the sex act are associated with nerves controlling other parts of the body, especially the mouth, the heart, and the organs of excretion. He can see how intimately the sex glands (gonads) are bound up with the other glands of internal secretion — the thyroid, the adrenals, the pituitary, and so on — which regulate bodily functions quite distinct from sex. The most cursory examination of the physiological substructure of the sex act shows how easily it can be facilitated or blocked by impulses coming from sources apparently quite remote from sexuality. The study of neurology shows how other bodily functions may become involved in the act or even supersede it. I cannot cram into a page or two enough information about anatomy and physiology to make clear the complex mechanism of sexuality. I shall not even try. If you have been bewildered by these few remarks, so much the better. I wish only to emphasize the fact that the sex drive is complex, exceedingly complex, so complex that it permits of the widest differences between one individual and the next both in the experiences which cause sexual tension and in its mode of expression. The anatomy charts we present to children and to the earnest bridegroom are over-simplified to the point of idiocy. The descriptions we give them of "normal intercourse" are even more grossly conventionalized. They are like a four-year-old's drawing of a man — a circle for a head and two straight lines to take care of body, arms, and legs. Everything that really matters is left out.

An analogy may help us clarify this conception of the relationship between sexual drives and the rest of our impulses. Suppose we were to import an expert from Europe to regulate the subway service of New York City from Times Square to the Bronx. We provide him with a map of the West Side branch of the subway only. He studies carefully the people who enter the subway from the street, estimates the number likely to get out at each station as the train moves through the residential districts, and supplies cars accordingly. Obviously his calculations will be completely off because he ignores the vast influx of people transferring from the East Side branch, and the outflow at other points of junction. The traffic load of any one branch of the subway can be understood only by studying the entire network of lines. Just so the physiological mechanism of the genital branch of the nervous system can be understood only in the light of knowledge about the entire array of nerves, glands, muscles, and internal organs which make up an individual.

Yet the physiological basis of sexuality is simplicity itself compared with its so-called psychological aspects. "The way of a man with a maid" is supposedly pretty familiar to us all, and pretty monotonously the same no matter who the man and who the maid. Several romances have been written on the situation of a man and a girl, grown to maturity in total isolation, falling in love on sight. The experiment, for certain obvious reasons, has never actually been tried. I have a notion that the romancers would be badly let down. I suspect that at first the young gentleman and the young lady would have no idea what to do about each other, that it would not even occur to them to do anything at all. Probably each one would have worked out some scheme for the release of sexual tensions and would at first continue the method without reference to the other. In the course of time an experimentally-minded pair might discover some value in co-operative enterprise. We can be sure, however, that the young man viewing for the first time a comely miss seductively clothed in a smile would not exclaim: "My mate!" and rush to enfold her in his arms. There is no set pattern for the expression of sexual drives. A flash of bright light will cause the pupil of your eye to contract whether you know anything about neurology or not. But the sight of a woman's body does not automatically arouse sexual desire without previous experience. The truth is that while the *need* for a sexual outlet is inborn, is as much a part of our body as our hair or teeth, the *choice* of outlet is learned just as laboriously as the multiplication table. Man is born to be hungry, but he does not know instinctively which objects in the world about him are edible. Through trial and error or through maternal precepts he learns that huckleberries make good eating and bayberries do not. Any mother will testify to the primitive omniverousness of the very young. Sex, too, is a native urge, but originally it is just as undiscriminating as infantile hunger. By experimentation, by example, and by instruction the child learns to focus his desire upon a member of the opposite sex.

We saw in the first chapter something of the course of this education. The child learns to respond to his parents, to servants, to playmates of the same sex, to a variety of specimens of the opposite sex. Small children often react with an erection to caresses from any quarter.[4] Education for heterosexual choice begins almost in the cradle, however. Parents jokingly tease their little boys about their sweethearts, encourage their baby daughters to tell whom they are going to marry, discuss the amorous affairs of older people, and, indeed, by the mere fact of their joint parenthood constantly present the child with a prime example of orthodox mating. With this training it is not surprising that the vast majority of children fall in love quite properly with a member of the opposite sex. In rough outline they follow the rules of normal sexual in-

---

[4] This phenomenon is more common than is generally believed since it is usually concealed by the child's clothing.

tercourse laid down in novels and textbooks, responding
to conventional " sex appeal " and receiving due satisfaction from the prescribed embrace. Their physical response
to parents and to friends remains diffuse — a generalized
glow of affection. Any tendency there might be toward
a localization of response in the genital organs is so
promptly suppressed that it never comes to consciousness
at all. Stimulation is transferred to non-sexual branches
of the nervous system, just as traffic on the subway or the
open highway spreads out in other directions when the
direct road is blocked. Only stimulation from a member
of the opposite sex is permitted right of way to the genital
areas.

This development is, of course, wholly to be desired.
The essential biological purpose of the sex mechanism is
the procreation of children, a purpose only attained by
heterosexual union. No one can doubt that both nature
and society are well served by the emphasis on " normal "
intercourse. In our enthusiasm for the end result, however, we must not forget the educational steps which have
brought it about. In the most orthodox sexual development earlier stages are not completely eliminated. They
are subordinated to and integrated with the final pattern.
The little boy who liked being cuddled by his mother still
survives in the bridegroom. The youngster who went hot
and cold when the captain of the school football team
asked him to run an errand has not wholly outgrown what
psychiatrists call his " homosexual component." Even the
baby who sucked his thumb with compelling passion and

wet his pants in spite of parental anger is alive and kicking. All the special experiences which created the particular physiological and psychological structure of one young man have left their mark upon his mature sex reactions. In short all of us are full of impulses, desires, and shames which have nothing to do with the simple diagram of " normal sex behaviour."

Study of the sex activity of relatively uninhibited happily married couples demonstrates very beautifully both the unorthodox nature of their impulses and the ease with which they are integrated into a " normal " heterosexual pattern. Sometimes the pair will be close and affectionate. Tenderness will pass into a rather solemn passion, a confirmation of their abiding love for each other. At other times their mood will be wholly frivolous. Intercourse then will be just a rattling good time without deeper implications. Or the husband will seek protection and cuddling at his wife's breast. Or he will lie like a girl while she takes possession of his body. At times he will vulgarize the act with smutty words or take a fine pleasure in hurting his wife and forcing her to his will. Or the couple may play at an illicit relationship, acting out a little seduction farce for their own benefit. They will try out odd positions and experiment with unusual parts of the body. Often, too, intercourse will be a routine satisfaction of a bodily need about as romantic as orange juice, toast, and coffee for breakfast. Our uninhibited happily married couples will take all of these variations and find them good.

Cynics have said that only ingenious modifications can

make tolerable the constant repetition of an act as simple as intercourse. In point of fact, however, these variations have a value far beyond mere spiciness. They provide a wholesome outlet for all the unacknowledged impulses of human nature. Through the medium of these intimate games a husband and wife can work out aspects of their relationship to each other and to the world which they cannot comfortably recognize as part of themselves. Attitudes too subtle or too painful or too self-contradictory for everyday use can be freely expressed in the abandon of sexual union. The form of expression is at the same time exceedingly direct and exceedingly well disguised as a game or an isolated moment of passion.

These submerged aspects of our personality which come out in sexual experimentation are not necessarily " bad." Some of them, of course, are incompatible with the moral standards of our society, but others are simply different from the dominant trend of our character. The man who prides himself on being strong to the point of ruthlessness cannot readily give expression in his daily routines to his yearning for a protective maternal love. No one is free from such yearnings, as we have seen, least of all the aggressively hard-boiled man. The tender, considerate husband also harbours somewhere in his nature resentment against those he loves and against his own weakness. This resentment is so foreign to his idea of himself that he cannot bring it out in his ordinary life. He can, half in play, half in passion, subdue and hurt the woman he loves during a sexual embrace. With this outlet he may be able to hold on to his job, which he might otherwise lose because of " unexplainable " displays of bad temper toward a superior.

. Any relationship is incomparably richer for the sounding of these overtones. The note of a piano is more beautiful than a pitch-pipe because of the simultaneous production of notes not wholly perceived by the ear. A marriage restricted to emotions consciously recognized and approved would be as thin as a pitch-pipe. Full marital union is achieved only by working out together any and all deep urges present in the personalities of both partners. While this union can and does take place every minute of the day, the sexual embrace offers the greatest freedom for the vivid expression of impulses commonly disguised beyond recognition.

Unfortunately most of us try conscientiously to cut out the overtones from our lives, and from our sex life in particular. Our efforts are due in part to misinformation about sex and in part to a fear, usually not recognized, that if the overtones once begin they will drown out the dominant note. Let us look more carefully into these two obstacles to free physical and spiritual intimacy.

The first difficulty need not concern us long. Sex practices deviating from the " normal " are often thought to be detrimental to health of body and mind. People fear that their behaviour in bed will " show in their faces," that they will develop nervous instabilities, trembling of the hands, shadows under the eyes, excessive pallor, insomnia, headaches, and so on. This fear is wholly unfounded. Every psychiatrist sees not only married couples whose sex life includes some of these practices, but also men and women whose sexual education has been such that they follow these practices exclusively. Organically they are as sound as anybody else. If they have been able to accept their difference in sexual enjoyment without strong feelings of guilt and remorse they do not suffer from nervous symptoms. On the other hand, many people who have never gratified their longing for unusual sex expression, or who have never even realized that they had such longing, show all the nervous signs associated with an unsanctioned sex life. In brief, sexual activity itself does not affect health, no matter what its form. Worry about it, like any worry, does lead to nervousness and even to straightforward physical symptoms.

Observation of those societies which approve of types of sex activity which we consider perverse will substantiate this point. The ancient Greeks were famous for their magnificent physique and for their athletic prowess. They are equally famous for the culture of homosexuality, which seems to have flourished especially well in the gymnasiums where the athletes congregated. Anthropologists tell us of a number of communities whose sexual habits are actually institutionalized around a form our society considers perverse. Among the Marindanim of New Guinea, for instance, homosexuality is the recognized norm. Heterosexual intercourse takes place only at intervals for purposes of reproduction. Yet the Marindanim are a strong people with a sturdy, workable social organization.

One type of homosexuality appears to be an exception to this contention that no physical results are to be observed. I refer to that small group of people who actually look either effeminate or masculine. The men may have characteristically female deposits of fat on the hips and breasts, the women a narrow pelvis, a deep voice, and facial hair. These people are suffering from well-recognized glandular disturbances. They do not appear effeminate because they indulge in homosexual activity. The truth is the other way round. Or rather their feminine appearance and their choice of a partner of the same sex are both due to a special physiological condition. Refraining from sexual activity would not affect their appearance one way or the other. Marriage does not cure them — in fact, merely increases their distress.

My emphasis has been upon homosexuality simply because it is the best-known form of sexual deviation. All the other variations of sex expression can be treated the same way. They do not in themselves affect general health. A few words about masturbation in particular will not be amiss, since it is so very common — indeed, almost universal. It has become quite fashionable to say that masturbation in moderation is all right, *but* — beware of its excessive use. It is my certain belief that the proviso is unnecessary. The child or the adult whose life is in general well ordered and wholesome will have no desire to masturbate to excess. We talk as if everyone would spend his entire leisure in the practice, once barriers of conscience or the threat of ill health were removed.

Nothing could be farther from the truth. The vast majority of people would simply not be interested. A child does not become addicted to sweets because he helps his father in the candy shop. Physical satiety sets a limit to masturbation just as it does to the eating of candy. Most children gorge on candy not because their real appetite for it is so enormous but because they have learned to consider it something special to be grabbed whenever possible. So long as masturbation is thought to be a pleasure stealthily indulged in against the wishes of a grudging morality, it, too, will be something to gorge on, regardless of appetite.

Masturbation is a perfectly valid form of sexual outlet. For young adolescents it is perhaps the outlet of choice. It not only provides for release of sexual tensions; it also helps localize sex feeling in the genital organs, thus paving the way for successful heterosexual intercourse later on. With marriage the desire for masturbation usually abates since other forms of expression are found more satisfying. During long periods of separation, or in those cases of extreme difference in sexual need mentioned above, some people again resort to this form of sexual activity. These people are very sensible. No harm can result from the practice. Fear and fear alone is responsible for ill effects which come from sexual behaviour of any sort. Worry over physical health can be cheerfully discarded.

Worry or anxiety also arises from the feeling that one's sexual experience — whatever it may be — is not " normal," even though the person does not fear illness. People try to measure up to various ideas they have formed of sexual adequacy. If they do not achieve orgasm in the precise manner described in the textbooks, if they do not achieve it at all, if they have only one orgasm instead of a number like the gentlemen in sundry jokes, if they prefer not recommended positions, etc., etc., they feel that they are missing something, that they are inadequate and contemptible. It is quite possible that our little discussion of the sex activity of many happily married couples, for instance, will make some people feel cheated because they do not indulge in the variations described. Now, it is quite impossible to prescribe sex activity for any couple. Variations are no more an essential feature of sex life than they are perversions to be stamped out. The only test of a good sex adjustment is whether or not a particular person finds it satisfying, not always, of course, but most of the time.

This statement brings us to the second difficulty I mentioned in the way of a full enjoyment of sexual partnership — namely, a profound distrust of the overtones in our own personalities. As we grow older our personality takes on a definite form which is very precious to us. For one reason or another in the course of our development we foster some impulses while we subordinate or ruthlessly stamp out other impulses. This selection is not made in accordance with a conscious, rational plan. The reasons for our choice lie in the whole complex of our emotional and social experiences from infancy onwards. We understand them very imperfectly. The rigour of our censorship of rejected impulses also proceeds from these childhood experiences. If we learned early to fear the results of certain impulses, if we have built our personality around the need for keeping them under stern control, we cannot easily give them even momentary and playful expression in sexual intimacy. Let us consider again the man whose personal ideal is strength. His ideal may be so precious to him, so essential a part of the character he lives by, that he dare not even for a moment, even in fun or in passion, permit an appearance of softness. His real dependency on his wife cannot be allowed even partial direct expression, because it threatens the defence he has built up against himself and the world. This type of uncompromising " strength " develops from a variety of causes. We can safely assume that masculinity so strong that it never melts into tenderness and never seeks tenderness from a woman is based upon unconscious fear. Fear of what? We cannot assume any particular fear without careful study of the man himself. The case of Joseph Lester shows one way that such attitudes develop. There are many others, of course, but one example will illustrate sufficiently how distrust of the overtones in our personality may limit the free expression of natural impulses.

It was Mrs. Lester who came to me, not Joseph himself. Mrs. Lester was a sweet, affectionate, pretty woman of thirty. She had been married for five years. She wanted to divorce her husband and marry a young artist. Her husband not only refused to give her a divorce but threatened her artist with violence. She wanted me to work her husband into a more reasonable frame of mind. As we talked, however, it became evident to me that her problem was by no means so simple. Indeed, I began to feel that she loved her husband deeply and that she had more than a notion that her artist was nothing but a pretty soft egg. I never saw Mr. Lester, but Mrs. Lester came to me regularly for several months. At the end of this period she had not only decided to stay with her husband, but was happily stitching wee garments in the approved movie style.

Mrs. Lester had a great deal of tenderness to give. The artist soaked up devotion like a sponge, but not Joseph. He was scrupulously fair in his dealings with her, but about as romantic as an ice cube. Their sex life was determined entirely by his wishes. He tolerated only a cool acquiescence from his wife. Once early in their married life she kissed his hand in a spontaneous flow of affection. Joseph turned white with rage and requested her to refrain from such foolishness. He apologized very correctly, of course, but the affectionate outburst was never repeated. Although he never expressed any love for his wife or permitted her to make love to him, Joseph was extremely jealous. He did not reproach her for attentions to other men, saying coldly that such behaviour was her own affair. But if she happened to be alone with a man for some trivial reason, if she danced more than once with the same man, or even listened with apparent pleasure to his conversation at a dinner table, Joseph would invariably work up a quarrel on some pretext or other. She was spending too much money, or the dinner was badly served, or she had been impolite to one of their guests.

Obviously Joseph is not really an ice cube, and obviously he is not indifferent to his wife. The violence of his reactions is an index of the depth of his feeling. A man who simply didn't care about tenderness would not reprove his wife for kissing his hand or mind her superficial attentions to other men. Joseph's history gives us a clue to his make-up. His father died before he was born. His mother was a sweet, affectionate woman, not unlike his wife. She was devoted to her little boy and he to her. The chances are that he was a typical spoiled child up to the age of six. Public school was difficult for him since it was disturbingly lacking in the tender indulgence he had learned to expect. By the time he reached the third grade he had learned to fight as well as the next one, and even a little better. When he was seven his mother married again — married very happily and presented Joseph with two charming little brothers. To a boy who had enjoyed the exclusive devotion of his mother for seven years, who was having a tough time at school, this marriage was a bitter betrayal. His mother continued to be affectionate with him as well as with her new babies. She was puzzled and hurt when Joseph refused her good-night kiss, when he no longer told her of his school adventures. Rebuffed by her oldest child, she turned more and more to the little ones for affection and comradeship — while Joseph quietly froze into the kind of person Mrs. Lester found so difficult as a husband. As a very small boy Joseph had learned to want and expect an excessive amount of protective, tender love. His babyish behaviour laid him open to more than average ridicule at school. His trusting expectation of tenderness made the actual indifference of the world seem actively hostile. He taught himself painfully to expect nothing from kindness, to be cold and self-contained, to return fancied hostility with real hostility. Many men under these circumstances retain a dependent relationship upon a woman — their mother and later their wife — behaviour often amusingly at variance with their arrogant attitude to outsiders. The defection of Joseph's mother, for so he interpreted her marriage, left him with a profound distrust of love and tenderness. Afraid of the world, afraid of love because it had brought him pain and disappointment, Joseph grew a protective shell of frigid self-sufficiency. A vicious circle developed. The more aloof he became from his mother and schoolfellows, the more they in turn let him alone and the deeper grew his resentments. By the time he married, this man's character had so crystallized in this mould of bitter repudiation of tenderness that he could not accept without anxiety the warm-hearted advances of his wife.

Joseph never came to me for treatment. Men who have built up such strong defences for themselves are very reluctant to break them down. They cannot admit their need for help without panic. Moreover, Joseph was a stable, efficient, moderately satisfied individual. His wife, less urgently in need, did receive treatment. She learned to understand her husband and to accept his coldness without pain. She learned that much of her own distress in her marriage came from her own resentment at the constant frustration her affectionate nature received. She was strongly maternal, unusually ready to give of herself to those she loved. Once she realized fully how much she really did give her husband, she was eager to continue her role. The marriage did not become an ideal union. Mrs. Lester, like any other woman, wanted emotional warmth. But she accepted her deprivation without bitterness, with sympathy, as she would have accepted physical invalidism in her husband. She was free to enjoy the many positive values in the relationship.

The advent of the baby will not be easy for Mr. Lester. The husband will be reassured against the threat of divorce, but he will be forced to repeat the experience of divided love first encountered with his mother's attention to his little half-brothers. No doubt he will behave badly at times, but his wife will be able to take it. It is even possible that the whole-hearted warmth of her love for him will ultimately give him enough security so that he can relax his defences somewhat and permit himself to receive and give more ordinary tenderness.

Perhaps this is the place to discuss in some detail what the psychiatrist tries to do for people who come to him in distress about their marriages. We can start with what he does *not* try to do. He does not give advice as to whether they should divorce or how they should behave toward each other. I did not, for example, tell Mrs. Lester that her artist was a sponge and urge her to stick to her worthy husband. Nor did I tell her to avoid expressions of tenderness or to force them upon Joseph. I did not recommend having a baby to hold the marriage together. Advice never works unless it comes from within. A wife may conscientiously go through all the paces suggested by her doctor and then by an ill-considered remark to her husband undo all the good she has tried to accomplish. In little ways of which she is not even aware her true attitudes will show through her well-intentioned pose — and the fat is in the fire, more sputtering and smelly than before. Honesty of feeling is the most important factor in successful marriage. The person who is acting upon the advice of someone else, however wise and just, does not have honesty of feeling.

The psychiatrist, as I have intimated before, does not try to remodel a marriage according to the pattern he fancies himself. He realizes that marriage means something different to every person who consults him. The struggles of two young artists from Bohemia to find a satisfying *modus vivendi* in common are quite different from those of the vice-president or even the president of the First National Bank of a small town trying to get along comfortably with his better half. The dominant trend of the first marriage may be comradeship. The youngsters may be in difficulty because an unforeseen competitiveness is forcing a bitter element into their relationship. The nucleus of the second union may be one of protection. The husband primarily wants a little girl to look after, but he is upset because his child wife is extravagant and ineffectual in running his house. The job of the psychiatrist is to help both of these couples work out the kind of relationship *they* want. His personal notion of what marriage should be is irrelevant.

Nor does the psychiatrist try to make over the people he sees. The broad outlines of character are pretty well fixed, both by constitution and by the early experiences of the patient. The psychiatrist cannot make an artist into a bank president — and he doesn't want to. He has no hierarchy of social values. He respects the basic personality he is dealing with. In fact, he respects it far more than the patient himself, and herein lies his real task. Most of us do not respect enough the kind of person we are. For one reason or another we are constantly pretending to be a different sort altogether. Or we set one part of ourselves the thankless task of keeping another part well out of sight. Play-acting is strenuous business, as anyone knows who has been on the stage. Trying to maintain a role in everyday life when we are actually afraid of being caught in the masquerade is still more exacting, even when we do it on purpose. You know the perennial movie about the pretty girl from the wrong side of the tracks who pretends to riches for a day and confesses her poverty at the end with such profound relief. Most of us are like that unfortunate girl, except that we haven't the advantage of knowing what we're about nor of the luxury of confession at the end. If we ever did confess we would find — as our heroine always finds — that all is forgiven. Very often other people have known all the time the kind of person we really are. Almost always they like us better in our true colours than in the false whiskers we have assumed.

As I said at the outset of the second chapter, nine tenths of our misery is sheer nonsense. Take our friend Joseph, who has put in a lifetime acting the part of a hard-boiled business man because he was afraid to be caught out in his native tenderness. Or Emily, who ran through one marriage after another because she didn't like herself as she was. Or you and me. If we could only learn to respect ourselves, to accept ourselves as ordinary human beings, instead of covering up and play-acting, we could put our energies into handling our real problems effectively.

So the job of the psychiatrist is to help married people work out their own particular aims freely and honestly. Very often treatment does not change a situation or the personalities of the people involved in any way apparent to an outsider. But instead of worrying about themselves and each other the people accept the relationship and go on from there. Sometimes a real change comes about because aspects of the personality previously put down with violence are permitted to find expression. Mrs. Lester changed very little under treatment. She had always acted pretty much in accord with the deeper trends of her personality. Only the resentment which she was building up toward her marriage was removed. Mr. Lester would, I think, show more change, since he would express openly a softness which now finds its outlet only in quarrels and bitter attacks on the person who calls forth his tender feelings.

Psychiatry often changes the sexual behaviour of the patient. An impotent man or a woman who objects to intercourse comes to enjoy normal sex expression. Milder disorders also frequently disappear. At times, however, the actual behaviour remains unchanged. If the patient learns to accept her behaviour, no matter what its form, the psychiatrist still feels that he has made a " cure." Mrs. Ellis, for instance, was not transformed into a cave-woman by treatment, but she did learn to enjoy the kind of sexual activity which was natural to her. With this change in attitude the *problem* aspects of her sex relationship disappeared. The psychiatrist sets no standard for the amount or kind of sexual activity. His point of view toward sex is simply that it should be satisfying and enjoyable.

CHAPTER V

༺ঞ৴

LIVING TOGETHER

A SHORT time ago I heard a worthy lawyer remark that he disapproved of women in business and the professions. " If a woman is capable and ambitious," he said, " let her marry a good man, stick to him, and push him to success. Let her rear fine, upstanding children. A woman in business is not a woman at all. She's a half-baked man in petticoats."

This vehement statement did not go unchallenged. A mild social gathering was abruptly converted into a forum on feminism versus the home, or the nature of woman, and finally on the function of marriage. Discussion rapidly became animated to the point of violent argument. A young anthropologist maintained that he would have neither love nor respect for a woman who subordinated herself to him. He wanted a strong partner who could stand on her own feet. He wanted his wife to have her own career. Only through economic independence could she preserve her independence of spirit and avoid clinging about his neck like a millstone.

"Millstone indeed!" protested another man indignantly. "Young fellow, you don't know the first thing about marriage. You ought to be glad to look after your wife. That's the trouble with marriage these days. We blame the girls for kicking over the traces, but we ought to blame the men. Young men won't take responsibility for a family. They want to keep all their independence and they think a good wife is a millstone. Well, I say, call her an anchor instead of a millstone. Stop drifting and take care of a woman and children. You'll get more solid satisfaction out of the devotion of a fine little woman than from all the equality in the world. And you'll pay for it by bringing home the bacon yourself and being the kind of man she can trust and admire. You'll both be happy. A woman wants to be shielded and cared for, and a man who is a man wants to do the protecting."

"But we don't want to be taken care of," said a young woman. "We have brains of our own and education. I want to go on with my own life and be something myself. The masterful male was all very well so long as women didn't know how to do anything but housework. I want a love life and children as much as anyone, but I'm no hothouse flower. I know the kind of life my mother led, and I don't want one like it. My husband and I will be friends. We'll work out a life together, and it'll be *our* life, not his."

"Don't be post-war," broke in another girl. "Feminism is out of date. What's a piddling little career anyhow? I don't want a love life. I want love. I want to marry a man

I can look up to and I want him to be crazy about me. You know what happens in these equality marriages. The wife wears herself out dashing around in business and cooking at the same time. No man on earth will do his share of housekeeping and baby-tending even if his wife is earning as much as he is. He gets sore because the meals are bad and he goes into a tail-spin if his wife gets ahead an inch faster than he does. Then he falls head over heels for an itsy bitsy girl who has time to look cute and sense enough to tell him what a great big wonderful man he is. Not for me. I'll be the itsy bitsy girl myself. Any rustling around I do to step up the income or live my own life the lord and master won't know anything about."

During the next two hours the discussion covered the questions of free divorce, of the double standard, of training in domestic science and sex relations, of economic opportunity and discrimination, even of fascism and war. It finally ended in an acrimonious dispute about who should wipe the dishes and whether a wife should take sides against her husband in an argument. In short, the problems, big and little, of living together in holy wedlock were very thoroughly canvassed. I am sure that the reader can cite similar discussions from his own experience. They are ages old and freshly exciting, because people continue to get married and run into difficulties in the conduct of their daily lives.

This chapter and the next, more specifically than the preceding ones, will be concerned with the business of ordering our everyday existence, of combining the distinct and often antagonistic needs of two individuals into a workable, satisfying union.

The reader is by now familiar with the point of view of this book. I have not taken sides with any of the disputants I have cited because I believe that abstract rules of conduct do not help a relationship. Its course is determined by the psychological needs and attitudes of the people involved. A wife may have a career or not; the husband may help her with the dishes or read the paper while she works in the kitchen. These bits of behaviour are not important in themselves. What is significant is their *meaning* to a particular couple. One wife considers washing the dishes alone an index of her slavery. Another feels that her dignity as a housekeeper is impaired if her husband helps her. If we are to understand the controversies which arise out of careers and household drudgery and budgeting and the like we must understand the fundamental relationship between husband and wife — the aims and longings and sore spots which each brings to marriage.

These aims and longings are as various as the people who take each other in marriage. They do, however, cluster about two major and opposing needs: the need for love and the need for self-fulfilment; the need to be sheltered and protected and adored and the need to feel ourselves independent and strong; the need for affection and the need for prestige. No human being is without both of these needs, though the balance between them changes from one individual to the next. The balance also changes at different periods of our lives. A man, no less than a woman, seeks in marriage refuge and reassurance. He is not very different from the adolescent who found it hard to give up the protection of the parental home. He still wants sheltering and protective love. And he still protests against his own very natural timidity and moments of weakness. He can rarely admit even to himself that he needs support from his wife. Just as the adolescent punished his parents for his own weakness, so the husband is apt to resent in his wife the strength he really demands.

The dominating behaviour of a man toward his wife is often the measure of his dependence upon her, a combination of his desire for strength and his need for protection. The blustering, masterful husbands are perhaps most frequently the jealous husbands who cannot without panic permit their wives a flirtatious glance or a temporary preoccupation with interests outside the home.

These tensions spring directly from the impact of two personalities upon each other. Every husband harbours as well a long series of wishes and ambitions which he strives to fulfil, and a number of sensitive areas which he must shield irrespective of his relationship to his wife. Marriage — living with another person according to the rules prescribed by our society — entails the sacrifice of many of these ambitions and the exposure of some sensitive areas. In so far as the aims are conscious, the sacrifice can be made in a straightforward manner with more or less good grace. A man may wish to play poker with his friends or take a chorus girl out to dinner or stay at the office to work, but he knows that he must often curtail these desires in the interests of his marriage or run the risk of marital discord. Very often, however, he is not aware of his real wishes. He may then unwittingly pursue them regardless of the cost to his marriage, or, if he is forced to give them up, he may suffer from a blind sense of frustration and annoyance. His business, for instance, may be far more important to him than he realizes. He does indeed come home from the office like a dutiful husband, but his conversation never leaves the problems of the day. He goes through the motions of being attentive to his wife in all good faith. It happens, though, that even during a moment of romantic tenderness he suddenly has to put in a phone call. His unconscious preoccupations destroy his well-intentioned efforts to be a good husband. Often the interruptions to the smooth flow of the love relationship are so subtle that the wife herself does not realize what is wrong. She knows only that she feels let down and neglected. In a thousand little ways, unbeknownst to themselves and each other, married people carry out their secret wishes at the expense of their union. Unconscious wishes are uncompromising in their demands. Trivial desires and vanities, of little moment in themselves, often assume major proportions when they are allowed to run their own course without conscious guidance. We will dwell upon this problem at some length in pages to follow.

The problem of the wife is essentially the same as that of her husband. She, too, needs the reassurance of a protective love and resents her need as an evidence of weakness. Like her husband she wants certain satisfactions for herself and defends herself against certain special terrors. Her self-seeking impulses, like his, are often unconscious and therefore uncontrolled, aiming at complete fulfilment without counting the cost. In our culture, however, women are better able than men to accept their need for love and protection, because they are traditionally the weaker vessel. Dependence is a sign of their womanhood of which they need not be ashamed. On the other hand, their personal ambitions are frowned upon by our society. For this reason their impulses toward self-aggrandizement, more frequently than those of men, are hidden from view and so removed from the possibility of rational control.

At the root of most marital difficulties lies, then, a deep fear of the loss of that love so necessary to our security and a feeling of frustration on behalf of the personal aims we have been compelled to renounce. There is a subterranean struggle for the uncompromising satisfaction of unacknowledged impulses; there is resentment against the partner who blocks our ambitions; and there is anxiety lest our hostile behaviour result in the loss of love we so urgently need. The trouble with the programs for the proper conduct of marriage briefly quoted at the beginning of this chapter is that none of them takes account of the to and fro movement between the desire for dominance and the need for protection characteristic of both men and women. The basic problems of marriage — and the basic satisfactions as well — are masked by an over-simplified conception of the needs of men and women. It happens too often that an antagonistic impulse, unimportant in itself, is given free and exaggerated expression because it can easily assume the disguise of a social virtue. Mr. Black, aged forty-five, enjoys cutting a bit of a figure with the ladies — in all innocence, be it said. His wife is not very attractive. She naturally resents a little his greater popularity and is slightly uneasy about her own status in his affections. Consciously, however, she repudiates any such petty jealousy. She never reproaches him for gallivanting around — but she does show an intense wifely solicitude for his lumbago, his heart condition, his figure, even, which serves to remind him and his lady friends of his advancing years. Outwardly she is within her rights as a conscientious helpmeet. Actually she makes constant, insidious little attacks upon him, without recognizing them as such for a moment. Mr. Black is more acute. He is beginning to be seriously annoyed by his wife. Her jealousy is indeed petty. She could handle it easily if she knew about it. So long as she conceals it from herself this series of antagonistic, socially acceptable acts is likely to continue. A person may wreck a precious marriage to gratify an insignificant bit of vanity because his conscious efforts unwittingly reinforce an unconscious impulse of destructive nature.

This discussion of basic problems in marriage has been extremely abstract and condensed. If the reader has found it confused and bewildering, let him cultivate the kindly virtue of patience. The rest of this chapter and the next one will be devoted to a clarification of the fundamental point of view by reference to the concrete instance. By showing how conflicting aims and anxieties have affected a particular marriage I hope we can cover the bare bones of didactic analysis with living flesh and blood. A good presentation of the complex interplay of impulse and behaviour I have briefly described requires a more detailed and intensive study of the illustrative marriage than any we have undertaken heretofore. I have chosen the Gordons as an example because their problems are, in essence, very common. With a slight transposition of the external circumstances, analysis of their difficulties and satisfactions would fit a great many marriages today. I trust, then, that the reader will not grow restive if I dwell upon their adventures at length and use them as a point of departure for the discussion of many facets of married life.

Jack Gordon was a self-made man. Without help from his father (a foreman in a small shoe-factory), without benefit of education beyond the eighth grade, he had won a solid position in the business and political world of his city. The rough edges left by his proletarian upbringing had received a pretty convincing polish. Although he was not an integral part of the best society, he was on a footing of familiarity with most of the important people of the town. His rendition of barber-shop ballads was spirited, his repertory of dialect stories extensive and pungent. Men of all classes respected him for his ability and liked him for his spontaneous good-fellowship. He was popular with women too. The most snobbish debutantes found him " terribly amusing."

Here and there eyebrows were raised ever so slightly when Barbara Haynes announced her engagement to

Jack Gordon, though no one considered the marriage unsuitable. The Hayneses had been one of the reigning families of the town for generations. They were not especially wealthy, but their social position was impregnable. Barbara herself was a small girl, with masses of soft dark hair and large brown eyes. She possessed a youthful, almost elfin beauty, more telling than mere smartness or prettiness, a beauty deliberately achieved by the careful selection of clothes and coiffure, for her features were not good in themselves. She was intelligent, well educated, and a gifted musician. Jack was deeply, romantically in love with this gentle, exquisite creature. He longed to cherish her and shield her from everything sordid.

Barbara's fragile appearance was, as a matter of fact, slightly deceptive. She was really an upstanding, ambitious young lady who had been encouraged to think of herself as a promising concert pianist. For years she had studied hard at her music, living independently in New York and in Paris. She had already achieved a small measure of success in public recitals, though at the time she fell in love with Jack the road to Carnegie Hall was beginning to look painfully long and stony. Her relations with people, her hours of work and fun, were planned as carefully and intelligently as her wardrobe.

Falling in love with Jack Gordon called a halt to her musical career. His business and rising political activities tied him to the town. Piano lessons for the young constituted the sole professional outlet for musical talent in the local scene. Barbara loved Jack Gordon. She liked his dynamic, driving personality and respected the fine achievement of his business success. Her imagination was caught by his political enthusiasm. She saw many ways in which she could help him — her social connections, her gift for entertaining, her knowledge of many subtle antagonisms and cross-currents of emotion in the townsfolk which she would know better how to handle than Jack, for all his vigour and ability. Moreover, she was tenderly aware of the rough edges in Jack's social approach. She felt that he needed a tactful wife to help him overcome the shortcomings of his education and breeding.

Both Jack and Barbara were thoroughly nice people, without vices and even without serious faults. They were very much in love. They were generously devoted to each other and eager to build a serene, beautiful, permanent life together. The marriage was full of promise.

Eight years later this promise seemed to have been disappointed. Mrs. Gordon was unhappy and sought psychiatric help. She was worrying about her marriage, although it was her son she came to talk about. The child at the age of seven had suddenly developed a nervous mannerism of screwing up his face. He often woke up at night screaming with fear from some nightmare, was making no progress in school, and had no friends of his own age. Mrs. Gordon wanted my professional support against her husband's arbitrary decision that the sensitive boy attend public school. As she talked, however, her personal distress about her marriage broke through repeatedly. Mr. Gordon's behaviour about the school was, she said, only one instance of his unreasonable attitude toward herself and the child. He attacked her even more than the child, she confessed finally. Everything she did or did not do was wrong. If she had friends in to dinner, her husband was often rude to them, told her that they were snobbish stuffed shirts and that she should have more consideration than to tire him out with such trivialities. " They're not stuffed shirts at all," she expostulated parenthetically — " they're interested in everything and they're much better informed than Jack is himself. But when I give up and decide not to entertain anyone for a time," she continued, " Jack's just as bad. He says that he needs relaxation and sociability. Once he even said I didn't ask a certain person to the house because I was ashamed of my husband. That was my old music-teacher. He gave a concert in town and came in for a lot of lionizing. I had lunch with him, but I didn't invite him to dinner. I couldn't have without asking a lot of the people Jack calls ' stuffed shirts ' too. Besides, I thought Jack wouldn't like him. And really, doctor, by now I am afraid that Jack will offend our guests. He can be perfectly charming, but he just won't be with the people that count. *They* don't care whether he went to college or not. Jack can't see it, though. He says they're pompous and dull and cold and narrow and can't see any good in a man who hasn't been to their stupid little colleges and is too busy to monkey with pictures and books.

" I worked so hard when we were first married getting a circle of friends who were fun and who could help Jack.

Jack liked them in the beginning. They liked him, too, and they did help him. Then people started telling him how much he owed his wife. And during one campaign the opposition published a cartoon of Jack lassoing with a wedding ring a bull labelled ' Public Office.' I told him it was just nonsense, the kind of thing any prominent man had to put up with. But I think he started being rude to me and our friends about that time. Another thing happened. Jack thought he would be made chairman of the organization committee the reform people got together, and he wasn't. They put in a chap who's awfully good at slapping everybody on the back and not much else. I thought they were right. Back-slapping was all that job needed, and Jack isn't good at it. Well, Jack felt terribly let down and said nobody believed in him, not even I. From then on he keeps saying I'm not loyal to him.

" You see how things are. Jack is gradually alienating all the people who are important for him politically. I've tried hard to show him what he is doing and explain to him the attitude of our friends. I want so much to help Jack, and I can — I really can, doctor — if he would only be sensible. But he fights me more than anyone else. It's not only that he won't let me work with him any more. He's terribly dictatorial about everything else. Take the boy, for instance. Jack has always left his training to me. He was so busy he scarcely saw the child. But he won't let me have a word to say about the school situation, and I *know* the public school is all wrong. We used to buy important things together. Now he won't be bothered about anything for the house. Why, he actually bought a yacht without even telling me. And expects me to live on it this summer instead of taking the boy to the mountains. He's absurdly jealous, too. I used to play duets with an old friend, but Jack made such a fuss that I had to stop seeing him altogether. I used to go to New York for concerts or opera alone or with mother once a week. Jack is too busy to go with me and he doesn't care for music. He acted so dismal and unpleasant every time I went, though, that I finally gave up my little trips. I don't know what to do. I love Jack more than anything in the world. Our marriage is the only thing that matters. My mother says I'm a fool to put up with the way he treats me, but I don't care. I'd do anything to make Jack happy. I can't. The more I try, the worse things get."

This was Mrs. Gordon's story — condensed from the flood of perplexed and bitter confidences she poured out at her first visit. Her account is accurate as far as it goes. She was sincere in her love and in her efforts to help her husband. She was genuinely bewildered by his antagonism and unreasonable behaviour. But her story doesn't make sense because it fails to take into account the underlying conflict between these two people and the confused, unconscious motivation behind their behaviour. Jack's reaction, irrational as it appeared to his wife, was a simple fight against domination and a growing feeling of personal inadequacy. Barbara's well-intentioned attempts to help him were a major threat to his self-esteem. Inevitably, then, the more she tried to do for him, the more threatened

he felt — and the more violently he fought back. You
remember that Jack entered marriage with a chivalrous
desire to cherish and protect his wife. This attitude was a
necessary defence for him against her social superiority.
Few men who have struggled upward from humble be-
ginnings can avoid feeling insecure about their limitations,
especially in the early days of victory before they are quite
sure of their new status. Before he met Barbara, Jack had
not come to grips with his social problem. He was naïvely
proud to associate with the elite of the town and did
not expect to be one of them. Paradoxically his humility
guarded him against a feeling of inferiority. His marriage
precipitated the problem. In a way it was a triumph, a
proof that the poor boy from the wrong side of the tracks
had finally arrived. He was now a full-fledged member of
the inner circle. But it also changed his point of view
toward himself. He was no longer a proletarian making
good in polite society. He was a gentleman who was not
quite a gentleman. His pride in having come so far was
changed to shame that he had not come all the way.
Barbara's breeding made him conscious of his own crudities, made him feel a little uneasy and gauche. Jack's
protective attitude toward his wife was his method of
handling his uncomfortable feeling that he was not quite
equal to her. Protection is a sign of strength. We can only
protect those weaker than ourselves. Jack could accept
Barbara's perfection so long as she was dependent upon
him. His mastery in the man's world of business and politics compensated him for his inferiority in the social sphere.

His picture of Barbara as an exquisite, helpless, feminine creature was necessary to his natural desire for masculine superiority.

This picture survived Barbara's enthusiastic talk about politics during their engagement. It could not survive her active and frequently successful efforts to promote his career after marriage. The more ably she helped him, the more his one line of superiority was undermined. He felt dominated and attacked, even though Barbara was fighting on his side. At the same time his consciousness of social inadequacy was intensified by Barbara's attempts to polish his manners and also by his now constant association with his social betters. Jack's position was, psychologically, very difficult, intolerable to a proud man not quite sure of himself underneath.

Jack Gordon was a fighter. A timid, deprecatory soul could never have battled his way up from the slums. His first impulse in the face of any affront to his ego was to take the offensive. He was not the kind of person who suffers quietly from a frank feeling of inferiority. He preserved his own self-respect by disparaging those who made him feel small. If he felt himself in danger of attack, he aimed the first blow himself. When his power was called into question, he affirmed his own strength by a vigorous display of force.

Unfortunately his battle with Barbara was the struggle of a blind man. He could not distinguish friend from foe, but lashed out wildly. His blows were badly aimed and struck himself and his allies as freely as the enemy. He did not know why he was fighting or against whom. He felt attacked and belittled, so he fought. The fact that he could not point to a real grievance, that he was often unreasonable even in his own eyes, made him increasingly unhappy and rebellious — against himself and everyone else. This confused, painful, blindly antagonistic state of mind naturally resulted in the whimsical bursts of anger and authority which Barbara found so incomprehensible. Yet he also turned to her for consolation and support, or was magnificently generous (witness the yacht) as another way of proving his power.

What of Barbara? Was she the innocent victim of a man in the grip of an inferiority complex? The relationship between two people is never so simple as that question implies. I have never seen a marriage where responsibility for conflict (note I do not say blame) could be laid exclusively or even primarily at the door of either partner. Barbara made her full contribution to the problems of the Gordon ménage. I said above that she was fighting on Jack's side. If that statement had been wholly true he might have been able to accept her help, or at least he would not have resented it so deeply. But Barbara was as human as Jack. She had needs and ambitions of her own. She was, you recall, a musician with good expectations of professional success. Her training and probably also her fundamental nature was oriented toward personal achievement. At the time of her marriage she did not give up her ambitions. She could not give them up, since they were deeply rooted in her personality. She merely substituted Jack's aims for her own musical career. She entered marriage with the full intention of playing a major role in his political life. She carried out her plan to the extent of receiving public recognition in the cartoon. Jack found the cartoon unbearable because it contained a measure of truth. He hated to be shoved and jockeyed into a position, however favourable. His masculine pride would not be beholden to a woman, especially not to that tender, helpless, well-bred child, his wife. Barbara, on the other hand, secretly relished the cartoon. She made a point of telling people how absurd it was — incidentally calling it to their attention. In countless small matters she not only pulled the strings, but managed — as if by chance or against her will — to let people know that she pulled them. Jack, necessarily, received the public acclaim and glory. Barbara wished it so. She had given up her own career and conscientiously denied herself all conspicuous success. Her job was to support Jack, to be the power behind the throne. Unfortunately Barbara (like Richelieu and Wolsey) could not wholly eliminate a need for personal recognition. Because of his own insecurity Jack frequently ignored or ridiculed her contribution to his achievements. Barbara resented his supercilious attitude without understanding its cause or indeed being fully aware of her own annoyance. Against her good judgment, against her real advantage, and *without knowing what she was doing,* she tried to exact homage from Jack and sought appreciation for herself from other people.

It is easy to censure Barbara for petty vanity and selfish

ambition. Yet I have never known a woman who could play effectively the role Barbara elected. A self-satisfaction so strong that it requires no recognition amounts almost to megalomania. Human beings need reassurance that their achievements are good. I have watched some of the best and most domestic of wives make a stealthy parade of their virtues and heard them suggest ever so subtly that they are in the main responsible for their husband's success. If the act is properly put on, the audience goes away remarking: " What a lucky man Mr. X is to have such a wonderful wife! No one would ever suspect it, but I believe she's the real business man in that house. Mr. X wouldn't amount to much without her." It is not quite fair to call this performance an act, because usually Mrs. X has no idea what she is about. Neither has Mr. X, though very often after the curtain falls he finds himself vaguely irritated. And the wife feels a little guilty without knowing why.

Now, the ambitions of Barbara and Mrs. X are perfectly legitimate. They are energetic, intelligent, executive women with a right to work and to feel that their work has value. The trouble is that they have no sanctioned outlet for their activity. Their partnership with their husbands is unacknowledged and in a way illicit. The men resent the encroachment upon their masculine domain, and the women resent the lack of recognition and frequent frustration attendant upon their cramped and hidden manœuvres. The upshot is too frequently a bitter, though largely unconscious, rivalry between husband and wife instead of fruitful co-operation. Mrs. Gordon's experience illustrates, I think, the inevitable discomfort of the position behind the throne. Most women who merge their ambitions with their husbands', who try to promote the man's career by working behind the scenes in a " feminine " manner, run into such resistance as Barbara encountered. Barbara was a little more ambitious, perhaps, than most women, and Jack a little less able to accept assistance because of his own problems. The conflict between them was therefore accentuated. The particular attitudes of every couple shape the conflict to an individual form. It remains a central problem in a great many marriages today. Active partnership between husband and wife is always difficult because of the peculiar touchiness of the modern male and the insecurity of the modern female. Of which more later on. The difficulties are not avoided by an attempt to hide them under feminine camouflage. On the contrary, they are intensified. In this connection I feel that for once I can step out of my psychiatric objectivity and give definite advice. A woman should never attempt to push her husband's career or reform his character or even modify his diet without his full knowledge and consent. Sir James M. Barrie notwithstanding, it doesn't work. A man cannot be helped against his will. The efforts of his wife, however well-intentioned and useful, however skilfully introduced, will lead to irritation and frequently to irrational destructive behaviour like Jack Gordon's.

Barbara's program included not only support in his political activities, but the transformation of his social presence. Barbara was perfectly aware of the covert gibes occasionally directed toward her husband. One of the tasks she set herself was the worldly education of her husband so that he should present not the slightest handle for ridicule. Another was to place him on a footing of absolute equality with the most snobbish. This pinnacle of social success she conceived to be of paramount importance both to Jack's personal satisfaction and to his political career. She overlooked the fact that it was also necessary for her own satisfaction. She was so identified with Jack, by marriage and by love, that any slight to him was also one to her. Yet she could not always resist the temptation to disengage herself from his inferiority — to show that, while she was loyal to her husband, she could also see his faults and laugh at them with the other side. The laughter of her friends was usually thoroughly good-natured, since they liked Jack and were free to ignore him if they didn't. Her own laughter was really not good-natured. It was constantly mixed with resentment — resentment at her friends for laughing, resentment at Jack for provoking laughter, resentment at the bond which subjected her to ridicule. If Jack candidly showed his ignorance of some little point — the identity of Œdipus, ancient and modern, of Koussevitzsky, of El Greco — Barbara somehow felt it necessary to prove her own knowledge by some little explanation to him and a deprecatory laugh at the one-track mind of these " captains of industry." She was given to making little comments — tolerant but barbed — whenever Jack was " cutting up " in a way that betrayed his different breeding. She would laugh with the rest at one of his ballads and remark charitably: " He's just a big silly boy. Pretty soon he'll grow into something sensible." After the party she would gently remonstrate with him for making himself conspicuous, quote reluctantly, and as if sparing him all but a hint of the truth, some disparaging remark she had overheard. He would protest that the whole crew of men sang quite as loudly. Barbara would then point out very tactfully that *their* song was their college hymn, quite a different matter from the vulgar ditty he had brought out. She was sure Mrs. Bradfield had been quite shocked. He must be more careful.

The result of these little disquisitions on taste and etiquette was wholly disastrous. Jack became self-conscious about his lack of college training and *savoir-faire*. The loss of his spontaneity left him merely awkward in groups where he had formerly been amusing in his own right. Barbara sensed the lamentable results of her training without grasping the cause. She redoubled her efforts to help her husband, but she succeeded only in increasing her hidden resentment against the feeling of social inferiority Jack forced upon her. Her little remarks became increasingly venomous in public and more definitely reproachful in private.

Jack was, as we have seen, the last man to be able to tolerate the role of dull schoolboy to which his wife's teaching was assigning him, and also the role of social inferior among his daily associates. His good-natured buffoonery rapidly gave way to a belligerent arrogance. He was acutely uncomfortable with his wife's guests, but he had learned to fight the world, not himself. Instead of bemoaning his own limitations, he naturally accused his guests of being stuffed shirts, dilettantes, and the like. He forestalled any snubs from them by being rude himself. Far from polishing a few rough edges in Jack's manner, Barbara succeeded in making him a first-class boor, and an angry husband into the bargain.

Just why did Barbara fail so pitiably in her enterprise? Most people conceive that " polishing " is within the province of wifely duty. A good wife is supposed to be responsible for her husband's health, appearance, and at any rate minor defects of character. Jack was, to be sure, unusually sensitive, but a tactful woman should be able to manage such a problem. Or so they say. I don't think so. Mrs. Gordon bears a reputation for unusual charm and skill in handling people. Superficially she was rarely at fault in her methods. I feel, however, that her use of tact was the substitution of a rapier for a bludgeon. Her weapon was no less dangerous because of its delicacy.

Incidentally, I am no great believer in the application of tact to major problems in marriage or any other human relationship. On the stage and between the covers of books I have seen women reform and transform their husbands by saying the right thing at the right moment, by skilfully playing upon the poor fellows' egotism, by dropping helpful suggestions which the husbands adopt as their own. I have also watched brilliant displays of tactful guidance in real life, but the results have not followed the expectations aroused by literature. The husband of one very charming

lady drinks heavily. Another divorced his wife after she
had groomed him for success as a writer. Almost always
the tactful wife has a very peppery husband. The casual
onlooker is impressed with her suave forbearance. The
psychiatrist often finds that the husband's irritability is a
result of tactful handling rather than its cause. The truth
is that no one likes to be " handled," no matter how skilfully. Husbands are justifiably annoyed when their righteous indignation is met with patronizing calm — with insincere and probably temporary acquiescence or with a
sweet reasonableness that never comes to grips with the
real problem at all. They resent being got into a good
mood for something unpleasant by a fine dinner, or, worse,
by a preliminary display of tender love. Tact is almost invariably patronizing and insincere. Its aim is to cover up
uncomfortable truths, or to push a man without his knowledge in a direction he doesn't want to go. Any dishonest
attitude, however praiseworthy its intention, is dangerous
in marriage. Daily contact under all vicissitudes of temper
puts too great a strain upon the tactful lady. Barbara could
correct Jack's *faux pas* with gaiety and subtlety most of
the time, but a very few slips into honest reproach when
she was tired or worried or vexed beyond endurance were
sufficient to make Jack aware of her real attitude. Moreover, we have seen how our unconscious impulses play
tricks on us. So long as Barbara is actually ashamed of her
husband and resentful about his behaviour she is in danger
of " accidentally " telling him the unvarnished truth even
though she has no intention of doing so. We saw how her

innocent remarks carried poison of which she herself knew nothing. The tactful wife who insidiously and painlessly cajoles her husband into good behaviour is a literary invention. Courtesy and kindliness are pleasant adjuncts to any relationship, but " tact " is too often a disguised hostility which cannot be used successfully to cure a husband's faults and get him to walk a path he doesn't like.

Barbara failed in her efforts to induct her husband into the higher reaches of society and social adequacy, not because her approach was insufficiently tactful, but because her fundamental attitude toward the problem was defensive and resentful and because Jack was not ready for the transformation. Since she was not aware of her attitude she was powerless to handle it. Nor could she understand Jack's resistance. Her belief that she could help him by polishing a few superficial crudities, effectively masked the real situation. She had never faced honestly the social implications of her marriage. She was not prepared for the loss of her accustomed prestige, for the discomforts of a less secure social position. Her natural impulse was to fight for her reputation as a cultivated, well-bred woman, but she did not realize that she was fighting, nor that her victory was necessarily won at her husband's expense. Neither did she realize that she herself disliked Jack's social and cultural limitations. During her engagement she accepted them as defects, to be eliminated after marriage. When she found that they did not disappear, but became accentuated under her guidance, she resented them very much indeed — again without being fully cognizant of her own feelings. Jack's antagonistic behaviour seemed to her a gratuitous insult, bewildering and unmerited.

If Barbara had been confronted with a clear choice between loyalty to her husband and the preservation of social amenities, she would have had no hesitation in renouncing the latter. She would stand by Jack Gordon against any open attack upon him and cheerfully accept poverty or disgrace out of devotion to her man. She was not offered a clear choice, but an apparent opportunity — nay, a duty — to reconcile her love for Jack with her desire for social approval. She begrudged Jack the small gift of her prestige because the sacrifice was forced upon her unawares. It was taken from her, not freely given. She fought automatically in the service of her personal vanity, not because vanity meant more to her than love, but because she did not realize the nature of the conflict. She could not forgive Jack's lack of breeding because she refused to recognize that she needed to forgive such a thing. Her snobbishness was as unconscious as her vanity, so she could not control either of them.

Snobbish and vain. These are unkind epithets to apply to a person as nice as Mrs. Gordon. I hasten to insist that Barbara was no more at fault than you or I or any other normal human being. Barbara had been trained from infancy to prize breeding and social position. These values were her heritage, as unconsidered as the air she breathed. It was inevitable that any crudeness in a person as close to her as a husband should jar upon her, and equally natural that she should not recognize her discomfort

clearly, for the idea of snobbishness was as repugnant to
her as to any of us. It was also inevitable that her efforts
to maintain her social position should not be consciously
formulated. Only a parvenu strives openly to climb the
ladder. The person who is born at the top accepts his
position without thinking. But he does automatically
struggle to keep his balance when the ladder starts to topple
under him. We are sympathetic with Jack's floundering
reaction against a sense of inferiority. We see clearly how
his resentments arise from the limitations of his background. Barbara's hidden resentments come just as naturally from the limitations of her early training.

The trouble in the Gordon ménage did not proceed
from cruelty and selfishness on the part of either Jack or
Barbara. Both of them were generous, loving people.
They were *people,* however; not ideal abstractions, but
human beings with the strength and frailty of their kind.
The elements of conflict implicit in every marriage led to
open distress for the Gordons because the blend was in
some respects unusually difficult to manage and because
both of them were unusually positive people. The difference in cultural background accentuated their difficulties,
certainly. Barbara's strength of mind and personal ambition were ill mated with Jack's defensive pride and desire
for mastery. Yet it would be a mistake to maintain that
" they should never have married in the first place." Jack's
state of mind at the time of his marriage was such that he
could scarcely have married anyone else. He had become
snobbish, if you like. Girls from his own class did not at-

tract him. He wanted the cachet of a successful marriage on his career. He was stimulated and excited by Barbara, not only in her own right, but also as a representative of her class. His marriage was often painful, but it does not follow that union with a woman with his own cultural limitations would have been more pleasant. I would guess that Jack — if he brought himself to marry such a girl at all — would find her very dull. He would be a little ashamed of her and believe that she hampered his career. He would long for exactly the kind of life Barbara gave him. I have known men with problems psychologically similar to Jack's who married simple-hearted, unpretentious girls, or who left their Barbaras for a less demanding mate. The form of their discontent changed, but not their discontent. Too often we assume that circumstances which play an important role in marital discord are the *cause* of the discord, that it might have been avoided by a different choice of circumstances. Sometimes we are right, especially if the couple is extremely young and immature or if the circumstances have been truly unforeseen. If the husband loses his legs in a train wreck, or the family fortune in an unpredictable crash of the stock market, one may safely opine that the marriage might have turned out differently (either better or worse) if the misadventure had not occured. But if an uneducated man marries a cultivated woman, or a short little fellow a tall willowy girl, we may be sure that he does so because of some need in his own being. Probably he could do no other and the consequent problems are already implicit in his choice.

Jack Gordon wanted to marry Barbara. He thought she was a gentle, acquiescent creature whom he could " protect " from the world. To be more accurate and certainly more clumsy, we might say that he thought he thought so. You remember that Barbara talked to him gravely about her music and her political projects. He appeared to ignore her plain warnings in his dream of exquisite helplessness. But did he? I suspect that Jack, in some area of his being, knew very well that he was marrying a strong, positive woman. And that he was well content. A fluttering, dependent social butterfly would have suited his deepest psychological need no better than a simple working girl. Barbara, the real Barbara, was a sort of sparring partner for him. He could prove his own strength by subduing hers. Jack was a highly competitive person, so competitive, indeed, that he needed a worthy opponent. Your champion chess-player has no satisfaction in easy victories. Jack needed a fight and a good fight. He also needed to win. The trouble with Barbara was not that she was strong and a fighter, but that she was sometimes too strong. Jack, cornered, forgot the rules of the game and sought victory through sheer pommelling. Yet Jack was not wholly the fighter. He was also a frightened little boy who wanted the strength and security of a strong partner. Barbara, again the real Barbara, was a refuge for his loneliness and timidity. A woman less vigorous and intelligent could not have offered him the bulwark he needed against his fear of the world.

The sensible reader has long since lifted his eyebrows at

such far-fetched analysis. How can a man marry a woman because she is frail and because she is strong, because he wants to fight her and because he seeks protection? It doesn't make sense. Nevertheless, to my certain knowledge, not only Jack but many of his fellows select their wives and conduct their marriages on just such an irrational basis. Human impulses are exceedingly weak in consistency. The unconscious does not trouble itself with logic, and the conscious mind is clever enough to carve out a passable syllogism from the most unlikely material by judicious omission of contradictory data.

Of course, these variegated demands would put Barbara in a very awkward position if she knew anything about them. A conscientious, affectionate, and omniscient wife could turn herself into a corkscrew to please her husband and then find him reproaching her for not being straight. Happily for her peace of mind, Barbara is unaware of all these complicated demands. She is too busy trying to fulfil her own. Like Jack she has a great number of incompatible desires. She, too, wants shelter and freedom, a strong dominating husband, and a child whom she can rule and comfort. She loves Jack because he is different from the men she has known — more direct, more vigorous. She admires him for his triumphant battle against his early poverty. Yet she is bothered by his failure to behave like everybody else and by his aggressiveness.

In spite of their quarrels and frequent misery I would classify the union of Barbara and Jack as a good marriage. The deepest needs of each of them found satisfaction in

the other. Both recognized the fundamental solidity of
their relationship. At no time did they consider divorce.
The question was only how they could make their marriage happier. How could they stop hurting each other
and themselves?

Now, I see no complete cure for their woes without a
thoroughgoing transformation of the character of both
Barbara and Jack. Just as we found no ideal solution of
sexual incompatibility or emotional entanglements with
outsiders, so we cannot put forward a perfect resolution of
the contradictory demands of two people for mastery and
protective love. But the distress can be diminished, the balance tipped toward satisfaction, in a marriage like the
Gordons. They cannot exorcize pain from their relationship, but they can relish it as a part of full-bodied living.
A good wine is a harmonious blend of sweet and bitter.
It is not sugar water with a specified alcoholic content. A
good marriage is a compound of struggle and peace.

If I were "treating" the Gordons (a privilege which
never came my way), my first effort would be in the direction of getting them to savour their marriage as it is,
with all its defects. Both of them were so tortured by a
sense of failure that they could not value what they had.
The struggles of their actual union were in such glaring
contrast to the high aspirations with which they entered
marriage and with popular conceptions of marital happiness that it never occurred to them to *enjoy* their real relationship. Yet if either of them had died, the remaining
partner would have been as lost as the bereaved member

of the most ideally mated couple. Absence of quarrels is too often regarded as the criterion of a successful marriage. Usually it means little more than indifference — a superficial placidity attained by shallow people or those whose real interests lie outside their home, or those who, with or without a day of reckoning, habitually bury their antagonism under a thick cotton pad of polite behaviour. The Gordon marriage, I repeat, was a good marriage, a rich, vital, satisfying union. Recognition of this fact would have helped them handle the painful discordant elements which bulked so large in their experience.

In passing let me remark that shocks and crises of all varieties very often serve the purpose of awakening appreciation of the value of an apparently discordant marriage quite as well as psychiatric treatment. Financial loss, sudden illness of husband or wife, the death of a child, even a quarrel so intense that it brings a couple to the verge of divorce may lead to a reaffirmation of love and a warm recognition of the basic satisfactions in their relationship. Of course if the marriage is not well grounded such calamities are likely to break it up entirely. It frequently happened that a smooth, apparently successful marriage collapsed under the strain of the depression, for instance. Husband and wife had been comfortably adjusted to their way of living, but not to each other. When the way of living changed, there was nothing left.

The trouble with " shock " treatment of a fundamentally good but superficially antagonistic marriage is that external circumstances may separate the couple before they have a chance to rebuild their relationship. You remember the Caswells. I suggested that Mrs. Caswell might have been pushed into divorce by social pressure and her own resentments so that reconciliation would be impossible. Or the antagonistic attitudes may be reinforced by accidental features of the critical situation so that the free flow of tenderness is prevented. Let us suppose that the Gordons' child had been kidnapped. The chances are that Barbara and Jack would have been reunited in their common anxiety over his fate. Suppose, however, he contracted scarlet fever at public school. Barbara's anxiety might then reinforce her resentment against Jack's insistence that the boy attend the school, while Jack, in the face of her more or less open reproach and his own feeling of responsibility, would become more violently defensive than before. So long as emotions are free and active it is easy for them to find a good resolution. If Jack could, during this crisis, just once relax his defences enough to show Barbara his terror, dependence, and guilt, her fundamental tenderness and loyalty could break through and the upshot might well be a firm acceptance of each other. But if the moment of strong emotion passes without understanding, resentments and defences may be yet more stiffly crystallized in the old mould.

The first step toward a happier marriage, however achieved, is freedom to value the relationship as it is. Barbara and Jack have come a long way when they can say with conviction: " Our marriage is not perfect; we often make each other miserable. Nevertheless we like living together. This life together, difficult as we find it, is still more satisfying than any other." Already their misery is less intense, because they do not have to keep their attention focused upon it. So long as they are struggling constantly to make their marriage better they are forced to concentrate on its problems. A quarrel is not only an acrimonious dispute about some concrete situation, but an illustration of the failure of their marriage. It is extended through every aspect of their relationship and protracted in time.

The observation of little children is a good antidote to adult strivings for continuous satisfaction in marriage. Two youngsters may fight frequently and bitterly and yet be warmly affectionate between battles. They hold no grudges for the periods of combat. However strenuous their quarrels, they think of themselves as friends and look forward to each meeting with eagerness. Adults cannot shift their moods as readily as children, but they can avoid deliberately fostering the persistence of disagreeable aspects of their relationship. The small daily bickerings and the inevitable shortcomings of any communal life are more devastating to a reflective, earnest, idealistic couple than to a pair who are more inclined to take things as they come. Every little unpleasantness is woven into a coherent pattern of disappointment and frustration instead of being dismissed promptly as an unimportant detail.

An optimistic, appreciative attitude toward marriage need not be based wholly on childish inconsequence or on a Pollyanna determination to look on the bright side of things. It can spring from a fine understanding of that central problem of married life which I outlined at the beginning of the chapter: two personalities with divergent and partially incompatible aims are engaged in the effort to satisfy these aims and at the same time make themselves completely one. They want absolute self-expression and absolute loyalty. Rationally we all admit that we can't have everything, that marriage demands compromise, and even, reluctantly, that love cannot be perfect. But we are quite irrationally annoyed when we find ourselves actually thwarted by marriage and irrationally hurt by any evidence of disloyalty. Now, it is impossible to be human without feeling this annoyance and this hurt. Instead of accepting our reactions as cheerfully as may be, however, as a necessary part of any close relationship, we are very prone to exaggerate them. We blame marriage, our partner, or ourselves for problems which are implicit in our very humanity. Jack suffered from the feeling that Barbara did not love him and was not loyal to him. She did indeed repudiate him at times when he encroached too heavily upon her own aims. But in the main she loved him with very great warmth and devotion. Jack threw away the riches he had because he did not have — and *could* not have — everything.

An animal psychologist once told me of an experiment with a chimpanzee. The experimenter put a banana under a box while the animal watched him. The animal was taken away for a few minutes. In the interim a piece of lettuce was substituted for the banana. Ordinarily the ape was very fond of lettuce, but when he was permitted to go to the box he was so upset by not finding the expected banana that he tore the lettuce to pieces and stamped on it. Married people frequently behave like this animal. We reject lettuce not because we dislike it but because it is not the banana which we anticipated. We reject the good marriage we have because it is not the perfect marriage which, consciously or unconsciously, we want. Our unconscious expectations are more dangerous than the naïve idealism we express. We can learn very readily to *say* that we don't expect much from marriage. To accept without bitterness the actual experience of imperfect devotion and the curtailment of our desires requires a much fuller understanding of the realities of wedlock.

Can the Gordons do more for themselves than relish the marriage they have? A less guilt-ridden and resentful attitude toward their problems would certainly relieve tension and diminish heartache, but can they not do something toward a more constructive handling of the specific points of conflict between them? I believe that they can. Again the method is understanding and respect for things as they are and people as they are, but this time the understanding applies to the particular aims and longings of Barbara and Jack. We saw how Barbara constantly intensified their difficulties by her course of action and how her belief in her wifely duty justified her misguided efforts. Jack's behaviour, too, was the result of a blind, misdirected attempt to handle the situation. Only by understanding each other and themselves could they work toward a fruit-

ful compromise rather than an intensification of antagonism. Rules of conduct, often very sound in themselves and
satisfactory for many marriages, may be actually harmful
if they are applied without reference to the problems of a
particular marriage. We are told, for instance, that it is
a good thing for married couples to take a vacation from
each other occasionally, that a short separation relieves
tension about trivialities and freshens the love relationship.
This happy result does often occur. Sometimes, however,
the " vacation " may be interpreted by one or the other
partner as punishment, as a rejection of the marriage bond.
Not infrequently the interpretation is in a measure correct.
Barbara's mother urged her to go off on a trip by herself,
telling her that every marriage was benefited by separation, that Jack would appreciate her more in her absence,
and that she owed herself a rest from his ill treatment of
her. The hostility to Jack was very thinly disguised by
the suggestion ostensibly designed to improve or at least
preserve the marriage. If Barbara had carried out her
mother's advice in anything like the spirit in which it
was given, the chances are that her husband would have
responded accurately to the basic hostility rather than to
the superficial " good sense." One would expect some sort
of retaliation from him and a further deterioration of their
relationship. No program for handling marital difficulties
can be successful unless it takes into account the *meaning*
of the difficulties to the particular people involved.

If I were " treating " Barbara and Jack, I would, of
course, help them understand the *meaning* of their diffi-

culties in terms of their deeper needs and desires. They would then be in a position to work out an intelligent, workable compromise between their conflicting aims instead of obscurely fighting for complete satisfaction of every impulse, however contradictory and realistically impossible. I have already explained what the psychiatrist tries to do in effecting an adjustment of divergent sexual needs. His aims and procedures are the same for these non-sexual needs of the personality.

But I did not treat the Gordons. Nor is it possible for every married couple in distress about their marriage (and that means — at one time or another — practically every married couple) to receive psychiatric treatment for their problems. Can psychiatry help them to help themselves without the constant individual guidance of the doctor?

I have already suggested from time to time — in connection with infidelity, with sexual differences, and now with these other problems of living together — that people try themselves to understand the *meaning* for their own marriage of the particular acts which bother them. I believe that this book and others of its kind, as well as the courses and study groups now available in most cities, can give untrained people a working insight into many of the deeper aspects of human nature. They can learn to recognize at least the more common unconscious impulses beneath the disguises thrown over them by a rationalizing, self-protective, naïvely idealistic ego. Psychiatry is not an esoteric mystery, but a body of principles and facts accessible to anyone who cares to study them. Just as the lay person can grasp in a general way the functioning of the human body, so he can understand the mind. He can also apply fruitfully a more extensive, though still unprofessional, knowledge of the commoner diseases and malfunctions, let us say tuberculosis.

There is, however, a grave possibility of danger in self-doctoring. The lay person may diagnose himself wrongly. Or he may be so confident of his ability to treat himself that he neglects a serious condition which can only be handled by expert knowledge. Or he may fancy himself the victim of diseases he does not really have, exaggerating the importance of symptoms he has read about.

Self-doctoring in the mental and emotional field carries the same risks. In fact they are even more serious, partly because of the difficulties inherent in the diagnosis and treatment of our own mental condition, and partly because of our attitude toward this branch of doctoring. The inherent difficulties I will discuss at length in a moment, but I want to say a few words first about this attitude toward self-help in handling emotional problems. Psychiatry is the youngest branch of medicine, especially as it applies to people who are not obviously mentally ill. Until a few years ago it did not occur to us that there might be a science of emotional control. We relied upon our own " will-power " to improve our behaviour and keep our emotions in hand. Traditionally, then, the field of the psychiatrist is the field of ordinary human endeavour. We all feel competent to handle malfunctioning in this field, while we would consult a doctor at once for a cold in the head. Thus many serious mental ailments which need expert attention are never referred to the psychiatrist because the lay person is over-confident of his own ability to handle them. This same tradition that anyone can be an expert in the matter of human emotions leads to the unbalanced application of imperfectly assimilated fragments of knowledge. The mother who has heard about the dangers of fixations denies her child expressions of affection, without any feeling that she is overstepping the limits of her knowledge and competence. She is like the mother who reads of the value of sunlight and suddenly exposes her infant to an hour of the noon sun with disastrous results, or feeds him so much well-advertised " roughage " that he develops an intestinal irritation. She wouldn't think of clipping out his tonsils by herself. Surgery is obviously a medical specialty requiring great knowledge and skill. The clothes we wear, the food we eat, and the expression of our emotions are traditionally within the province of the layman, so we cheerfully adopt as a popular fad any bit of specialized knowledge that comes our way, without any feeling for its possible seriousness. The traditional, common-sense way of doing things is usually faulty, but by and large it works. In the course of generations people have learned not the best procedures, but passable ones. Any radical change from the past fashion, whether of diet or of the conduct of marriage, may entail grave consequences which the layman with his limited knowledge of physical or emotional functioning would never anticipate. Doctors make mistakes too. There are medical fads as well as popular ones. In general, however, the wider knowledge of the physician protects him against the uncritical and exaggerated application of a new idea in his own field. The trained psychiatrist is much more cautious about making interpretations and suggesting changes in conduct than is the lay person who has learned a little psychology.

Now for the difficulties inherent in applying psychiatric knowledge to our own problems. Nothing is more inaccessible to us than our own deepest impulses, in so far as these run counter to the ones we consciously accept. It is very hard to gain insight into the part of ourselves we have always tried to keep from view, and very easy to reach a partial understanding which still protects us from full recognition of impulses we cannot tolerate. The possibility of a wrong diagnosis does not worry me very much. It is unlikely to work serious harm — even if made by a psychiatrist! The important question is what we do with our self-knowledge. Too often we use it only to torture ourselves, when we are left to our own not too tender mercies. The psychiatrist's task is only begun with the bringing to light of hidden impulses. His main work is to effect a reconciliation between these impulses and the conscious ideal of the personality. The impulses are hidden in the first place to relieve the individual of an intolerable burden of guilt and distress about them. Left to himself, the patient would be devastated by self-reproach after he is forced to recognize their existence. The psychiatrist is not reproachful. He accepts these impulses as natural human qualities which have their rightful place in any personality. They work serious hardship only because they are unacknowledged and so function in isolation without the corrective influence of the whole personality. From the psychiatrist the patient gets not only recognition of his repressed aims, but also tolerance for them. Through the friendly, sympathetic, objective attitude of the psychiatrist he learns to accept and *like* himself as he is, to integrate all his impulses into a smooth, working whole.

Married people, applying by themselves the techniques they have learned for the recognition of unconscious impulses, too frequently lack this friendly attitude. Their problems are increased rather than relieved by their own analysis. I have seen people with very good psychiatric training torment themselves and each other by a constant hunt for unconscious hostility beneath superficially pleasant or indifferent behaviour. These people had not serenely and affectionately accepted each other and themselves, so their understanding was purely destructive. I have particularly in mind the case of a colleague who came to me in very great distress. The husband felt unloved to an extreme degree. He analysed very acutely the hostilities underlying his wife's behaviour, suffered from them himself, and pointed them out very freely to her. The wife, on her side, recognized the validity of his analysis and developed an almost obsessive feeling of guilt about her behaviour. She also recognized the mechanism of projection (see page 13) in her husband and realized, with equal pain, that he had a great deal of hostility toward her. The fundamental conflict in this marriage was not unlike that of the Gordons. It was not changed, except for the worse, by the sophisticated " understanding " of unconscious motives.

It is not enough, then, to learn the existence and contours of deeper impulses in oneself and one's wife. One must at the same time learn tolerance for them. Without a spirit of sympathy and acceptance the practice of tracking down latent hostilities is thoroughly bad. The more skilfully it is done, the more catastrophic the results. I have said repeatedly and I say again that every human being, by virtue of his humanity, has mingled with generous, altruistic feelings, self-seeking aims, petty vanities and ambitions, hostilities, resentments, and competitive attitudes even toward those he loves best, as well as a variety of erotic impulses. If the reader finds this statement cynical or bitter or shameful, he had best close the book at once and forget what he has read. Any effort he may make to apply the knowledge here expressed will be dangerous to his marriage rather than helpful. But if he can accept with comfort, even with gusto, the idea that he is a full man with a man's quota of selfishness and fear and love and courage, then he can, I think, profitably examine the particular array of impulses with which he and his wife have to deal.

Here is another little clinical test for the reader to apply to determine his fitness for self-doctoring. As you read about Jack's arrogant weakness and Barbara's disloyal vanity and ambition, do you think what hateful, mean, stupid people they are? Do you feel complacent because you are not such as they? Do you, with horror and dismay, see yourself in the description of their behaviour, or wonder whether you have qualities as bad? You have, of course, but if you wince at the thought you had better preserve your illusions. If you feel that you could not love so pitiable a creature as Jack and that no one could love Barbara as she really is, it would be a mistake to view your own marriage with greater clarity. We must never forget that our illusions about ourselves and our partners are primarily a defence against a reality which we condemn. Psychologically they are very useful. We can safely let down our defences only if we simultaneously renounce our condemnatory attitude.

This point is so crucial that I labour it still further. I have noticed that most people confronted with such an analysis of human frailty remark promptly: " But I don't expect to be perfect. Of course I have faults." An admirable admission. Unfortunately if one is so incautious as to mention a specific fault to them they are at once on the defensive. Either they prove that the fault does not exist, or they are very much cast down. This reaction of repudiation, indignation, or hurt follows upon the pointing out of any behaviour whatsoever which they consider undesirable. There is a very great difference between the blanket statement: " I have faults " and the comfortable recognition of a particular defect. Obviously the first statement means nothing at all, psychologically. Indeed, one's feeling of virtue is enhanced by the expression of humility. We must be able to accept without distress the concrete re-statements and hatreds and disloyalties and pettinesses of our everyday selves before we can handle them adequately.

Ideally we should, of course, be aware of all our impulses and need no defences against our real selves. In practice we must be as tolerant of our inability to achieve perfect integration of our impulses, good and " bad," as of the fact that we have " bad " impulses at all. Some of our attitudes, irrational and defensive though they may be, are built into our personality so firmly that we cannot recognize the impulses they cover, much less tolerate them, without a complete reformation of our character. They must be accepted as they are, by ourselves and our partner in marriage. The burden of adjustment must lie with the other fellow or with our handling of external circum-stances. In time, of course, attitudes shift. At some future date we may be able to gain an insight and acceptance im-possible at present. No part of the personality is absolutely fixed, but some aspects are more flexible than others. I would guess that Jack's defensive, belligerent attitude to-ward his social superiors was pretty stiff at the time Mrs. Gordon came to my office. It was thoroughly irrational, to be sure, a nuisance to his friends, a serious threat to his wife, a source of suffering to Jack, and a practical handicap to his career. Nevertheless the knowledge that he desper-ately wanted social prestige and was personally inadequate to achieve it was too painful for Jack to assimilate at that time of his life. Barbara's resentments about her social insecurities were, on the other hand, less deep-seated. Social position did not mean a great deal to her. Loss of prestige because of her marriage was not a blow to her ego — she was in a position to choose whether or not she would remain at the top of the ladder. The impulses which led her to struggle to maintain herself and to repudiate her husband were relatively superficial. She could, I believe, readily come to recognize both her own feelings and the basis of Jack's problem. Her own reactions she could accept as natural enough under the circumstances. I feel sure that her annoyance at Jack's behaviour would be greatly tempered by sympathetic understanding. She would, I think, see that her efforts to teach him merely intensified his feeling of difference, and realize clearly that her marriage exacted the sacrifice of her former social position. Not a very difficult sacrifice, once she knew that it must be made and gave up the unconscious struggle to have *everything*. At times, certainly, she would find herself again conniving to place herself in a favourable light in some awkward social situation. She would smile at her failure and begin anew.

Barbara's insight and gradual shift in attitude would not solve the problem of social adjustment completely. Jack would remain difficult and unhappy. Barbara would have periods of regret and lapses into her former resentful feelings. But she would be throwing her weight toward a solution rather than against it. In time she would come to accept Jack very fully and warmly as the kind of fellow he was, his crudities and sensitivities along with his vigour and love. Their social life she would take as it came — as Jack prescribed it — without caring for prestige and position. I believe that in the course of months or years Jack himself would gain enough reassurance from her love and her sincere indifference to the social problem to relax his defences. Barbara would help Jack precisely because she made no effort to do so, because she liked him the way he was. This happy result would be strictly a by-product however. The moment Barbara sets out to help Jack socially, she places herself on a superior footing and rouses his antagonism.

Barbara's desire to accomplish something obviously "worth while," on the other hand, appears to be a more fundamental part of her character. She needs to feel that she is somebody and that her work is valued. This need, already very marked, would become increasingly strong as she gave up her reputation as a skilled hostess and charming woman of the world. We saw how this need expressed itself in her effort to be the power behind the throne and how she felt frustrated and unappreciated. Barbara, like most women in our society, was unable to accept her ambition frankly. It seemed to her "unfeminine." She was afraid of failure, and at the same time afraid of success, since a wife must not be more successful that her husband. I should not expect her to understand fully her very complicated attitude toward her ambition, still less the impulses which fed the ambition itself. She could, however, come to realize that, unfeminine or not, she wanted to make something of herself and accept herself as that kind of woman. Again she would not be able to handle the problem perfectly. She would continue to defeat herself at times and go through periods of distress about her work and its relationship to her husband and to her own conception of her wifely role. But her conscious efforts would be more nearly in line with her deeper impulses, instead of being directed against them.

Jack, I think, could learn to accept Barbara's competition in the field of a career more readily than her dominance in their social life. In this field he was already successful and felt relatively secure. We saw that his desire to " protect " Barbara was a product of his feeling of social inferiority. It did not spring directly from his personal ambitions. We saw also that he really wanted a strong woman for a wife. It would not be easy for him to renounce his full masculine superiority. He would want to remain absolutely preeminent. But he could go pretty far toward understanding his conflicting desires to be the boss and to have a strong partner. Still more readily could he learn that Barbara needed a legitimate outlet for her energy and ambition. Competition between them would persist. Once more, however, they would be working toward a realistic compromise instead of blindly fighting each other.

The practical solution of the career problem is not so important. Barbara might continue to work side by side with her husband as his acknowledged partner, or she might return to her music. Probably the latter course would be preferable. A woman in politics has an anomalous position, while music is a socially acceptable career for her. Moreover, Barbara's chief contribution to Jack's political activities lay in her ability to handle influential people, and this ability touched upon Jack's most acute sensitivities.

These suggestions for specific insights and adjustments are, I need hardly remind you, merely illustrative. I am guessing at the type of understanding the Gordons would find easiest. They might attack their problem from a different angle and reach as happy a compromise. Another couple with a different array of basic impulses would arrive at a very different solution. It might happen, for instance, that the husband's insecurities centred primarily on his ability to make money. His wife's competition in this field would be especially devastating, while her greater social success would be relatively easy to assimilate. In the next chapter we will consider briefly a variety of marriages to illustrate further the basic problems underlying superficial conflicts and the possible resolution of the conflict through understanding.

CHAPTER VI

⌇

WORK AND MONEY

MARGARET WESTLEY is a second or third cousin of my wife. She lives in a small New York town, Townsville, well outside the orbit of any larger city. We see her at rare intervals, but with the special intimacy granted to relatives, and we are well supplied with family anecdote about her from a variety of aunts, uncles, and cousins. I have watched the course of her marriage for a dozen years now with increasing respect and admiration. I like to think that Margaret is typical of a great many wives throughout the country.

My wife's grandmother was born and bred in Townsville. She married a minister of the gospel who led the slightly nomadic life so common in his profession and finally settled down in a large city. The old lady's sisters and brothers and most of her childhood friends remained in Townsville. The town has gone its quiet way with little lending or borrowing of population and ideas for nearly a century. Fifteen years ago a nationally known concern established a factory in the town, bringing with it an influx of strange workmen and unfamiliar executives, who are beginning to exert an influence on local manners and ways of thinking. Only within the last decade has it become proper to send the young people away to the big universities, whence they seldom return.

Margaret and her husband, George, attended a small denominational college twenty miles away from Townsville. Margaret was pretty and popular and frankly much more interested in parties than in the tedious verbosity of Cicero or the campaigns of Gustavus Adolphus. The town was firmly American in its reverence for education, however, so Margaret did her assignments conscientiously in a spirit of good-natured and unreflective obedience. George was more serious-minded. He was ambitious — ambitious to become a vice-president of the Townsville Savings Bank and perhaps also a selectman. He read his Cicero earnestly for the sake of the mental training he was told to expect from following his tortuous sentences; he studied mathematics, history, and political science for their practical value, and the classics of English literature for " culture."

In the natural course of events George and Margaret fell in love and were married, to the great satisfaction of their parents and with the complete approval of the whole town. For two years they rented a small house on Elm Street. Margaret did all the housework, including laundry, as a matter of course. She made her own clothes, a charming layette for the infant which arrived promptly after the first year, her husband's shirts, and of course her curtains, drapes, and household linens. Her friends were engaged in approximately the same activities, though a few of them had a hired girl to help, and many were neither as skilled nor as ambitious as Margaret in fulfilling their household tasks. The " girls " met weekly for bridge or sewing circle, each one entertaining the crowd in turn. Less frequently couples exchanged visits in the evening. All were active in church work. Occasionally a large dance was held in the Grange Hall. As a young matron Margaret continued to be as popular as she had been as a girl. If George was so preoccupied with his work that he sometimes protested against the social whirl his wife seemed to crave (a dinner engagement or two each week and a visit to the movies), if he left even the heavy work of furnace-tending to her, his behaviour was not strikingly different from that of his fellow husbands. Moreover, Margaret believed in the importance of his work and — outside of certain moments of exasperation or fatigue — accepted the added limitations and burdens of her life cheerfully enough.

After two years it became evident that even with Margaret's careful and efficient managing George's meagre salary as assistant cashier of the bank could not be stretched to cover the rent of the house, doctor's bills, and the living-expenses of four people — the fourth member of the family due to arrive in two months' time. Besides, George's father died, leaving his mother alone in the big house. She needed care and company, the young Westleys needed financial aid. The obvious, indeed the only, solution of both problems was to move the young family bag and baggage to the elder Mrs. Westley's home.

My wife and I made our first joint visit to the Westleys three years later. My wife was rather apologetic. She hoped I wouldn't be too bored — the visit would be short — it meant a great deal to her family — the Westleys were really quite sweet in their way. At that time we were both young sprouts fresh from a big university, " advanced " in our ideas, " Bohemian " in our way of living, arrogant and provincial after the manner of our kind. Looking back, it seems to me that the Westley clan was more tolerant and worldly-wise about us than we were about them. They were, I think, shocked and surprised by many of our remarks, but sensibly put them down to our " city " background and perhaps to our youth. It never occurred to them to take our ideas as a real challenge to theirs, or to abate their affection and loyalty to members of the family, however eccentric. We found George pompous and absurdly self-important about his little bank and his election to a minor office in the town. My wife was deeply indignant about his " neglect " of Margaret, and his lack of common consideration — she was still furnace man and laundress although she was expecting her fourth child. Margaret, in her intimate talks with my wife, complained freely about her isolation from her friends. The old Westley home was on the very edge of town. She could not leave the children long enough for visits to them, and when the girls came to her house Mother Westley was always around, disapproving of bridge, putting a damper on cheerful gossip. Mother Westley spoiled the little boys dreadfully and nagged the life out of the little girl. Margaret did all the work, but not in her own way. She had to follow her mother-in-law's fussy economies and pet ways of doing things. There was a lot of work, too. The house was big and old-fashioned — a pump in the kitchen, a wood range, no bathtubs. George stayed downtown half the time to work in the evening. They were never alone. Margaret felt also that George and his mother seemed to support each other against her on many small but vexing issues.

My wife was full of sympathy and good advice. She instructed her cousin carefully in birth-control methods superior to the one the Westleys were using with such indifferent success. She told Margaret that she should have a home of her own, a tiny one if necessary, and insist that her mother-in-law pay for a companion out of her small capital. The young should not be sacrificed to the old. As for George, he should be made to look after the furnace and wipe the dishes and take care of the kids a few hours on Sunday. Why should he loaf with the newspaper when Margaret worked ten times harder than he did any day and every day, with no thanks from anyone? Marriage, my wife said, and I agreed, should be share and share alike. It was a wicked shame for George to have everything his own way just because he was a man. The children should be in a nursery school to develop their social instincts and leave Margaret more time for herself. Townsville had never heard of nursery schools, but we thought Margaret could easily organize a group of mothers in a co-operative plan of some sort — with one full-time worker and the mothers taking turns as assistants.

My wife reported to me these conversations with impatient pity. Margaret, she said, was so *spineless* about her troubles. She simply refused to stand up for her rights and the rights of her children, to be intelligent and realistic about money. She had promised very readily to try the new contraceptives, but she laughed at the idea of getting Mother Westley a companion. No one in Townsville would think of using *capital* to live on. Also Mother Westley needed her family, not a paid stranger. Everyone would say she was being neglected if her children moved away, and everyone would be right. Margaret took to defending her mother-in-law as actively as she had complained about her previously. Of course she was difficult at times. She was an old woman, too old to change her ways. Naturally she still felt like the boss in her own house. She adored her son and she had always preferred boys to girls. It wouldn't hurt the children or herself the least little bit, Margaret said, to put up with her ways for a few years. People always had something to put up with and just now it was Mother Westley for Margaret. It wasn't even a question of putting up with her, really, because as a matter of fact Margaret was very fond of the old lady. They understood each other well enough. Wives and mothers-in-law were always a bit jealous, but what of it?

And George. George wasn't the kind of man who could help with the dishes and mind the babies. He would feel ridiculous and he hated that more than anything in the world. " George," she said, " is a very good husband and a sweet boy, but you have to take him as he comes. I know he seems to you kind of stiff and sober and narrow and maybe conceited. I guess he is. There are lots of things about him, though, that you don't see. You say he doesn't thank me for doing the housework. Why should he? I don't thank him for working at the bank either. We take it for granted that each of us does as good a job as he can. You talk as if housework was so dreary I should have a medal for doing it. Until you started talking I hadn't thought of it one way or the other, but now I can tell you that I *like* housework. So do my friends. We complain sometimes. So does George and anybody else. That doesn't mean anything. Housework is our job. I don't think it matters so much what you do so long as it's important, and you can't say looking after a family isn't important. Just now my job is extra hard. Two years ago George was working almost every night, and having trouble with a man at the bank. What's the difference? Anything you do has easy times and hard times. Maybe," Margaret added with some asperity, " when you have a family of your own you'll see that some things just have to be done and you can't push people around to suit yourself."

It took a good many years for my wife and me to " see," but gradually our zeal for reform in the Westley family turned to admiration, and our condescension toward the narrowness of their small-town views changed to a certain envy that their sense of values could be so secure and un-troubled by winds of doctrine and attitude. Old Mrs. Westley died a year or two after our visit. The old home was sold and the family moved closer to the centre of town. With the small inheritance and a higher salary Margaret was able to have a part-time hired girl herself. As the years went on and the children grew older, she took an increas-ingly active and important part in community affairs. There was no organized social service in the town, but there were plenty of families who needed special care. The church depended for its very existence on the bazaars and similar ventures she and the other ladies engineered. The small hospital in a remodelled frame building was so hoplessly inadequate that the drive for a building fund was urgently necessary. In short, Margaret has no lack of legitimate outlet for her executive talents. She receives her full meed of recognition both as a public-spirited woman and as a good housewife.

George becomes more " substantial " year by year. My wife and I find his unswerving political conservatism a little hard to take. We still smile at his undiminished self-importance. We cannot help feeling that he and his kind are rather dangerously attached to a cause already lost. Margaret has taught us to recognize his personal worth, however, and we no longer attempt to incite rebellion in his family against his dictatorial ways. We suspect that Margaret smiles at him as often as we do, but in a very different spirit. She doesn't care whether he is pompous and opinionated or not. He's a good man whom she has lived with for twenty years and whom she loves.

I consider the Westleys' an excellent marriage, though I have lived with them enough to hear vociferous quarrels between all the members of the family. I have listened to many complaints and recriminations expressed individually and collectively. But I have noticed even among the children the same kind of basic affection and respect for the other fellow just as he happens to be made, which is so striking in Margaret's attitude toward her husband. Young Bob was writing verse the last time we visited in Townsville. The family teased him about it, frequently and thoroughly, but they all seemed to feel that the pursuit of poetry was a perfectly legitimate occupation. As a little boy Bob was a timid youngster. I remember, in those salad days of my career as a child-psychologist, discussing his " problem " with my wife and carefully approaching Margaret with suggestions for handling it. " Oh, yes," she said, " Bobby's very shy. He's sweet, isn't he? Going to kindergarten might be a good idea if he wants to." Bob is still a quiet, unobtrusive chap, but he is very unselfconscious and easy in his relationship to people. His present poise grows, I am sure, much more from Margaret's appreciative " He's sweet " than from the social training of the kindergarten. She has been more ready to *like* the distinct personalities of her children than to *handle* their different problems.

George and Margaret and the children have all had to make sacrifices. Measles and chicken pox and whooping cough have laid them low. The littlest girl nearly died of scarlet fever and retains a rheumatic heart in memory of the occasion. There have been broken bones in variety. The children have had not only the usual ailments of their age group but the typical jealousies and rebellions as well. Money is always scarce. Everybody works hard. But everybody feels that he belongs where he is, that he is loved and valued, and that his job is important, from George in the vice-president's office at the bank to the girls washing up in the kitchen.

Not all small-town marriages are so excellent. George is a thoroughly responsible and capable person. Margaret has more than her share of human kindness and self-reliance, with few areas of hypersensitivity either exposed or defensively covered up. I think, though, that Townsville has contributed its share to the success of her marriage. Until recently she has been immune from many of the problems which confront those of us who have wider contacts with the troubled events and attitudes of our time. Marriage in Townsville still follows a well-defined pattern. Divorce is almost unheard-of. So is the careerist woman. The roles of husband and wife are clearly outlined by a sturdy tradition to which there are few exceptions. Margaret and George had no trouble accepting marriage as the permanent framework of their lives, because it could scarcely be anything else. They built up no elaborate expectations of special personal values to be won. Marriage, a particular kind of marriage, was too much a matter of course to occasion a great deal of reflection about its merits and demerits. Margaret's philosophy of cheerfully taking the circumstances of her wedded life as they came to her seemed to me original and mature, but I dare say that her attitude is not uncommon in Townsville. We all grumble about the weather, but only those of us who, vicariously or at first hand, have become aware of the winter cruise feel that we suffer beyond our due. The person who is preoccupied with the delights of basking on Bermuda sands is unlikely to make the most of the facilities a northern winter offers for a good time. The extended possibilities of our contemporary world, both emotional and material, increase our fun, it may be. They also increase our discontent. What we have not keeps pace with what we have.

Both Margaret and George knew from childhood the kind of lives they were likely to lead, at least in their broad outlines. Their expectations were not challenged by more glittering possibilities, but constantly reinforced by the dicta and behaviour of everyone about them. They were not eccentric individuals, such as may be encountered in any society, however close-knit. The scheme of living imposed by the community was moderately satisfying to their human needs. Small wonder, then, that the Westleys, along with most of their acquaintances, settled down to a stable union, reasonably harmonious both in itself and in its relation to the community.

Moderately satisfying to human needs. This phrase applies, I think, especially to Margaret in contrast to women from more sophisticated communities. I said that

Margaret did not lack for a legitimate outlet for her energies and recognition of their value. She led a busy, responsible life, in contact with her fellows. Her activities were labelled feminine by her environment. They did not bring her into competition with her husband or raise the cry that she was a "half-baked man in petticoats." On the contrary, the harder and more successfully she worked, the more impressive was her standing *as a woman*. She earned no money for herself. She had no political or economic opinions. She did not intrude in any way upon the so-called masculine world. Nor did she have any desire to do so. Her own work was of recognized value. The women around her set no example of personal ambition except in the purely feminine realm of sewing, cards, and church socials. Her education had done nothing to awaken broader interests, much less a need for active participation in the world of politics or business or the professions. No one had suggested that housework was a menial occupation or that she was frittering away her time in church bazaars. She was given the opportunity for work generally recognized as important and she won prestige by doing it well.

I do not know how many little towns like Townsville survive in America, still preserving so clear-cut a pattern of marriage and the separate duties of man and wife. The general pattern undoubtedly persists throughout the country, even in Greenwich Village, but in many sections an infiltration of new attitudes and modes of behaviour has blurred its contours. Margaret's life has come to seem a little stuffy and limited, not only to the feministic college graduate who spoke her piece at the beginning of the last chapter, but also to the suburban housewife with her more sophisticated social and cultural interests. The distinction between the masculine and feminine world is no longer so rigid. There is a great deal of interplay between them. Lines of demarcation remain, but they have become very fluid. One community differs from the next in its conception of what is womanly or manly. One set of people within a community differs from its neighbours, one person from his friends, and finally our individual attitudes vary almost from one moment to the next. The trouble is that these attitudes, so subtle and incalculable, are closely tied up with our sense of personal worth. We accept social judgment of the kind of work we do as a true judgment of ourselves. The woman who works outside the home is not quite sure that she is a good wife and mother. The man who needs help from his wife in supporting the family is apt to think himself a poor sort of fellow, a failure.

I cannot see myself that it makes very much difference actually what a woman does. Margaret Westley was just as busy with matters not concerned with the personal welfare of her husband and children as many women who spend their afternoons on the golf course or at some kind of professional work. What does matter is the *attitude* a woman and her husband have toward their activities. Margaret's attitude was free and unafraid because her type of life was thoroughly approved by the community, her husband, and herself. It is much more difficult to achieve such an attitude when social and personal values are confused, when the mode of life consciously pursued is at variance with prevailing mores and often with the unconscious attitude of the woman herself.

Mrs. Harmon suffered from such a confusion of values. She came from a sturdy New England family which practised to an almost excessive degree the virtues of sobriety, thrift, and hard work. She was herself an excellent housekeeper and a devoted wife. She enjoyed her home and her children. Paradoxically she fell in love with a man of gayer, less responsible disposition. Perhaps this occurrence was not so remarkable after all. Mrs. Harmon, like most of us, was not made all of a piece. She had her moments of rebellion against the staid idealism of her youth, together with an uncomfortable feeling that she was missing a good deal in life. Very probably she loved her husband for precisely the qualities she disapproved of. His light-heartedness and generosity sprang from the same source as his instability and extravagance.

Mrs. Harmon had a very difficult time during the vivid boom days of the '20s. Her husband was making a good salary and was, like so many in those happy years, lucky in his investments. He bought a home in one of New York's more fashionable suburbs — a more pretentious house than his wife felt they could afford — and plunged the family into the rather hectic gaiety of that era. In competition with the chic, sophisticated women who were her "friends," Mrs. Harmon felt herself mousy and unattractive. They were an interesting lot — intelligent, well-informed, able to drink and talk with the men on their own level. A few of them even worked with the men, earning fabulous sums as buyers, dress-designers or copy-writers. Mrs. Harmon's domestic concerns seemed trivial, her ideas old-fashioned and a little childish by comparison. She began to believe that she was rather stupid and to wish that she had gone to college instead of the finishing school which had seemed so suitable at the time for a girl who had no idea of taking up any sort of career. Her husband accused her of being a kill-joy with her saving ways and prudish demeanour. Her efforts to maintain the family stability and to rear the children according to " decent " standards merely brought her into conflict with the community in which she lived and with her husband.

This difficult situation was only the setting for Mrs. Harmon's main problem, which was distrust of herself. Doing the same things as Margaret Westley, she had not her serene attitude toward herself and her work. She could scarcely be expected to stand up against so much social pressure, and indeed she did at times make a conscious effort to mend her ways. She tried getting tight on several occasions, but alcohol made her gloomy instead of gay and she suffered a severe attack of conscience the next day. Occasionally she bought herself an expensive and modish dress, only to feel self-conscious when she wore it and absurdly guilty when the bills came in. Moreover, her husband, although he reproached her for being goody-goody and close, showed definite signs of annoyance at these attempts to fall in line with his ideas of how life should be lived. In reaction to these splurges she would become more virtuous than ever. Unfortunately even then she felt guilty and frustrated, first because she liked being a wet blanket no better than the rest of us, and secondly because of a sneaking belief that she was losing a great deal of fun and a disquieting sense that it was wrong to be so serious. She had not only the criticism of her set to bear, but also the rebellious side of her own nature.

Once she gave up entirely and went home to her mother on a long visit which she had half decided to make permanent. She was surprised to find herself bored by the stiff solemnity of her former home and considerably irritated by the narrow views of her old friends and their ponderous earnestness. Her husband soon came running after her, penitent and distressed. They returned home together, full of bright expectations of a happier way of life — only to slip back into the old groove within a month's time.

The depression came to Mrs. Harmon as a welcome release. With the collapse of the stock market and a reduced salary, her sparing, housewifely talents were given full play. During the early months of loss her husband was pleasantly appreciative, glad enough to rely on his stable wife. As time went on, the old problems reasserted themselves, but in a lower key, not so far out of her range. Her husband teased her for counting quarters instead of dollars. His high spirits and the free behaviour of their friends, even though they met at the delicatessen for beer after the movies instead of in a New York speakeasy, still made her feel half envious, half disapproving. But at least she was permitted to work hard for her home and family, with honour instead of disdain. She recovered more confidence in herself as a valuable, dignified person. Her own attitudes were once again relatively in harmony with the attitude of her group.

It is easy to see a vindication of Mrs. Harmon's stable home-loving character in the reaction of the family to the depression. One might view the episode as a modern version of the fable about the grasshopper and the ant. For the psychiatrist the story has a different moral. Mrs. Harmon was lucky in having the depression come along to relieve the acute strain in her marriage, but her problems go much deeper than Æsop's tale. One problem is the purely personal one of handling a husband more easygoing than herself. There is, I think, only one solution — the very partial solution suggested so many times in this book — namely, a clear recognition and acceptance of the conflict and the values of their relationship. Mrs. Harmon loved her husband in part because he represented a strain in her own nature to which she dared not give free expression. She actually liked his instability, I am sure, and was as annoyed at herself for liking it as at him for being irresponsible. Mr. Harmon, for his part, was well content with his wife's more solid virtues. His vanity suffered a little from having a wife less dashing than the other women in their group. He rebelled at times against her firmness and what he called, not without reason, her nagging. But she was necessary to him just as she was, ballast to his light-hearted disposition. Naturally he was annoyed when she tried to change herself and distracted when she left him. Both of them consciously wanted to change the other person, tried to do so, and succeeded only in creating serious tension between them. Unconsciously each one got a great deal of satisfaction from the relationship as it was. A better understanding of this situation would lead to a more workable compromise between their conflicting tastes, some such compromise perhaps as the depression ultimately forced upon them. Through the tense months of 1930 Mr. Harmon learned how much he needed his wife's stability and Mrs. Harmon gave free expression to her maternal affection for her gay, irresponsible husband.

The other problem Mrs. Harmon shares with a great many women — the adaptation of her own ambitions to the circumstances of her marriage and her social surroundings. Margaret Westley had no such problem because her wishes coincided with the requirements of her life. Barbara Gordon had difficulty reconciling a desire for accomplishment in the so-called man's world of politics or professional music with the needs of her marriage. She was cast for the role of housewife, but her training and talents lay elsewhere. Mrs. Harmon wanted to devote herself to her home. She was fitted by her education and background and tastes for efficient, gracious household management. The anti-domestic atmosphere in which she lived prevented the free exercise of her truest interest. Both Barbara and Mrs. Harmon felt apologetic and frustrated.

Neither one was permitted to follow the kind of life naturally satisfying to her, because of social attitudes.

The influence of social attitudes on work, incidentally, is not confined to women. A few years ago Fred, the head mechanic of the garage in the town where we spend our summers, told me a little about his problem. He is a charming young fellow, educated as well as anyone in the town. He fell in love with the daughter of the town's leading merchant. She loved him, his salary was adequate, and his prospects good. The family, however, and to a lesser extent the girl herself, objected to the match because Fred wore greasy overalls and worked with his hands. Out of consideration for this attitude Fred tried the more acceptable occupation of salesman for several months. He couldn't "stick it." It had no future, he said, and was terribly dull for a man accustomed to the excitement of diagnosing and treating the ailments of automobiles. He returned to his old position — to my great satisfaction as a car-owner — regardless of his wife's protests. Last year he took over the ownership of the garage. I hope that his status as proprietor compensates his good lady for the fact that he still wears overalls.

Fred knew well enough what he wanted to do. So did Mrs. Harmon. Their conflict was an open struggle with opposing attitudes. Very often, nowadays, the conflict is not so clear to the people involved. They have themselves adopted social attitudes disparaging the work to which they are naturally inclined or which for some reason they are forced to undertake.

A colleague at the university recently asked me to see one of his students, a Miss Whitford. Her major problem appeared to be just such a conflict between her own attitudes and the job she had. Her job was housekeeping and the care of a year-old baby, while her attitude was one of scorn and repudiation for all domestic activities.

Josephine Whitford graduated only five years ago from one of our more dynamic women's colleges. She and her friends were the " intellectuals " of their year. They had plunged enthusiastically into contemporary social and æsthetic movements and determined never to subject themselves to the stultifying routine of housework and bridge. For two years Josephine had kept the flame of intellect alight by working at Macy's, but the third year she married the section manager of her department. In spite of their decision to keep their marriage " modern," Josephine soon fell into the toils of motherhood, from which she found it impossible to extricate herself. Her husband's salary did not run to nursemaids and housekeepers. Josephine tried desperately to pay for a maid out of her own earnings, but the practical difficulties proved to be insuperable. The only job she could get combined long hours with small remuneration. Her employers showed a chill intolerance for occasional necessary absences when the precariously adjusted household machinery bogged down in some emergency. When I saw her, a single evening course at the university while her husband stayed home with the infant was the only bit of intellectuality she had been able to salvage from the wreck of her aspirations.

She was tense and resentful and very, very sorry for herself.

As she talked I was struck by two things: the superficiality of her intellectual interests and the undercurrent of stability evident in her remarks about her little family. She was indiscriminate in her desire for a job — any sort of job outside the home was sufficient. She had picked her course at the university because the professor was famous and " intriguing," not because of a mature, consecutive interest in the subject matter. Her college record was not brilliant and her performance at Macy's, though creditable, had been undistinguished. On the other hand there was no question of her fundamental loyalty to her husband. While she referred slightingly to her offspring as " the brat " and asserted frequently that she could wring his neck, it was also plain that her care of him had been conscientious and tender. In short, it appeared to me that Josephine's natural inclinations were by no means averse to a domestic life, but that she was unable to accept them because of the scornful attitude she had adopted toward " old-fashioned " home-making under the influence of her particular social group. I think she knew, dimly, how artificial her intellectuality really was, and was quite justifiably afraid that if she once gave in to her housewifely duties her " interests " would vanish into thin air. So long as she identified worth-while activities with activities outside the home, this possibility was a crushing blow to her ego.

I have no doubt that Josephine would have come to terms with her problem by herself, but I like to think that our few talks together hastened the process and relieved her of a nagging sense of failure. She rapidly gained a better perspective toward jobs, within the home and without. The glory that had become incongruously attached to the task of selling sportswear faded a little and the business of caring for two very dear people grew proportionately more significant. Reassured as to the value of her work at home, she began to find it more satisfying than anything she had previously attempted. Her pretence of absorbing intellectuality simmered down to an interest in some phases of music and art and economics, less intense but far more genuine than the feverish concern she had expressed before. The gibes of her old friends were disquieting, but she developed a good line of argument in defence of her position and was on the whole relieved to be free of competition with girls more brilliant than herself. Gradually she built up a new circle of friends whose point of view and activities were more similar to her own. One great advantage of living in a metropolis like New York is that, with luck and a little effort, it is possible to find a group of people who share your attitudes no matter how odd they may be. By the time her second child was born, Miss Josephine Whitford had become frankly Mrs. Louis Morton, a reasonably contented wife and mother.

Josephine was fortunate. Her problem lay in the discrepancy between notions she had acquired about the indignity of housework and the part she was called upon to play. She was in fact better fitted to the role of housewife and mother than to the career from which she was ex-

cluded by the practical necessities of her life. A shift in
attitude toward herself and her job was enough to make
possible a harmonious relationship between her aspirations
and the activities forced upon her. Many women today are
in no such favorable position. The work they do, either at
home or in business, is more fundamentally at variance
with their own desires, so that reconciliation cannot be
attained so readily.

Our colleges and even our high schools turn out with
increasing frequency women who have developed strong
and perfectly genuine specialized interests, in art, in design,
in mathematics, medicine, or business. They are well
trained. Their education and the years of independent
work which often precede marriage have oriented their
personal ambition toward tangible achievement. It often
happens that they make the acquaintance of their future
husbands through their studies or through their work.
During the courtship period they are colleagues or fellow
students. The modern young lady no longer passes from
the protection of her father to the guardianship of her
husband. Whether she continues professional work or not,
she wants to " make something of herself " as an independent human being. Her husband is often very sympathetic to these aspirations. He, too, repudiates the carpet-
sweeping, sock-darning ideal of womanhood and respects
his wife for her intelligence, her efficiency, her upstanding,
vigorous concern with matters outside the petty household routine.

It is true that the practical difficulties of running a home and a job are manifold, especially while the children are young. I have observed, however, that young people who have thoroughly accepted themselves and their relationship on the basis of mutual freedom in their professional life handle these problems very well. The woman realizes that she must compromise to a certain extent with her desire for vocational success. Her husband is not above attending to household chores when need arises. They face the vexations and trials of their joint enterprise with equanimity — just as Margaret Westley and George put up with their hardships without rancour.

Unfortunately such happy working partnerships are rare. They are more difficult to achieve than the kind of union enjoyed by the Westleys, not so much because of the practical problems involved as because of the complicated attitudes which both men and women have toward woman's work. Beneath the brave protestations of equality and independence, learned in modern schools and under modern economic conditions, runs the age-old tradition that woman's place is in the home, while her husband is the master and the provider. We are so steeped in this tradition that the attitudes it fosters are deeply rooted in our personality. Our adherence to newer modes of thinking is apt to be very partial and superficial. Certain activities and characteristics are identified in our society with womanliness, others with masculinity. The woman who engages in so-called masculine activities, who has a " man's " mind and ambition, can scarcely help being influenced by this judgment, even though she has rationally rejected it.

She is often uncertain about her status as a woman, as a wife and mother. Sometimes she affects scorn of the whole problem, wearing aggressively " sensible " clothes and the manner appropriate to them. She is brazenly practical about her children and very hale-fellow-well-met with her husband. Again, she may try to cover her efficiency with frills and ruffles and be more stridently feminine than her home-keeping sisters. Since she is not wholly sure of herself, she is very sensitive to any imputation of neglect for her household.

Margaret Westley dished up warmed-over food on wash-days and confidently expected her family to be tolerant. Her children often replaced missing buttons with safety pins. No one criticized her for the occasional shortcomings of her housekeeping, least of all herself, because she was obviously too busy to get everything done. The woman who works outside the home may neglect her family no more than Margaret, but she is apt to blame herself for every little mishap. The neighbours and her husband are also likely to be unduly censorious. Trivial domestic crises, common to every household, become important because they touch off the wife's feeling of guilt about her un-womanly behaviour.

At the same time she tends to resent the handicap her home duties lay upon her professional efforts. Under the most favourable conditions a woman's time, attention, and emotion are so divided between her home and her job that she cannot compete on equal terms with either men or unmarried women. In proportion to her concern about

her job she is naturally annoyed at the inevitable interruptions and uncompromising demands of her domestic
responsibilities. Nor can she help feeling guilty about her
annoyance and concealing it as far as possible from the
world at large and herself.

The husband, on his side, has a great many sensitivities
which grow out of an unacknowledged desire for old-
fashioned masculine prestige. He is disturbed by the fact
that his wife has allegiances and preoccupations which take
her away from him. Wanting complete love and devotion,
he finds his wife's emotional self-sufficiency unpleasant, if
not actually threatening. He expresses the belief that marriage is an equal partnership, but his emotional ideal for
himself, taught subtly and insistently from his earliest
childhood, is that of the masterful male. His naïve self-
esteem asks a blind admiration from his wife and full authority over the household. In spite of his mature intellectual viewpoint he tends to feel diminished in his capacity
as male head of the family by his wife's participation in
matters which are traditionally his sole responsibility.

Most men, I believe, handle this conflict of attitude by
developing a patronizing tolerance toward their wives'
career. Let the little woman amuse herself! This formula
is very successful so long as the wife's work remains on a
dilettante level. His old-fashioned masculine ego is kept
intact and his modern broad-mindedness is flattered. The
wife, too, unless she takes her work very seriously, finds
this flippant justification of her activities acceptable. The
moment she carries forward her job in all earnestness,

however, the flimsy compromise falls to pieces. She resents the indignity of viewing her work as an amusement. As she becomes more definitely absorbed in her own affairs and especially when she becomes successful, her husband's egotism is again painfully exposed. He is almost inevitably thrown into competition with her work, on two counts. One is his feeling that he is losing her love and devotion. The other is that she may beat him at his own game. Few men can stand being married to a woman more eminent than themselves. One gentleman of average attainments who wed a recognized female genius and frankly devoted himself to her career found himself enough of an oddity to be " written up " in a number of popular magazines. Nobody enjoys being outdistanced by another person, but the husband who is outdistanced by his wife is especially vulnerable. Society considers him a pathetic and ridiculous figure. If the natural American male is to preserve his self-respect, his wife must stay a good distance behind him, or at the very least win her prestige in some sort of " woman's work " for which the husband can cultivate a healthy disdain. The threat of wifely pre-eminence is so severe that competition begins very early in the race, inevitably introducing disturbing elements into the marriage.

It is not easy for men and women to admit the existence of this competitive factor. We do not like to be jealous of people we love, nor try to get the better of people with whom, theoretically, we should not be in competition. I know very few men who can face this situation frankly and openly. Women are somewhat more conscious of it, but as a rule only when the circumstances are obviously difficult. I am reminded of an acquaintance of mine, a very successful publicity woman, who gave up her job at the time of her marriage simply because she felt that she could not ask her husband to tolerate her high salary. She worked in a small town, dominated by a single business. Her employers offered to make a place for her new husband in order to keep her on their staff. Nevertheless in the midst of the depression both young people migrated to New York to hunt for jobs together. I think they were wise, though I am not too confident that the marriage will be happy even so. Mrs. Brown is a dynamic, ambitious, gifted person, ten times as capable as her husband will ever be. Mr. Brown is neither so weak that he enjoys being taken care of nor so strong that he can face frankly his wife's intellectual superiority. The move to New York will relieve their problem temporarily, but in the long run such a marriage will endure only if both the Browns are willing to accept themselves as they are — a difficult assignment for people brought up in the emotional attitudes of our society.

Fortunately the Browns are a very special case. Usually married people are more evenly matched and the wife's double duties keep her well in check. The problem is typically merely the husband's *fear* of his wife's competition in work, and it is acute chiefly because it is unrecognized. The husband does not know that he is jealous. He tries to be encouraging and helpful, but his unconscious desire to defeat his wife and have her all to himself leads him to place stumbling-blocks, carefully camouflaged, in her path. He is perfectly willing to have her work, but why must she be late to dinner or come home fagged out? His kindly efforts to keep her from tiring herself often effectively prevent her accomplishing anything which might threaten his prestige. He teases her in the most good-humoured — and thoroughly malicious — manner possible, skilfully undermining her confidence in herself and the value of her work. He calls to her attention the dirty thumb-marks on the woodwork and agrees with Junior that it's just too bad the child has been struggling with broken shoe-strings for two weeks, but he remarks — too sweetly — that mother can't be expected to see to the house while she is so busy with her job. His wife retaliates, with equal self-deception. Since the value of her work has been called into question, she sets herself to prove that her husband has similar limitations. She is quick to notice and emphasize any procrastination in the fulfilment of his household duties — she has been waiting for weeks to have him fix the electric iron and glue the rung of that dining-room chair. And shouldn't a father spend *some* time with his children? In short, because of their basic competition and personal insecurity each partner in marriage is eager to put the other in the wrong, simply as a means of self-justification.

As a rule these domestic bickerings, like those which arise in every type of marriage, do no one very much harm. My recommendation for handling them is no more elaborate than a cheerful shrug of the shoulders. They are sandwiched in between moments of companionability, very often the richer for the sharing of interests and point of view between two individuals of similar tastes. At times, however, the sly attacks become so bitter on both sides that they are a real menace to the happiness of the union. In these cases it is perhaps necessary for one or both people to face the real issues involved more honestly. Once a man is willing to grant himself a natural jealousy of his wife's achievements, he limits its influence. Usually the jealousy is absurd, the product of an ego still nourishing itself in secret upon traditions the conscious mind has rejected. Once a woman looks openly at her fear of being unfeminine and recognizes the competitive aspects of her relationship with her husband, she too is in a position to control her insecurities and resentments and envies instead of being at their mercy. Not all at once, of course, and not with complete success. The conflicts go too deep to be resolved in a day or by one couple in opposition to a whole society. But the conflicts can be diminished, limited in scope and relieved of much bitterness.

Not infrequently a woman works not because she wants to but because she must. Economic conditions are so confused and so poorly adjusted to contemporary needs that it is often impossible for a man to support his family by his own efforts according to the standard of living we think proper. It is sometimes easier for a woman than a man to find a job during these days of depression. The practical situation may call for a reversal of the roles customarily allotted to husband and wife. So far as their abilities, training, and temperament go, individual couples may be

well able to make this adjustment. An unreasonable society, however, having fitted women for jobs and having,
on occasion, forced them to take over the financial support
of the home in whole or in part, refuses to grant emotional
sanction to a family organized on such a basis. The woman
who makes her contribution to the household in dollars
and cents is given leave to consider herself a martyr, even
though she does not work half as hard as Margaret Westley. The man who cannot maintain his family adequately
alone is ranked as a failure. If, deprived of the opportunity
of earning money himself, he tries to carry his share of the
burden by doing housework, he is not respected as an
honourable man, but pointed to as a comic figure.

It is hard indeed for any man to stand up against the
gibes of society, or for his wife to guard herself against
the feeling that her husband has failed her. In those not
uncommon instances where the husband has no talent
for making money, where he is lacking in initiative or
even stamina for hard work, the marriage withstands
social criticism only with the greatest difficulty if at all.
A man may possess every virtue under heaven, may be
the most charming and lovable of husbands, but if he fails
to convert his virtues and his charm into gold, he is looked
upon as worthless. The adjustment can be made, however.
The Blackwells made it. Mrs. Blackwell was a personnel
manager for a large insurance company. Mr. Blackwell
was called an architect and he did occasionally build a
garage for friendly neighbours. His chef-d'œuvre was the
house he built for his own family with his wife's money.

They lived in a small town near the city. During the week Mr. Blackwell had full charge of the three boys. Their mother appeared on Saturday afternoon and left early Monday morning, with occasional evenings in between. She was not wholly free from sporadic feelings of guilt about her " masculine " role — she asked me whether she should not resign and force her husband for his own good to be more industrious. I dare say Mr. Blackwell was sometimes a little uneasy about his financial dependence. On the whole, though, this family was one of the happiest I have known. The father combined a gentle, easy-going, comradely affection for the boys with enough firmness to keep them reasonably in hand. He loved puttering around the house and garden. Mrs. Blackwell's ambitious, energetic nature would have been restless and discontented in the confines of her home. This couple had drifted into a very suitable alignment of their specific desires and temperaments. They were fond enough of each other and happy enough in their respective jobs to thumb their noses at a carping society. Indeed, their friends and neighbours had become so accustomed to their way of life and had so long witnessed its patent success that they forgot to jeer.

In this connection, too, I think of the parents of a good friend of mine, country people who managed a similar compromise with even less social criticism. The husband was an artist and a dreamer, albeit ostensibly a farmer. He played his violin and waved his hand delicately toward the fields which next year he would plant to wheat and potatoes. Next year never arrived. His wife taught a one-room school for fifty years and reared six children, three of whom have made their mark in the sophisticated city world. I suspect that in former times, and even now in rural areas, the wife not uncommonly ran the farm and contributed the lion's share of executive talent. Indeed, in all the country families I know, the wife works very hard, not only on housework and baby-tending, but on such productive enterprises as poultry farming, care of the milk when it is marketed, even truck gardening. Only in the towns is it necessary for her to help out conspicuously by leaving her home daily for office, school, or factory. Only under modern business conditions does the problem of the wifely contribution to family maintenance become acute. The woman's place can be in the home only if she can *work* there, can carry her part of the economic burden without leaving its walls. With the development of mass production she is often forced into industry to accomplish the same things which were formerly her responsibilities at home.

Society is gradually adjusting itself to this shift in "woman's place." The number of women, and especially of married women, who have employment outside the home is constantly increasing. Families caught during this transition period between new necessities and old traditions must simply make the best of it. The man and woman who can understand and discount these old traditional feelings, who can accept the present requirements of their lives, are on the way to enjoying themselves and each other regardless of the kind of work each is called upon to perform.

What of the modern woman who stays home? Does she side-step all these problems connected with work? Is her husband's ego secure from competition and her own nature satisfied in doing woman's work? We can divide such women into two classes for the purpose of this analysis: those who have never thought of carrying on independent work, and those who are educated for a career, who have personal ambitions which they have renounced. The second class is no better off, I have found, than those women who do try for a career. They are subject to more or less open feelings of frustration. They tend to be jealous of their husbands because of the greater freedom men enjoy and resentful toward the children who have put a stop to their own efforts. I am always a little worried when a forceful, ambitious woman decides to put all her energies into her home, especially if she is so comfortably situated that she cannot let off steam scrubbing floors. It is very hard for her to avoid dominating the family and participating too vigorously in the lives of her husband and children. Their natural independence and selfishness seem to her a repudiation of her devoted love, their shortcomings an index of her failure. She cannot tolerate her own periods of impatience and temper because her relationship to her family is mixed up with her ideal of personal success. She has given up so much to be a wife and mother that she expects an unhealthy perfection by way of reward. The discontents any of us feel with ourselves and our existence are ascribed, not always consciously, to the idea that important talents are being thwarted. In giving up work a wife is apt to feel obscurely defeated, defeated by her husband and her family and by her own lack of courage in pursuing aims she has learned to consider important.

The home-keeping woman who has always accepted a domestic role for herself does, I think, feel somewhat more comfortable in her own skin because her conscious aims are usually more in harmony with the traditions and expectations of the people around her. Of course, like Mrs. Harmon, she may have the misfortune to live among " intellectual " women, or she may have a husband who craves stimulation and companionship at home. I was interested to discover that my friend Professor Barton, though he is very fond of his wife, finds his home boring to the point of exasperation. My own feeling for Mrs. Barton has always been one of affection and admiration. She is a warm, generous, vivid little person. She has a kind of wholeness and genuineness rare in our generation, and she is completely wrapped up in her family. An academic salary does not provide adequate maid service for the household. Entertaining is so much of a strain on the family purse and Mrs. Barton's time that most evenings are spent quietly at home *en famille*. Mrs. Barton's talk rarely touches upon topics beyond the small adventures of the children or her altercations with the storekeepers of the neighbourhood. Since she is alone a great deal during the day, she does like to talk at night. When guests are present she sometimes feels

" out of it " or else distresses her husband by the triviality of her conversation. Barton has enough good sense to feel no more than a passing irritation at his wife's cultural limitations. Mrs. Barton certainly has twinges of jealousy toward those women — or men — with whom her husband bursts into animated, excited discussion, but on the whole she is so happily busy with her family and so confident of her husband's basic affection that she does not worry very much about herself. The only real problem the Bartons have is the one we all have. We want everything and we cannot have it. Barton is in possession of the jewel so many men seek after — a wife who makes him the centre of her universe. He cannot at the same time have an independent intellectual. Mrs. Barton enjoys her husband's superiority. She cannot then reasonably expect to be his mental equal and to monopolize his interest.

Some women, less secure than Mrs. Barton, are plagued beyond endurance by their jealousy of their husband's work and outside contacts. The other woman is not the only rival a wife fears. The siren who lures her husband away may be no more glamorous than a row of filing-cases or a pudgy new " prospect " for life insurance. A husband's absorption in his work may leave his wife as forlorn and unhappy as his infatuation for another woman.

We are accustomed by now to look beyond the apparent circumstances for the explanation of any particular disturbance in marriage. Jealousy of a husband's work depends on more than the number of hours he spends at the office. Probably all women have some negative feelings

toward the interests and activities which break in upon
their close relationship with their husbands. Every woman
knows that she cannot monopolize a man; that he needs
his work; that she has no respect for complete dependence
upon her; that she herself becomes bored and irritated if he
is constantly underfoot. None the less, beneath this sensible appreciation of the facts of marriage, runs a natural
and unreasonable longing to be all in all to her man. We
saw that men were hurt by their wives' preoccupation with
the demands of a job. Women are hurt in exactly the
same way. Such feelings are nonsensical, of course. None
the less, the words whispered by moonlight — " Nothing
matters but you, you're all the world to me " — echo rather
hollowly the next morning when our hero concentrates on
the stock-market reports over breakfast and rushes to the
office after the most perfunctory kiss.

One woman said to me plaintively: " If I could just once
get my husband so crazy about me that he'd miss an office
appointment I'd be satisfied. I don't really want to interfere with his work, I want him to be a success, for himself
and for me. What I hate is the knowledge that his job
always comes first. He'll break any date with me, leave me
flat any minute, if his boss just crooks his little finger."

This lady was unusually honest about her feelings perhaps, but her reaction is very common. Most women try
in little ways to prove that they come first and nourish
little resentments against the demands, all too faithfully
satisfied, of their husbands' work. Since such behaviour
is patently absurd and heartily condemned by society, the

good wife masks her jealousy under concern for her husband's health or any other apparently legitimate reason for curbing his activities. The man senses vaguely her antagonism to his work and feels his independence undermined. He fights back with a more pronounced concentration on the job. As domestic bitterness grows, he may use his work as a means of punishing his wife and as a relief from the strain of his life at home.

Now, in most marriages these little jealousies and resentments remain little. They are the cause of minor squabbles and discontents, without serious effect upon the relationship. It does sometimes happen, however, that they swell to unmanageable proportions. Some wives like Emily Bowen, whom I described in the second chapter, may be so lacking in self-confidence that they need more than their share of affectionate reassurance. At the opposite pole are girls of unusual beauty or charm, accustomed to a great deal of adulation. They may find the normal " neglect " of a busy man in such contrast to the fervent adoration of earlier years that they exaggerate its importance. Ordinary wifeliness is an unfamiliar role, a flat, uninteresting role after the excitement of being the reigning belle.

In this category of jealous wives we must also put those who have sacrificed a great deal for marriage. I know a certain rather spoiled young lady who married against her parents' wishes a nice young man who had neither money nor prospects. He was really such a nice young man that he set himself seriously to work to earn money for his wife. The marriage was to her a romantic adventure. She was unprepared emotionally for the long hours of loneliness which fell to her lot. Having given up so much for her man, she felt he should be wholly hers, and could not share him even with his job. She craved intense and constant love as compensation for the lost luxury of her parental home.

Some women who lead a monotonous, starved existence by day are also likely to be exacting when their husbands come home. The daily trip to business seems to them so much more exciting and pleasurable than their own household routine that they somehow feel their husbands are under obligation to them. The least a man can do, they argue, is help with the dishes and take them to the movies. He should show *some* consideration for the dull, shut-in life he forces a woman to lead. Such women are often thoroughly unreasonable. They plague their husbands for providing so little money, but object strenuously to any evening work the men may undertake in order to " get ahead." But these reactions are very natural. The home-keeping wife with little money does have a pretty thin time of it, and most of us tend to find our own miseries more severe than those of the other fellow.

On the whole, though, women accept pretty well the fact that men must work. The little jealousies intrinsic in this situation are more often intensified by the husband's over-emphasis on his work than by the wife's special problems. Sometimes the husband is so taken up by his work that he doesn't have very much emotion left over for his wife. Note I say emotion, not time. Women can stand being left alone a great deal if they are given warmth and genuine affection when they are with their husbands. Some men do not give their wives such warmth, cannot give it because their business means so much to them. There are a great many possible reasons for intense absorption in work. It may be the expression of an unhealthy self-love, a desire to extend the ego by multiplying possessions and heaping up the riches which apparently bring respect and power. Such men have little to give a woman in any case, since they love only themselves. Or efforts to accumulate wealth may be the result of fear of coming too close to people. The man does not dare trust himself to personal relationships for fear of being let down or destroyed. His work is a protection against an intimacy with his wife of which he is afraid. It does not matter whether the protection is really needed or not. Sometimes the husband is afraid of poverty itself, so panicky on the subject that everything else must be subordinated to guarding himself against financial loss. Boys who have been poor in their childhood or who have seen too vividly the consequences of financial failure occasionally develop such terrors. Other men prize the masculine contacts which accompany their working activities. They are happier with their business associates than with any woman, and therefore find it difficult to relax at home.

American society lays such stress upon vocational success for men that these attitudes are likely to be intensified. The wife herself, though she suffers from her husband's neglect, is frequently a party to the forces which drive him to anxious striving for pre-eminence. In most communities the status of the family depends to a large extent upon the money and position of the husband. Living in the right house in the right neighbourhood, observing the local niceties in entertaining, wearing smart clothes, sending the children to the best schools, and belonging to the proper clubs — all these items are tremendously important. The normal home-keeping woman, well adapted to her community, naturally wants to take part in the activities of her friends. Her own prestige rests upon her ability to have things as nice as her neighbours or a little nicer. Good management, ingenuity, and personal charm can help to eke out a limited income, but income there must be, roughly equivalent to the typical income of the community. Since only the husband can supply this income, the most devoted of wives can scarcely help being a bit of a slave-driver. She does not have to urge him to make more money or make a fuss about poverty to stir up feelings of guilt in her husband if he fails to keep the family in line with the standards of the neighbourhood. So long as she wants very much the things she does not have, she will manage in little ways, against her own wishes, to make her husband aware of his limitations as a provider.

Money is regrettably important in contemporary society. A man is not judged by the excellence of the thing he produces, but by the amount he can sell it for. His achievement, we may almost say his character, is measured in terms of income. No matter how stable he may be, how worthy a citizen, how excellent a father and husband, he cannot give his family the advantage of a secure and respectable social position unless he earns the proper salary. Indeed, too often the man's chief, almost his only, contribution to the running of the home is financial. His time and energy are so absorbed by his work that he leaves the management of the home and the children entirely to his wife, retaining his headship of the family only by virtue of his ability to pay the bills. Because money has come to stand for success and authority, the manipulation of the family budget takes to itself emotions appropriate to other more personal relationships. For this reason the admirable systems for family financing frequently proposed in books of advice to the married cannot always function according to schedule. The husband may need to feel the reins of government in his own hands. He may have to prove his authority over the family by making his wife come to him for every little expenditure. Or he may be unduly sensitive about the size of his income. The most matter-of-fact discussion of ways and means — can we afford to take a cottage at the shore? — can we buy a new car this spring? — is interpreted as an attack upon his manliness. His pride suffers from his inability to supply every desire of his family. He is obscurely vexed by his wife for putting him in the position of having to recognize the limits of his success. The actual size of income is not important. The man whose salary is only twenty thousand instead of thirty or forty like his friends' feels just as inferior as the man who has two thousand instead of three.

The wife of today is as dependent upon money for her personal satisfactions as her husband. Margaret Westley could pride herself upon her embroidered tablecloths and fluffy cakes. Women in more sophisticated communities do not set much store by hand work. My wife gets out her elaborately tatted piano throw only when the donor comes for a visit. She does make a few jellies herself during the summer and " put up " beans from our garden, but she tells me that this domestic activity is just a gesture. She can buy jellies and canned vegetables cheaper and better at the A. & P. Most women who are interested in beautifying their homes nowadays feel that they must buy smart linens, tailored drapes, and professionally upholstered chairs. The era of hand work is closing even in the home. Sociological studies of the contemporary family point out the enormous increase in bakeries, restaurants, laundries, and other commercial substitutes for home products and activities. A good home-maker today is the woman who can buy with economy and taste, not the skilled needlewoman and cook. It is interesting in this connection to note the recent growth of consumers' organizations whose purpose is to teach women how to judge the products they purchase. Inexpensive home entertainment, even for children, is also on the wane. More and more the wife is dependent on money, on her husband's income, for the desirable conduct of her home. It is hard for her to be tolerant of a straitened budget when her own position in the community and the social adjustment of her children is so directly affected. She brings to the budgetary discussions the uneasy knowledge that her personal prestige is at stake. A new fur coat is not a matter of sartorial vanity, but a badge of her social status.

The Sibleys have, I think, handled the money question very well. Mr. Sibley is anxious about money. He does not feel secure unless he is " putting by " several thousand dollars a year, enough to care for any possible emergency in the years to come. His wife naturally wants to furnish her home pleasantly and to have nice clothes for herself and the children. She believes justifiably that her husband's thrift is excessive. Nevertheless she has come to realize that his saving policy is very important to him, and that he cannot be reasoned out of it. Experience has told her that he gets worried and irritable as his bank balance diminishes. Looking at her marriage in the large, she has sensibly decided that new furniture and clothes are things she must do without even though rationally the family could well afford them. She has her rewards — a serene husband and a pleasant home atmosphere. Moreover, Mr. Sibley has enough understanding of the situation to see that he is asking more of his wife than most husbands and that his peace of mind depends upon her acquiescence. His appreciation of her concession to his needs makes him unusually considerate of her wishes in other matters.

Mrs. Sibley is perfectly right. Money matters cannot always be handled rationally. Psychological attitudes toward money are just as real as the money itself. Successful family budgeting cannot be based merely upon a rigid allocation of funds to rent, food, recreation, savings, and so on.

It must also take into account the emotional needs of the family. Budgeting in my own household is very whimsical. We spend when we happen to be in funds and economize when we are out of funds. Usually we're economizing! I am sure that a more systematically planned spending program would be more advantageous from a practical standpoint. We are willing to be less efficient and more comfortable. Other couples are uneasy unless they know the destination of every dollar they earn. Money, in short, is not only dollars and cents, but a symbol of personal attitudes toward marriage and toward life. Budgets must be devised to satisfy not only the butcher and the baker but the husband and wife themselves.

Work and money! They are the very tissue of our everyday lives. For all of us they mean not only a forty-hour week and a minimum wage, but a tangle of emotions, some satisfying, some disrupting. Social traditions, childhood patterns, grim necessities, are all thrown together in a brew more or less palatable according to the harmony of the original ingredients. People like the Westleys whose early training coincides with the expectations of their social group and the requirements of their present life are lucky. Most of us, nowadays, have to work out a concoction to our own taste. We must learn to discount certain preconceived notions of what our work *should* be. We cannot entirely eliminate them, but we can make ourselves aware of their existence and so bring them under control. The woman who works, knowing her basic anxieties about her feminine role, can smile at them. The man whose income does not meet the needs and desires of his family can scarcely help being disquieted, but he need not lose his self-respect. Every type of work relationship, every level of income, every kind of budget has its problems — and its advantages. We can achieve a happy family life in so far as we are willing to live with our own special problems and satisfactions, instead of yearning after those of our neighbours.

༄

CHAPTER VII

CHILDREN: THE CONSUM-
MATION OF MARRIAGE

BABIES are a symbol of the permanence of any marriage.
They are its chief anchor. More divorces have been prevented by a youngster's cry or smile than by any legis-
lature. There is something more compelling in the movements of any one of the ten toes of a six-months-old infant
than in the activity of the United States Supreme Court.
Statistics show that divorces diminish in direct proportion
to the number of children in the family. Sixty-three per
cent of all divorces in the United States occur in childless
marriages. Even one child is frequently enough to save
a marriage. Three times as many childless couples separate as couples with one child. Only two per cent of all
divorces in this country take place when the parents have
to consider the welfare of four children. Psychiatrists
working with discontented married couples smile happily
to themselves when husband or wife talk in the course of
treatment for the first time about plans " to have a baby."
In this connection I am reminded of the Dalton family.

Mr. and Mrs. Dalton could not live together, nor could they live apart. They had already been divorced from each other once. A second separation seemed imminent. The husband was preoccupied with Wall Street during the day, and detective stories at night. The wife gave most of her devotion to a handsome bull terrier. Her reason for not having children was disgust with her parents' treatment of her. " It does not seem fair to bring children into the world and make them suffer as I did in childhood," she said. In the course of treatment the wife overcame these attitudes. The change was first suspected when Mrs. Dalton got rid of the dog. It was confirmed by her subsequent pregnancy. Mr. Dalton has no time or inclination to read detective stories now. Keeping up with the development of a three-months-old baby is much more exciting.

I do not wish to suggest by this story that making a family is the way out of an unsuccessful marriage. " Having a baby " is in itself no solution for the sufferings of mismated couples. Adults need to have accepted the general problems of their marriage before they are able to assume the added demands of parenthood. Marriage should already have given to husband and wife a feeling of security before the baby is conceived. Some disappointed young people start a family to capture for the first time the joys of marriage, or to recapture lost joys of a romantic courtship. These unhappy couples make married life more unhappy in this way. They only add to the difficulties of mating. The best way I know of breaking up a young marriage already going sour is to subject it to the very heavy burdens and responsibilities of childbearing and child-rearing. One does not cure a sprained ankle by running on it, or make larger a skimpy portion of food by cutting it in smaller pieces.

Only recently I ran into a couple whose unfortunate experiences illustrate this point. Mr. Bath is a young dreamer about twenty-five years old. His wife, a couple of years older, is active, ambitious, and energetic. They have been married about three years, but not very successfully. The very serious differences in their temperaments have made for quarrels and dissension. The husband lacks the go-getting qualities of his wife. He has a poor money sense and is more interested in his work as an inventor than in getting paid for his ideas. Mrs. Bath, efficient and adequate, naturally gets impatient with what she considers her husband's dilatory ways. She nags and scolds in an effort to get him to make good according to her standards. Both husband and wife have had a difficult time. Mrs. Bath, tired of feeling she was getting nowhere, decided to have a baby. It seemed to be a good way of encouraging her husband to assume more responsibility for earning a larger income. And she liked babies. Her easy-going man put up no objections to her plan. At least not until after the baby was born. When the baby was beginning to crawl Mr. Bath picked up the toddler to fondle it. Mrs. Bath went into a violent rage. " I won't have you playing with the child that way," she screamed. " The doctor says you'll over-stimulate it." She did not add what was also in her mind: " and you'll make

it just like yourself." Even if she had added these words
it is hardly likely her husband would have heard them.
He had put the baby in its crib and had walked out the
door. He did not come back.

No matter how going a concern a marriage may be,
the advent of children causes severe strain between parents.
Newborn babies cannot be taken in their stride; they
have none. Their very physical disorganization sets the
pace for their influence on marriage ties. Children are
as disturbing to marriage as their own physical eccentric-
ities. Any orderly, smooth, satisfactory relationship carefully worked out between husband and wife is broken up
the very first night the child is home from the hospital.
The inability of a child to do anything for itself means
that demands are made on parents which create a new
relationship between husband and wife. Their time and
energy are no longer their own for companionship or
intimacy. The little tyrant need only raise its voice a tiny
bit to break up the parents' closest embrace. The warmth
of the adult relationship is for ever being disturbed by
the child's demands for physical attention. At any hour
of the night the newborn youngster can separate husband
and wife without repaying them for their loss with even
a friendly smile. The child's physical requirements have
the right of way over their feelings toward each other
and toward the child. No matter how much one or both
of them may resent this intrusion, their only choice is
to obey the child's call and sacrifice their own need for
each other. Babies are tyrants.

Children come between parents; they also help to unite them. A peek into almost any American home, such as the Coopers', will demonstrate both these points. The husband has come home early to spend some time with the children before they go to bed. The children are playing in the living-room with their parents. It is a jolly, happy scene. Father is helping his son build a bridge from the pieces of a Mechano set. The daughter is dressing her doll. Mother looks on smilingly, occasionally making comments to her husband or to the children. She looks at her watch. It is time for the children's bath. " Bath, children! " she announces. No one pays any attention to her. She stands up, walks over to the boy, holding out her hand as an invitation to him to accompany her to the bathroom. " Just five minutes more," he pleads. " How about it, daddy? " he asks. " I think the children might go without their bath tonight, dear," father answers, remembering his own childhood days and his rage at having to go to bed just as his soldiers were capturing the enemy's fort. " Now, Henry," mother replies, with a slight crispness in her voice, " you know those children are supposed to get a bath every night. And I do think you might support me in this." It is not necessary to elaborate upon this little story. The reader has already sensed the beginning of a family quarrel. The quarrel develops. The children are pushed off to bed. Husband and wife sit down to supper and go through the meal with heavy hearts and hardly a friendly word between them.

Husband's and wife's differences in this instance, as on

so many other occasions, arise from a common interest in the children and an earnest desire to spare them many of the crippling experiences connected with their own early training. Each parent has brought into marriage the conviction that his own parents' methods of raising him have handicapped his development. The husband is sure he would now be the president of his firm instead of its treasurer if he had only been given more independence in childhood. The wife on the other hand is convinced that her present inefficiencies as a housekeeper can be traced back to childhood, when she never had to do anything she didn't like. Both parents are agreed that their own children shall not be penalized in these ways, even if they have to fight each other to prevent it.

As a child I remember suffering severe punishment while my mother was bathing me. She was tantalizingly slow — so it seemed to me — about handing me a towel to wipe away the soap that had got into my eyes. Later on I liked to hang around the bathroom while my wife bathed the children. I had to give up this pleasure, however. My vexation with my wife for taking an interminably long time — so it seemed to me — to hand the children a towel when they got soap in their eyes was too disturbing to both of us.

My wife, on the other hand, was never allowed as a child to have friends in to meals. I notice that she encourages the youngsters to bring home to dinner loads of small friends oblivious of my concern for the poorhouse that I am sure awaits our old age as a result of her extravagance.

This mutual concern with the children's upbringing which one moment separates the parents fortunately brings them together again a moment later. Let us return to the Cooper family. Supper being over, the wife cannot keep to herself any longer the story the teacher told her about Johnny. And the husband needs to know from his wife what her plans are for the children's summer so that he can arrange his budget. Both of them have to get together on deciding whether the daughter should have music lessons and whether the boy should be allowed to spend the coming week-end with a friend in the country.

But behind the scenes of this little family drama there is sometimes a more serious problem making for family discord. The advent of children into a home naturally stirs up a good deal of jealousy between parents. Husband and wife have heretofore given all their love to each other. As soon as a woman becomes pregnant, her interests, in part at any rate, become centred on her child. The husband is perforce denied his wife's complete devotion. This withdrawal of the wife's love can be of varying degrees. In some cases it can go pretty far. I knew one mother preoccupied with the joys of bearing a child who openly encouraged her husband to sleep with her sister. This is a rare example, to be sure. But over and over again the psychiatrist learns, in reviewing the history of families in difficulties, that their troubles started with the birth or even pregnancy of the first child. It is not at all unusual to discover that the husband entered into extramarital relations for the first time during his wife's pregnancy. The husband jealous of his rival, the prospective baby, seeks solace in a little creative affair of his own.

This problem of parents' jealousies of their own children becomes much more complex as the size of the family increases. In the course of time one parent has become more attached to a certain child; the other parent to another. Every time one of the parents — the husband, let us say — lavishes affection on a child of his choice, the wife, feeling she is denied her husband's love, retaliates by disliking the child her husband prefers and increasing her display of affection for her own favourite. A continual battle between the parents takes place around the children. Sometimes the battle is an obvious one, sometimes it is very subtly carried on. In the Cowan family the fight was of both kinds.

Mr. and Mrs. Cowan had two children, an older girl and a younger boy. The mother was devoted to her son; the father acted as though there were only one child in the family, his daughter. Mr. Cowan could always find good reasons for encouraging anything his daughter wanted to do and good excuses for discouraging his son's needs. He could always find time to take the girl to the movies, but he was too busy to help the boy with his lessons. Mrs. Cowan, on the other hand, enjoyed going to the museum with Junior, but housework prevented her from making clothes for sister's doll. Husband and wife frequently called attention to the other's display of favouritism toward the children. Denials, excuses, counter-charges followed. Resentments and even bitterness accumulated between the parents.

One can cite many examples of children making their parents' relationship to each other more difficult. Mrs. Ellis almost died during her third pregnancy and Mr. Ellis has never forgiven the youngster for it. On the other hand the wife feels especially devoted to the little fellow and is extremely solicitous about his needs. The husband accuses her of spoiling the boy and excuses his own severity as a necessary antidote to mother's coddling. The child is frequently ill. Mrs. Ellis neglects the family to nurse the boy herself. She will hardly allow anyone else in the sickroom — even her husband. A feud which temporarily threatens to break up the family develops whenever the boy is ill.

The Ellis family has something in common with the Mannings. Mrs. Manning's fourth child is a depression baby. Mrs. Manning was not anxious to have another child just at that time. She felt, she said, " too insecure " about her husband's " financial future " to go through with it. Mr. Manning wanted a girl and was sure he was going to get it this time — " depression or no depression." He was right and his devotion to the baby is as strong as his wife's resentment against the economic sacrifices the family has to make to pay off the doctor's bills for her confinement. Naturally she can't help expressing some of these hostile feelings. Without consciously wishing to be destructive to her husband's morale she unfortunately reminds him of these debts when he is struggling with the monthly budget and having a difficult time meeting all his obligations.

I hope the reader contemplating marriage or the married couple contemplating having a family will not become discouraged at this point by what may seem to them a dismal picture of family life. I hope they will not decide, from these little stories about the difficulties of family life, to embrace more tightly their present unhampered happiness. They need not be discouraged from continuing their own development and the richness of their experience by excursions into marriage and child-rearing. As they will learn a little later on, the emotions children stir up in and between parents are the feelings all human beings have. It is as human to be jealous as it is to love. And the deeper the feelings, the more human the personality. Children make adults human. They do it by forcing parents to express and bring out in the open the very natural feelings society tries to get adults to hide.

Children are medicine for society's repressive attitudes. In our culture all of us have been taught "to spare the other fellow's feelings," and incidentally our own. Behind politeness formulas, good manners, jokes, fibs, half-hearted compliments, and evasions we have learned to hide our natural impulses. The keynote of the emotional quality of our society is poise. Now, dignity and poise are extremely artificial commodities. There are moments when any of my best friends make me sick. I would enjoy most heartily punching them on the nose. Yes, the women too! There are other times when I feel a deep warmth and affection toward these same people. Yes, the women too! If I want to keep my friends I am not allowed — except within very narrow limits — to let them know how I feel. And this dictum applies to the expression of affection almost as much as it does to a display of hostility. Our dealings with adults have become pretty well institutionalized. Society has well-defined rules and regulations for handling emotional traffic. Human feelings are as channelled as cars on a four-lane highway.

On the other hand, in our relationship to children we are given the opportunity for much more freedom. Adults are allowed to be practically as tender as they like with babies. Society permits even older children to be " loved almost to death." And *provided we can find a good excuse,* children can be disliked as heartily as they can be loved. The " Spare the rod and spoil the child " era of child-training is an example of this rationalized attempt of society to permit adults to come out with a native hostility toward children. Of course, society would not sanction a " Spare the resentment and spoil the friendship " era of adult emotional training. It lacks the courage for that. Between adults feelings must be buried. Between adults and children feelings, within a much, much wider range, may be expressed. Since some correctives against society's repressive taboos are necessary to prevent adults from drying up, thank God for children.

While dealing with these disturbances between society's attitudes and our own emotional life, I should like permission to work off a few pet peeves on the subject of society's attitude toward motherhood.

It is my conviction that our civilization, by its over-solicitous concern for the pregnant woman, has made childbearing an abnormally anxious and difficult period for everybody concerned. Having a baby becomes a period of strain and anxiety instead of a normal biological process. Under the disguise of protecting the expectant mother, society has surrounded her with fears and prohibitions which literally frighten to death many mothers-to-be. Mothers are warned on all sides against the dangers of leading a normal life. Their friends, and frequently their doctors, tell them what they must not eat and drink, what shows to see, what books to read, and even what emotions to have. These deep-seated prejudices infiltrate the most well-informed circles. I remember a professional colleague, pregnant with her first child, asking me to tell her about the mental hygiene of childbearing. By this she meant: what feelings should I have about becoming a mother? I am afraid my suggestion to enjoy the event in any way she could did not do much good. She had been too well indoctrinated with the idea that she was suffering a medical, and hence pathological, experience. Little wonder the apprehensive lady had vomiting attacks and spells of high blood-pressure while carrying the baby.

Fears surrounding pregnancy can on occasion become severe enough to make it necessary for a doctor to terminate the woman's unfortunate suffering. These fears are frequently hidden behind the physical symptom for which the patient seeks medical help. In this way the fears are kept from the mother's knowledge. I once knew a young student who went through this unhappy history. During her pregnancy she turned up at classes accompanied by her husband. She failed to appear at examination time. I was told she was in the hospital being treated for pernicious vomiting. The vomiting became so bad the doctors decided to interrupt the pregnancy. Following this abortive attempt to become a mother, Mrs. Lewis sought psychological advice. For the first time she learned how frightened she had been. And for a very good reason. As soon as she had told her husband and family about conception, they began passing through a fine-mesh sieve every detail of her life. The harassed mother was not even allowed to attend classes alone. The husband was afraid his wife might be distressed by something she heard.

Sometimes it is unnecessary under these circumstances of extreme fear for the doctor to stop the pregnancy. Nature does it for him. Many miscarriages caused supposedly by falls, frights, and other accidents are of this origin. An obstetrical friend of mine cites the following examples. An expert horsewoman who had never fallen from a horse before had her first mishap during the second month of pregnancy. She lost her seat, and with it her baby. In another instance a pregnant woman living in Boston decided she had to be taken care of by an obstetrician living in Arizona. In order to avoid the dangerous bumps of a train ride she went by aeroplane. She became so frightened that she aborted *en route*.

A particularly regrettable aspect of the problem of child-bearing is this: the more " civilized " the group in which the pregnant mother finds herself, the greater her difficulties. In direct proportion to her sensitivities a woman is surrounded with numerous worries, fears, and prohibitions about the dangerous process of becoming a mother. The more primitive the group, the easier and happier time women have bringing children into the world. Good evidence of this point is found in the easy style in which Indian tribes go through childbirth. Among the Pawnee Indians, for example, mothers work — and work hard — up to within a few minutes of the time for the child's delivery. Nor is anxiety manifested by other members of the tribe during the earlier months of her pregnancy. On the contrary, the pregnant woman is looked upon with special favour as an example of healthiness and robustness. Her physical health is considered to be outstandingly good. Her pregnancy proves it. In our American society fertility has no such prized status. The more cultivated the woman, the greater the anxiety about her childbearing ability.

Nor does society's dirty work stop when it discourages motherhood and scares the pregnant mother to death. If she survives these two hazards she is confronted with another anguishing cry in the night: the fear of labour pains. One of my professional colleagues, impressed by the easy time Jamaican coloured folk had giving birth to babies, investigated from a psychological point of view the problem of labour pains among white women. He came to the conclusion that the pain of delivering a child was caused by the contraction and spasm of muscles which carried out the job of pushing the baby into the world. The spasm of the muscles, however, was out of proportion to the work they had to do. The muscles were functioning like a twelve-cylinder motor on a four-cylinder job. The unnecessary work the muscles were doing was a response to the fear of pain, and hence helped to increase it. The women whom he studied admitted they were approaching oncoming labour as though it were a sort of punishment and something very definitely to be afraid of. Society had so loaded them with anxiety that they anticipated — and experienced — a greater degree of pain than was physiologically necessary. By psychologically preparing these women for labour — that is, by reducing their fears — this psychiatrist lessened their labour pains.

But let us assume now that a woman has successfully turned her back on society's over-anxious attitudes toward pregnancy and labour and is now a mother, looking forward to the fun of being a parent. Let us assume, too, that the warmth and flexibility of the husband's and wife's relationship to each other permit their happy acceptance of a change in the family constellation. Unfortunately, even now society cannot leave the wife alone to have a good time with her family. She is not permitted to enjoy her baby in her own way. As soon as the child is born she runs up against a whole series of social attitudes which seriously interfere with her happiness. One of the most devastating of these is the attitude of society toward motherhood.

In middle-class circles the concept of motherhood is so inflated with high-hat ideologies and distorted by unnatural trimmings as to make it impossible for most women to live up to. A woman as a mother is supposed to see herself as possessing all the qualities and virtues possessed by the Virgin Mary, Queen Mary of England, and Whistler's Mother. To admit that she might be as human as a Mrs. Simpson is unthinkable. A mother in our group is by definition the embodiment of sacrifice, love, and tenderness. She lives only for her children and their complete development. She is never permitted a hostile gesture toward any of her offspring, no matter how brattish they may be acting. If she does discipline a child, it is only for his own good and hurts her more than it hurts little Johnny. Should she have a number of children, a mother has to love each child to exactly the same degree, irrespective of sex, age, personality, or constitution. Should one child be handicapped by a clubbed foot or mental deficiency or any other disability, she is permitted and expected to love that child even more than the others and demand from herself and the other children greater sacrifices in its favour. A good example of this behaviour is seen in the Brighton family.

Mr. and Mrs. Brighton have five children. Four of them — two boys and two girls — are fine and healthy. The fifth, the oldest boy, is suffering from a permanently damaged brain, the result of an automobile accident. Unfortunately medical science is impotent in such conditions. At present there is no way of replacing destroyed brain tissue with fresh, clean brain substance. To make matters worse, the boy has from time to time spells of an epileptic nature. He shakes, throws himself on the floor, and becomes unconscious. He will never be any better. Mrs. Brighton, however, is not permitted to give up her efforts to make this boy as healthy as the other children, even though each doctor she visits tells her the same unhappy story. Mrs. Brighton cannot accept this verdict. As a good mother she must struggle on, trying to help her son. If she were a rich woman the only danger in her behaviour would come from her preoccupation with this handicapped child and a corresponding withdrawal of interest from the other children. Unfortunately, the Brightons are not rich. The family has to make sacrifices to take elaborate care of this boy. Doctors, nurses, special training procedures are expensive, expensive enough to rob the other children of educational opportunities which would surely get them somewhere. Mrs. Brighton has a fine courage, but it is the courage demanded by an intolerant social order evaluating a mother's job.

These concepts of motherhood which society asks our womenfolk to live up to are quite unpsychological and even harmful. Women even as mothers are human beings and not statues of the Madonna. They have in their dealings with their own children likes and dislikes, loves and hates, preferences and choices, as they have toward all other human beings. There is nothing in being a child's mother that changes this fundamental psychology. To be sure, society asks mothers to act as though there were some special God-given feeling inherent in motherhood and in no other human relationship. This point of view is not only nonsense, it is dangerous. It is harmful to mother and child alike. It calls upon mothers to hide their very natural feelings toward their children, especially the natural antagonism all mothers feel toward any child at times. A mother is not allowed to express her annoyance if, for example, the child develops a temperature of 101° just as she is getting off for a long anticipated restful weekend with her husband. She is allowed to express only tenderness and solicitude. She is expected to give up her trip with a smile.

Because of what society expects from them in their relationship to children, parents sometimes go to unnecessary and painful lengths in their efforts to hide from themselves disappointments, antagonisms, and hostilities they must as human beings experience toward other human beings, even their own children. If a father wants a son and gets a daughter he is not permitted disappointment. He must consider himself blessed, nevertheless. His feelings toward his daughter are expected to be only the most positive. Any wishes he may have that she were a boy have to be wiped out like bad debts on his ledgers. Now, while he may become very, very fond of his daughter, he can still legitimately wish she were a son and at times resent her sex. Of course, as a good father he is not allowed to do this openly. To get around this dilemma he may be driven to change her sex by bringing up his daughter as though she were a boy. He will teach her all his own masculine interests, encourage her to make his choice of college courses, and even attempt to direct her career along lines of his own profession.

Mothers, too, can have a similar problem, as we will see from a brief review of the experiences of the Clow family. Mr. and Mrs. Clow were extremely well-meaning people, anxious to do everything for their only child, an adolescent boy. Mrs. Clow, without knowing it, had never forgiven him for being a boy. She tried to hide his sexual identity behind the name of Francis. Now, Mrs. Clow, in all fairness to her own psychology and needs, had justification for feeling disappointed because her only child was not a girl. Unfortunately she was unable to admit to herself this disappointment, a mother being expected to consider herself rewarded by having children irrespective of their sex. Without knowing why she was doing it, Mrs. Clow set to work to make Francis into Frances. "Frances" grew up to be a sissy. During adolescence he got into trouble, stealing money to run off to Hollywood to join the movie colony. He travelled only as far as Broadway and the movie houses; when his money gave out he returned home, but not to stay long. Mrs. Clow, recognizing something had to be done for her son, decided at last she was going to make a man out of him. He was packed off to a military school. Life there was, of course, too harsh for him. Francis had been roughly dropped off the deep end by his parents' efforts to help him. He got into some unfortunate habits at military school and was more disturbed than ever.

It is not necessary at this point to follow Francis' progress. He is going to come out all right eventually. I am more worried about Mrs. Clow, who so unnecessarily seems to have punished herself because she did not find herself in harmony with the attitude that mothers must only love their children under all circumstances. If she had known that all mothers, including Cornelia, the very proud mother of the Gracchi, and Gertrude, the distraught mother of Hamlet, and Mrs. Roosevelt, the gracious mother of many successful children, have at times hostile emotions toward their children, she would have been spared much anguish and unnecessary feelings of guilt.

It is just as human for parents to hate children as to love them. A combination of hate and love toward our offspring is the normal parental attitude. This normal mixture of positive and negative feelings is found in all close personal contacts: whether the tie is between parent and child, husband and wife, brother and sister, friend and friend. It was nicely and emotionally described by my own ten-year-old son, who came to me one day saying: " Daddy, sometimes I feel like kissing Abby " (his six-year-old sister), " other times I could wring her neck all the way downtown."

One asks, of course, why there should be this normal and universal resentment against parenthood on the part of mothers and fathers. I think the answer is as simple as this: There are many aspects of parenthood which cause us definite pain, discomfort, and displeasure. The human reaction to any painful experience, whether it be getting

up in the middle of the night to heat the baby's bottle or
listening to the boss bawl us out for coming in late, is
resentment. As already indicated, the fact that we are
dealing with our child does not change our own instinctual
natures. Blood relationship only helps to make our hates
and loves more intense. When all the desirable romance is
stripped from the joys of parenthood, there is left a whole
series of painful debts that mothers and fathers have
to pay as the price of a family. And only morons enjoy
debts.

To make the subject more concrete, it might be a good
idea to take a brisk look at some of the costs adults have to
pay for the privilege of joining the ranks of parents. There
is, of course, the economic burden. This load has become
much heavier in the last generation. And for two reasons.
Parents have to support children in better and better style.
The duration of this support has been extended. When
Matthew Vassar endowed his college, the only provision
he made for taking care of the girls' clothes was three nails
on the wall. One was to hang a nightgown on, the second
was for a day dress, and the third took care of a Sunday
frock. My private office being near a girls' finishing school,
I have the opportunity of seeing the young ladies' trunks
arrive at the beginning of the school year. Any one of
these boxes — and most students have two or three —
would be big enough to take care of all the clothes, belong-
ings, and personal possessions with which my parents
migrated from England to this continent with two children.

The increased economic strain of supporting children does not begin or end with the adolescents' clothes. It begins as soon as the child is born and is encouraged by a combination of respect for science and fads between which we harassed and guilt-ridden parents are naturally unable to distinguish. Aside from the expenses of all kinds of medical specialists — gynecologist, pediatrician, orthopedist, orthopsychiatrist (with whose very heavy fees I have, of course, an understandable sympathy) — to help bring the child into the world and to advise upon the conditions under which it should remain here, there are special outfits to be bought for the toddler. The gifts of layettes, blankets, rattles, etc., that most mothers used to rely upon to take care of their children's needs during the first few months of life can no longer be depended upon. Not only must these early requirements come up to scientific standards, but they must also fit in with the child's special personality needs, so we are told! Moreover, the cost of even a young baby's food has to be reckoned with now. It is not enough to feed a child orange juice and cod-liver oil, we have to make sure the oranges come from — is it Florida or California? And the oil from the right one of the three Scandinavian countries. Of course, the child needs not only a special room, but one with the right exposure to sunshine. You may have to move out of your own bedroom to satisfy the little tyrant, but that's just your hard luck as a parent. Of course, if you happen to live in an apartment you can't expect to be a successful parent unless you are lucky enough to be able to afford a special set of stairs for teaching the right kind of infantile muscular co-ordinations. It is not necessary to elaborate much further this problem of the increased expensiveness of raising children. A word must be said, however, about the greater costs of education. Formal education now begins at eighteen months and lasts until father's bank account runs out. I remember a patient telling me how red her face became when she entered her two-year-old boy in nursery school. She was told that since she had been so tardy about arranging for his education it might be too late now! And there is a cute little anecdote in this connection in our own family. My son had been to nursery school from the age of two to four and we decided to give him a sabbatical year. When he was five a conference with a prospective school took place to discuss details for admittance. The school official inquired very carefully about his earlier educational background. She was rightly interested in what he had done between the ages of four and five after he had graduated from nursery shool. It was explained to her that he had been having a good time with young friends in the neighbourhood. "Yes," she responded, "that's all right, but I can see you would be anxious now to have him back in school. I can see you wouldn't want him to mark time any longer."

But economic strain is only one of the discomforts of parenthood. There is the further factor of conflict between a woman's career and babies. We have already dealt with the more general aspects of marriage and a woman's career. We are now interested in women who would like to work outside the home and have a family too. The fact that some women give up a promising career to marry and have babies also helps to account for the presence of normal negative feelings that these mothers have toward their children. No human being likes sacrificing something she enjoys and looks forward to if she is at all normal. True enough, she may be making a good exchange in turning in a job for a family. Nevertheless in having a family she is jeopardizing her chances of advancing along the road of a successful career. Children are a hindrance to a woman's professional ambitions. She is giving up something by assuming the responsibilities of a family. And there is no one I know who has ever reached that stage of maturity who doesn't prefer to keep her cake as well as to eat it. Women who had opportunities of amounting to something in the outside world can't help resenting the limitations placed upon their worth-while interests and activities by a brood of squalling, demanding youngsters.

When I tell this to my feminist lady friends they all jump up in a body and yell — without worrying about their usual politeness: " Nonsense." They point out with what seems like unnecessary vigour that they have given up chances of being successful in business or in academic careers and don't mind it a bit. And as for resenting their children, " How ridiculous! " All I can say to them is " How fortunate! " but neither of us really believes it. It is my conviction that women who have given up a career for marriage and babies resent their choice and express some of this resentment in antagonistic attitudes toward the children who have helped to make the decision ir-revocable.

Now, the interesting aspect of this problem is that these women really need not feel as they do. They are just as well off as their college mates who went ahead with both a career and the creation of a family. Mothers who give up a career feel resentful, but women who elect to have both a job and a family feel guilty about neglecting their children. They think of themselves as bad mothers and resent the children as the cause of their own guilt feelings. I have never met a working mother in middle-class family life who did not have these disrupting emotions toward herself and her children.

To be sure, these feelings are not always recognized by the working mother. She may unknowingly go to great lengths to hide behind over-solicitude her negative feelings. She may be unnecessarily generous in her gifts of toys, she may give the child an over-abundance of freedom, she may make all kinds of sacrifices to send the child to the right school. Or she may show on the slightest provocation ex-treme anxiety about the child. For the mildest cold the child is kept in bed for days. The youngster may never be allowed to cross the safest streets without an adult com-panion, or even to play with other children in the park be-cause of the danger of germs. In all these ways does the working mother betray her unhappy guilt about being away from the house so much. In all these ways, and in many others, does she attempt to " make weight " for what she unnecessarily considers the child's deprivations and misfortune.

One can't help at this point commenting on the jealous attitudes of a masculine society toward the working mother. These attitudes have a good deal to do with the guilt these mothers feel. The liberalizing influences of the last century, which make it possible for women to compete with men on a more equal basis, have done nothing to make women feel more comfortable in their skins when they become mothers as well as working women. On the contrary, a mean society which opens up jobs for women and invites them to play a man's game seems to treat these women like guests who have overstayed their invitations as soon as they get babies.

This conflict between work and parenthood is not limited to mothers. It affects fathers, too, but to a lesser degree. Among white-collar families fathers are permitted to occupy themselves with business more and their homes less. Women are still considered primarily responsible for the home and the personal amenities of the family. But fathers do not get off scot free. There is the week-end, free from business pursuits, during which they are expected to dedicate their time to the happiness of the children: pulling Freddie around while he learns to roller-skate, holding Mary on her new bicycle, taking Harry swimming and the whole family for a Sunday picnic.[1] Fathers, however, have

[1] The introduction of a car into every middle-class family's home has made family social life more available. It has also helped to increase the emotional discomfort of fathers who do not "follow the leader," as it were, and give the family a good time.

a good excuse — and it is frequently only an excuse — for getting out of these chores. The emphasis today on economic security and earning a large enough living to make possible the satisfaction of all material needs of the children gives him a good excuse when he would rather stay downtown in the late afternoon than run around the block chasing after his daughter on a scooter. He can, without feeling too uncomfortable, get away to the country club with his cronies over the week-end on the very acceptable plea that a day or so of relaxation makes him more fit for Monday morning's business crises. And it is an actual clinical fact, supported by contact with and study of fathers and mothers in a psychiatrist's office and in clinics, that fathers feel much less guilty than mothers about their relationship to children.

At this point I am not primarily concerned with the social implications of these conflicts and the reasons why mothers feel more guilty than fathers about their children. I am more interested in those individual parents of both sexes who suffer from these fights in their inner mental life, those parents who cannot decide how much time to devote to home and children, to what extent a sincere and laudable interest in work should be allowed to compete — and it does always compete to some extent — with the demands of child-raising. My job is to help mothers (and fathers) like Mrs. Robertson, who had two full-time jobs: one as mother of her own three children, one as mother of fifty schoolchildren in the capacity of teacher. She worried so much about not doing a good job either at home or at school that she had periodic nervous breakdowns. Or like Mrs. Evans, who had a talent for music. So frightened about neglecting her children if she took time off to develop her piano-playing, this unhappy lady suffered severe cramps in her left hand whenever she played her instrument more than fifteen or twenty minutes. And Mrs. French, whose superlative research mind was lost to the world. She turned down job after job because she was afraid of being considered a bad mother if she worked outside the home.

It seems too bad that so much destructive feeling should have been built up on society's part around the supposed dangers of neglecting our children. Not only is a good deal of achievement lost to the world in general by parents' inabilities to enjoy their own accomplishments and ambitions because of fear of neglecting the children, but the family is no better off for this self-denial. If parents are made to feel they are not devoting enough time to their homes, they feel guilty. If they give up some of their own interests to give more time to the children, they feel resentful about the high price paid for parenthood. Between guilt and resentment as constructive emotions there is very little to choose. When we feel guilty we punish ourselves, when we feel resentful we punish the other fellow. In the end both solutions get nowhere. Now, the interesting — and I hope helpful — observation a psychiatrist has to make from his contacts with mothers who do not work or have serious interests outside the home and with mothers who do is this: It does not seem to make any difference to the welfare of the children whether a mother gives all her time to her family or not. Mothers who give all their attention to the family have as many difficulties with children as mothers who do not. And mothers who work on jobs are apparently just as capable of enjoying their children as mothers who spend more time with them. The point is that the conflict between job and babies is not nearly so important as the conflict between what society says mothers should be and what they really are. Mothers who can thumb their noses at destructive social attitudes about motherhood have a much happier time, whether being a mother is a full-time or only a part-time job.

In connection with the origins of parental resentments toward children it will do no harm to review by way of the Huston family what was said earlier in this chapter: children interfere with the adjustments husbands and wives have already at some cost established to each other. One can take it for granted that when a new baby is born into a family there is going to be some change in the feelings of all other members of the household toward each other. These changes are not easy for any normal person to make. Over and over again I have seen families almost at the breaking-point because of the demands on their feelings the new child makes. It is most understandable that the cause of these difficult readjustments, the new child, is going to be resented as well as loved. A healthy resentment toward the child is inevitable. And so we find it in the Huston family.

Mr. and Mrs. Huston had had a rough economic and

psychological struggle before marriage, and during the first three or four years of married life too. Mr. Huston had got through high school by dint of perseverance and money earned after school hours. Mrs. Huston's people were better off, but she had worked her way through college because her father did not approve of a college education for women. When Mr. Huston married his wife she was working as a school-teacher; he, as a mechanic. Mrs. Huston felt her husband was meant for bigger things and continued to work during early married life to enable him to get more training. Following the completion of Mr. Huston's education and the landing of a good job, Mrs. Huston resigned from her work to take care of the home and prepare for motherhood. The next eighteen months were a happy period for both of them. For the first time in their lives they were relieved of strain and were free to have a good time. While Mrs. Huston on occasion missed her independent job, she got a good deal of satisfaction from her husband's success. She had been so much part of it. Moreover, she had time now to build up the family's social life. The home took on the atmosphere of her personality and she liked what she was creating. The husband did too. He behaved more and more like a successful person. His work caught the spirit of his home life and he started to receive recognition and a large salary. Increasing the size of the family was the next psychological step for expansion. Two children — a boy and a girl — were born in rapid succession. During the first few years following the births of these children both Mr. and Mrs. Huston had

been too closely tied up with these new experiences to
notice any difference in their own feelings and behaviour
toward each other. These differences started to come out
as the children's personalities took more definite shape
and the children began to make on the parents independent demands. No longer was it possible for the adults to go
off together for a week-end alone, the children insisting on
going along. Even an evening together at the theatre was
spoiled before it began by the fuss the children made
about being left at home with the maid. Neither Mr. nor
Mrs. Huston liked having to give up good times with
friends at the house because their daughter was a light
sleeper and woke up with nightmares whenever the party
got a little hilarious. Around this period quarrels developed between husband and wife for the first time. In these
quarrels a good deal of resentment toward each other was
expressed. When the heat of battle had subsided and a
reconciliation was being effected, both parents admitted
that what really bothered them was the way they now had
to share each other with the children. They did not recognize so clearly, however, that the resentment they had felt
toward one another was resentment toward the children
for coming between them. The true origin of these feelings they dared not admit even to themselves.

The Hustons are no different in their fundamental
natures from all parents. In so far as children come between husband and wife they arouse parental antagonisms.
In so far as they constitute a common bond between husband and wife they intensify the love between the adults.

All children create for all parents both sets of reactions. Sometimes these negative and positive feelings are expressed toward the children directly, sometimes the parents try to protect the children from these impacts and spend on each other the more hostile emotions. No matter which way parents express their feelings, strong hates and equally strong loves toward their children are a normal part of a parent-child relationship.

In the last few paragraphs I have talked mostly about the way society manages by its exalted ideas of parenthood, of motherhood especially, to make parents feel guilty about a normal hostility toward children. Unfortunately, it makes them feel guilty too about their love for their own children. Strange as it may sound, as many parents are worried about loving their children too much as too little. The psychiatrist specializing in the treatment of children's behaviour difficulties is consulted by many mothers and fathers whose chief problem is fear of loving their children too much. These are parents with strong human sympathies who " hold back " their affection because, as one mother phrased it, " my child might get a complex if I show him too much tenderness." For example, Mrs. Fletcher's particular worry, as she saw it herself, was her seven-year-old son's fondness for coming into her bed in the morning after Mr. Fletcher had got up. She was worried by the ardour her son displayed during these morning visits and did not know how to handle it. Her natural impulse was to respond affectionately. She did not want to give the boy a " complex," though, and solved her dilemma by getting up and dressing. The boy never did get the affection he craved and his mother wanted so much to give. Because of Mrs. Fletcher's guilt both mother and son were denied an opportunity of enjoying their relationship.

I am afraid it must be admitted that much of this guilt parents have about loving their children too much has been stirred up by modern psychological literature. " Psychologizing " has made parents so apprehensive about the dangers of coddling children that they have fallen over backwards and have become afraid even to love them. We have been told that the trouble with Hamlet was his love for his mother, so intense as to drive him mad. The implication from this experience either given by or inferred from educators is that a mother had better watch out if she does not want this to happen to her son. Mothers get the impression from much popular and some less popular literature that if tenderness expressed frankly and openly toward children does not make her boy a Hamlet, it will at least make a sissy out of him. And apparently, judging by our attitudes toward sissies, that is almost as bad! Parents are certainly put in a difficult position. They are not allowed to express openly their love for children and they are not allowed to express hatred toward them. Little wonder that parents caught up in this modern psychological dilemma ask for a heavy ritual of dos and don'ts written out as concretely as the Ten Commandments with which to guide their relationships to their children twenty-four hours a day. Inasmuch as our own instincts (positive or negative) left to act by themselves would be too destructive to childhood, so we are told, it has become necessary to surround ourselves and our children with protective layers of accredited prohibitions and sanctions carefully card-indexed and available for every occasion. My contact with this kind of " child-guidance " training has taught me detailed answers to such problems as:

1. What to do when Johnny says " Shut up " to you:
   (a) when nobody is around,
   (b) when visitors are on the scene,
   (c) when his teacher is visiting.

2. How to say something nice about your child so she will not become conceited:
   (a) when her brothers and sisters are around,
   (b) when mother is alone with her,
   (c) when her father is home.

There are other modern " child-guides " who take us all the way back to Plato's ideas to get around the fact that parents have feelings. Plato, it will be remembered, arranged in his Republic for all children to be segregated from parents at birth. Aldous Huxley in his playful way has improved on that solution. In his brave new world parents would not even have the function of turning out the original protoplasm necessary to start the child on its way to life. A mixture of the right ingredients selected from carefully labelled bottles by a competent clerk would do away with parents altogether!

If I were not facetious about this kind of training of parental emotions, I should be quite angry. And for good reason. The effects of calling attention to the dangers to children of parental emotions and of giving parents carefully indexed guide-books for handling their feelings seem to have been this: It has made parents think they must compete with St. Anthony or St. Anne as guides of children's lives and has succeeded in leaving them feeling defeated and frustrated when their own standards of behaviour fall below heavenly example. Many modern child-training authorities are doing their best to give parents the idea they have to be angels if they want to raise children successfully. Disturbed mortals get the impression that following a concrete and explicit code of instructions is the only path to successful parenthood. The instructions aim to direct parental emotions as a policeman directs traffic. But the penalties for infringement of rules are much more severe. Parents are left feeling like the devil at their inevitable failures.

This is not all the damage this kind of parental training does. By giving parents the idea that there are very definite wrong ways and right ways of handling children, educators help to increase the anxieties and tension they set out to alleviate. Since all parents have feelings that at times break through the best conceived set of rules on child-guidance, it does not help them to know what they could have done to avoid losing their temper, showing their anger, or expressing an outburst of affection for the child they genuinely prefer. On the contrary, this knowledge only makes parents feel more guilty and miserable. These rules, even if organized by Horace Mann himself, would be harmful because they cannot humanly be followed. Parents' feelings toward children are stronger than law and would break through a constitutional amendment. It does not help parents to know what experts consider the best course of action in handling children. Because of human emotions adults are helpless in *sincerely* carrying out any rules, no matter how well conceived. To know what we think we should do and be unable to do it leaves us feeling more impotent and defeated than ever. Under these circumstances I should much rather trust the straight-forward expression by parents of normal resentments and affections than the most perfect set of guidance rules.

One of the biggest reasons why I believe that these carefully thought-out sets of rules on child-training are more harmful than helpful is this: Some of the happiest children I know are children of parents who do not know any of these rules or, if they do know them, break them all.

Hidden away in the New Hampshire hills is a young lady of forty-five of whom I am very fond. To be sure, she has red hair, but this is not the only or even the chief reason for my affection. Mrs. Fuller is the mother of twelve happy children. In the summer I take the opportunity of calling on her and her brood frequently. She moves about among her youngsters in an easy-going way and is no more concerned about her feelings toward them than toward the chickens in the yard. Her children are the best-adjusted children I know, and I like to have my own youngsters play with them in the hope that there is something con-tagious about children's happy behaviour. Mrs. Fuller's success as a mother is not due to training. It could not be. She has never attended a parents' discussion group. And I have an idea she has never read a book. She does not hold with too much " larning."

There is another mother I know who lives in the Middle West. Everybody is surprised to learn she is a college graduate, so successfully has she parted with all her earlier education. She has been too busy raising a family of five children on about thirty dollars a week to keep up with her earlier background. She screams at her brats, cuffs them, and loves them until they are now recognized by their state as one of its most promising groups of adolescents. One of them recently won a college scholarship in a state-wide competition in which maturity and future promise as well as scholarship were carefully evaluated.

But these two mothers are more fortunate than most parents. They are not afraid to accept feelings which we as parents are unnecessarily afraid to face. Parents tend to think of themselves as "bad" when they feel hostile toward their children. Hence their fear of recognizing their own hostilities lest they consider themselves lacking in parental love — the worst kind of condemnation in our civilization. My conviction is that there are never good or bad parents. There are only parents who behave like all human beings. Sometimes they love their children. Sometimes they hate them. Any parent who cuddles and hugs his offspring on some occasions would at other times gladly turn him in for a new Ford in which he and his wife could resume the sweet courtship that was taking place before the advent of a noisy interruption. If this fact could be generally accepted, much destructive and painful anxiety would be taken out of parent-child relationships. To recognize our own feelings toward the family — whatever they may be — with a " So what? — all parents have them " attitude would spare both parents and children many unhappy experiences. And the " So what? " attitude should come out of realizing that all parents are in the same boat. They all have hostile feelings as well as feelings of love for their children. They all have moments of feeling angry, irritated, annoyed with them, as well as periods of feeling very tender. We are all, in other words, normal human beings, albeit parents.

Furthermore, were this attitude generally accepted it would be no longer necessary to hide our negative feelings behind many detailed activities aimed at improving the child. For that is what we unconsciously do. Instead of being able to admit to ourselves that we have hostile feelings toward our children, we disguise them as efforts to make our children healthy, wealthy, and wise. Were the " So what? " attitude a part of our psychology — and it becomes harder and harder to make it so as child-raising becomes a more and more specialized occupation — one of the areas of parent-child contact to show first the impact of a fresh attitude would be the highly emotionalized field of physical hygiene. Good physical hygiene is helpful to a child's healthy development. It probably matters at what hour a youngster goes to bed, whether he eats sufficient fruit and vegetables, and whether he receives an adequate amount of sunshine and fresh air. At the same time I have a very definite idea that these rituals frequently get entangled with feelings that tend to destroy their value. If a father becomes so anxious about loving or hating his daughter, let us say, that he is afraid to make any suggestion about her physical care without consulting a doctor, then the doctor, no matter how great his knowledge of physical hygiene, is not able to help the child, or the parent very much. It is not the child's physical hygiene but the father's mental hygiene that needs help. If the father could say to himself: " I am worried about my feelings toward my child and that is why I am so concerned about her physical hygiene," he would be much happier, and the child much healthier. If the father could now go one step further and add: " So are all other parents anxious about their sentiments toward their children; I guess that proves I'm a normal parent," we psychiatrists specializing in mental hygiene or preventive psychiatry would be looking for W. P. A. work, along with a good many very able pediatricians. The child, freed from the burden of parental anxiety incorporated in a rigid physical routine, would no longer need a doctor's help. Children react more favourably to freely expressed parental feelings than to the same feelings in disguise, whatever form the disguise may take. And whatever form the freely expressed emotion takes.

A hard-working father once came to a semi-private child-guidance clinic because he thought his four-year-old boy was slow in learning to talk. He quite rightly pointed out to me how difficult it was for him to understand why his child should be backward. The parents were intelligent and had brought up the child according to the best approved methods. Before the depression the boy had had a nurse, who had seen to it that the child was never disturbed from the regularity of his routine. No one was allowed in the nursery during meal-time, company was restricted during social hours to prevent over-excitement and fatigue. Intelligence tests showed the child to be of average mental level. The little boy's backwardness in talking was not due to lack of mentality. Nor to physical disabilities. The careful physical routine had taken care of the child's body very adequately. But it had not taken care of his emotional growth. He had become overburdened with anxiety about himself, and this anxiety had blocked the development of his speech. His emotions had got in the way of his ability to talk, as happens so frequently with adults making a first public speech before a group of strangers. This boy was suffering chronically from " public-speaking difficulties." His anxiety about appearing before the public, as it were, was directly traceable to the rigidity of earlier physical routine. The more concern others about him showed, the more the boy became concerned about himself. But whence the harsh routine? From the nurse, it might appear. The nurse, however, was only taking the father's place and had been selected by him for her strict disciplinary qualities. To handle his strong feelings toward his son he unfortunately had felt the need of a strong hand. Not being able to trust his own human impulses — and quite likely being ashamed of them — he had separated his son from himself and his own feelings by a strict nurse and an ironclad set of rules. The child had responded to the separation by backwardness in speech, thus separating father and son further and making the relationship between them more tense and painful.

The relationship between this father and son was a punishing one for both of them. The father without knowing it had resorted to punishment to relieve his own guilty feelings. By organizing a painfully over-strict routine for the boy, he was also punishing himself. All parents use punishment in one form or another to handle the uncomfortable feelings created by ties to their children. Punishment serves the useful purpose of diminishing the painful tensions caused by our emotions. Not all parents are aware of utilizing this purge. Many of us may hide punishing behaviour behind such disguises as sending the child to a military school to learn manliness or to a boarding school to learn independence. Strange as it may sound, it is nevertheless true that giving in to all its wishes is another disguise for punishing the child. (But more about this later.) If we desire to punish our children, and every normal parent should have that desire from time to time, it seems to me that a spanking has much to commend it. It is undisguised hostility, therefore understandable to parent and child, and it is self-limiting. The disturbing relationship terminates with the spanking. Children, given a choice, prefer this form of punishment. I remember once overhearing a boy of nine say to his mother: " I wish you would lick me instead of refusing to talk to me." By a licking the slate is cleaned; adults and children alike get a fresh start. Another advantage of a spanking is the psychological truth that it hurts daddy as much as Jimmy. Inasmuch as daddy loves Jimmy as much as he dislikes him at the moment, Jimmy's tears are as painful to his father as the spanking is to his son. And since fathers punish children to punish themselves too, both adult and youngster re-establish swiftly and effectively by this method emotional equilibrium. A spanking straightens both of them out. A few less rules of conduct and a few more physical contacts — take your choice! — would have made our backward boy more articulate.

It is interesting to observe that physical punishment has gone out of style as child-training techniques have become more and more elaborate. This change is related to developments in our culture. As already mentioned, emotional poise is now the prized possession of a supposedly well-adjusted adult and parent. Adults today are not allowed to show feeling. An unnatural condition of life. That is why the movie and the theatre have become more and more popular. Here you can see feeling freely and publicly expressed. You may with the aid of group singing express yourself. We are working toward the hopeful day when the audience will be an active and emotional part of the show. As it has become less and less refined to show feeling, especially toward our own children, techniques for hiding it have become more and more necessary. This is one function of good techniques (diets, routines, methods for handling temper tantrums) for raising children. As morphine masks pain and discomfort, child-training rules cover up our angers, our resentments, and our loves. The hairbrush of last century has been replaced by spinach. Instead of scolding a child we give him a " rest period " to relieve fatigue — that is, the adult's. Or an enema for his " toxic condition."

Over-elaborated child-training efforts sometimes go further than hiding adults' feelings. They frequently aim — unconsciously, to be sure — at preventing the youngster from having too good a time. This fact was brought forcibly to my attention recently when I overheard the following conversation between a friend and his four-year-old son. Harry came into the house eating acorns. His father met him in the hall and noticed the little boy was eating.

Father: " What's that you have there, sonny? "

Son: " Oh, nothing, daddy."

Father: " Mummy is going to be angry if she sees you eating between meals. You know you are not allowed to do that, fellow."

Son: " It's all right, daddy," looking up into his father's face with a smile, " they don't taste good."

Harry had realized much more clearly than we adults that behind our strict management of children's routine is frequently the unconscious purpose of seeing that children do not enjoy themselves too much.

Teachers, as well as parents, unknowingly fall into the same pitfall of using routine child-training methods as a punishment. I remember being in a classroom one morning as some five-year-old children were returning to their studies from a visit to the bathroom. The teacher, although a kindly soul, was quite disturbed. Even the presence of a visitor in the room was not sufficient on this occasion to prevent the young lady from losing her poise. She called out to the first two children as soon as they appeared: "You've been loafing in the bathroom. I can see by your faces you've been having a very good time. You know that's not allowed."

CHAPTER VIII

꒰ꔛ꒱

ALL CHILDREN HAVE
DIFFICULTIES

ADULTS, by hiding their feelings behind the " musts " and " must-nots " of an overdone routine, make life less enjoyable for children. The fact that children suffer from these restrictions does not worry me so much. Children's personalities are as elastic as the rubber balls they play with. Youngsters have natural powers of recuperation which resist most adults' well-intentioned misdirection. I am much more worried about the grown-ups. They have no such resiliency. Because of very close ties to children, adults, whether parents or teachers, receive the full imprint of blows apparently aimed at youngsters. It is they who truly suffer for what outwardly appear like efforts to protect the young and the innocent.

I was once working with a family in which a seven-year-old boy was seemingly making a poor school adjustment. One day the teacher sent the boy home from school with instructions not to return until his father had visited the school. The father being out of town, I, as the family psychiatrist, visited the school *in loco parentis*. The teacher, Miss Snowdon, a very attractive lady of thirty-five with a nice big bosom and plenty of feeling, explained what had happened. Tommy was " getting too much for her " and there had to be a showdown. The lad was disrupting the class by his clownlike behaviour. He was one of the most popular children in the group. All the other children, boys and girls, were extremely fond of Tom and protected him on all occasions. Unless she took matters in hand she was afraid the boy would disintegrate the morale of the room. Moreover, he was not learning anything. The teacher's sympathy and friendliness much more than her words impressed me as she spoke. I got the impression from listening that the teacher was going through a more painful experience than the youngster. From all she had said, it would appear that Tom was having a very good time. One could take it for granted that the most popular boy in the class was not likely to be especially unhappy. Miss Snowdon reacted to my impressions and, I hope, an unexpressed understanding of her. " You're a psychiatrist," she said. " I want to tell you about a dream I had, doctor. Last night I dreamed I was holding Tom in my arms. We were travelling down a hill very fast on a scooter. The scooter was very close to the ground, but I was afraid Tom would fall off. I hung on to him for dear life." I commented: " You are very fond of Tom, aren't you? " " Yes. You see, it's near the end of the year and he will be going on to the next class." " Don't be afraid to enjoy him while you have the chance," I suggested.

This whole episode is a very real illustration of how adults apply to children discipline of one kind or another to get rid of their own anxieties. Miss Snowdon, Tommy's teacher — we could just as aptly be talking about Tommy's mother — was very fond of the boy. Fond enough, in fact, to be afraid of her love for him. She was afraid she loved him too much; she was afraid, too, that the end of the school year would see the termination of their relationship. On the one hand she wanted to hold on to him; on the other she was alarmed by what she considered the dangerous nature of their close companionship. As revealed by her dream, Miss Snowdon unconsciously believed her love was leading Tom rapidly downhill to destruction; she made herself feel guilty and unhappy about her affection for him. On occasions like these a person instinctively reaches out for punishment or discipline as a means of relieving guilt. The punishment, however, has to be double-edged. The punishment should appear to be directed at the child who is consciously considered at fault. In the process of disciplining the child the adult should be made to pay a bigger penalty. Miss Snowdon's psyche handled both these aspects of her dilemma. The boy was sent home from school in mild disgrace. The teacher was robbed of her enjoyment of the child in the meantime. Both child and adult were, from the point of view of Miss Snowdon's conflicts, appropriately punished.

The teacher's efforts to straighten out her disturbing emotional ties to the boy make a psychiatrist in more sentimental and reflective moments a little unhappy. And for this reason: In so far as native love for the youngster is considered, the teacher's influence on her pupil was very wholesome. The boy's personality was flourishing under her treatment. He was happy, his classmates were happy with him, the teacher alone was dismayed. Her fondness for Tommy made her consider her influence harmful — even though, as Tommy's excellent personality adjustment and her own dream indicated, she really had nothing to worry about. Supposing Tommy had fallen off the scooter, it would have been almost impossible for him to have got badly hurt. On a scooter one is pretty close to the ground. It was not the teacher's tie to the boy that was creating mischief. The bond between them was most beneficial. It was Miss Snowdon's concern about society's attitude toward their relationship that was kicking up the fuss. That is why she sent for the father. The teacher needed reassurance about her own conduct. She wanted to learn from the father that he approved of her conduct with Tommy and her positive feelings toward him. It is encouraging and pleasant for me to be able to report that the authority psychiatry carries in some situations was in this instance effective in helping Miss Snowdon enjoy Tommy as much as he enjoyed her. The blessing of the doctor permitted the teacher to behave like the very human person she was afraid of being.

I would like at this point to light my pipe and take a few pages off to chat about one aspect of this school situation which interests me very much. I refer to Tommy's academic adjustment. Tommy was doing poor school work.

His marks were low. His reading was unsatisfactory; he read " was " for " saw," " no " for " on," " tap " for " pat." Arithmetic came hard for him; he could not add 8 and 3 without using his fingers. A good many parents who send children to school to learn something might point out very cogently that Tommy (and perhaps his teacher) did not seem to know what school was for. Neither of them was especially worried about how much he had learned. Problems of personality development appeared to be the major and perhaps the only issues at that school. Would it not be better, it might be asked, to send Tom to another school where, although less popular, he would be forced to learn something? These are important questions for any parent to consider. They bring out in the open one aspect of how a child's mind — and an adult's, too — functions.

Most people believe — and they have a good many psychologists on their side — that any intelligent youngster should be able to learn to read, to add or subtract, to spell,[1] and to write at a certain age provided he is adequately taught. If Tommy does not learn these subjects as quickly as his classmates, he is either unintelligent or there is something wrong with the school or his teachers. None of these reasons explains Tommy's scholastic backwardness. The school is recognized by liberal and conservative educators alike as outstandingly good. It is used as a training school for teachers by a leading teachers' training college. Tommy's teacher has been in the school many years and

---

[1] A little more tolerance is shown children who cannot readily learn to spell — so many adults are bad spellers.

has a reputation for ability national in scope. Tommy is not dull. If all the thirty children in his class were graded on the basis of intelligence Tommy would rank about sixth from the top. He has an intelligence quotient (I.Q.) of 130. This means that he has a mental age of nine years, although he has only just celebrated his seventh birthday party. (If his mental age were seven years and his chronological age seven his I.Q. would be 100.)

It is necessary to look in some other direction to discover reasons for this boy's scholastic retardation. It has been my experience that poor schools and children's limited intelligence are not the most important causes of poor school work. In a white-collar population they are the least important basis for a child's educational backwardness. Nor are physical conditions — bad tonsils, decayed teeth, sinus trouble, glandular disturbances, headaches, fatigue — any more important in explaining why a child lags behind his peers in making good school grades. When a child belonging to a middle-class family is doing poor school work the first place to look for an explanation of this disability is among his emotions. Eight times out of ten the answer will be found there. On the other two occasions something wrong with the child's intelligence or physical condition or his teachers will be found.

A child whose father earns at least fifty dollars a week [2] fails in school most usually because he is unhappy about something. Good intelligence and good physique and

---

[2] This point of view would not be as applicable to poorer children. They are handicapped in school work to a larger extent by the conditions I have just discounted: low intelligence, physical hazards, or poor instruction.

good schools can only produce good scholastic results among children who are able to enjoy school work. Boys and girls get their motive power to concentrate and study not from their intelligence but from their feelings. If they are worried, angry, or unhappy they cannot, no matter how hard they may try, put their intelligence to work. Intelligence is the motor with which the human machine is equipped for mental work; emotions are the gasoline which supply the power to run the machine. It can be taken for granted that the children in Tom's school have adequate intelligence. They have been carefully selected on admission from this point of view. Their intelligence, however, is no guarantee that they are contented and satisfied with their lot. Unless intelligence is free to function, liberated by a sense of well-being and security, a child may behave like a mental defective.

It is not unusual to come across children failing in school work whose native intelligence puts them many grades higher than their grade placement. They may be doing poor fifth-grade work, although, from the point of view of their intelligence alone, able to make good eighth-grade showing. They are sometimes referred to clinics by schools, for suspected mental deficiency. I remember one such junior-high-school boy twelve years of age with a mental age of seventeen. (His I.Q. was around 150.) He was about to be expelled from school as lacking high-school calibre. Objective tests soon showed he was inherently capable of doing work four grades ahead of that in which he was miserably failing. Nor would it have done any good to promote him in the hope of stimulating greater effort. This boy's intelligence, good as it was, was not able to function. For all practical purposes he was unable to use more intelligence than a ten-year-old child. His intelligence was blocked. Barriers had been placed across the free flow of his mentality like a dam of concrete across a reservoir. And not by any physical illness either. The boy's intelligence had been tied up in knots by his disturbed and confused hates and loves of mother and father, of sister and brother, securely enough to take a psychiatric Houdini to unravel them.

But these are the kinds of problems a psychiatrist working with children likes to unravel. Given adequate time, sometimes amounting to a year or even two or three, the therapist is frequently able to obtain results that make him feel he is hobnobbing with God. He sees a boy almost dismissed from school as a dumbbell now making the honour fraternity. He has had some responsibility for the change. He is justified in feeling proud of his patient and proud of the branch of medicine he practises. While he recognizes the job has taken a long time, he honestly realizes that there is no quicker way out in the long run.

I have made the point that children's intellectual difficulties as a rule are not problems of intelligence at all, but emotional problems. The youngsters are suffering from " sick feelings." Their brains are well; their sympathies, sensitivities, sentiments, and attitudes are sick. These sick feelings interfere with powers of concentration, ability to memorize and recall what they have learned, skill in making wise decisions, and the exercise of good judgment. Their span of attention is short; restlessness and boredom and fatigue soon overtake efforts to persevere at their work. To a lay observer it looks as though these children lacked only good work habits. And so they do. They flitter around from one job to another in schools where freedom prevails. In more rigid institutions they sit in their seats looking at the teacher but daydreaming about who made God, pitching a no-hit baseball game, or could the moon conceivably be made of green cheese. Since these speculations do not disturb the class routine, teachers may not discover their deficiencies until examination time. Their poor marks are such a shock to the teacher's self-esteem and pride in her work that she then has to make a diagnosis of mental deficiency to maintain her own morale. Now, while it is true that these children lack good work habits, this complaint is an effect and not the cause of their difficulties. They are unable to work steadily because their sick feelings interfere with steady effort. They try to work but find it as difficult as a one-legged man finds running. To say that these children need only disciplining in good work habits is as helpful as pointing out that the one-legged man only needs the right training to make him a champion runner.

In these situations treatment of the child's disturbed feelings has to precede improvement in school work. A head-on attack on the scholastic situation is likely to be futile when it is not distinctly harmful. When a child is backward in school subjects, it seems most logical to obtain a good tutor to help him out. This procedure may be logical, it is seldom psychological. Most children who are having difficulties in school learn in their own good time once their emotional life has been straightened out. There is little we can do to hasten the process by applying pressure of a disciplinary or tutorial nature. All the evidence points to continued failure and an intensification of feelings of frustration and defeat from the application of pressure. Inasmuch as these children's difficulties do not lie in the realm of their intelligence, putting pressure on their intellects is like trying to paint a house white with black paint and being surprised at the result. If a child who finds himself in this scholastic mess is nevertheless happy at school — of course very few of them are — the very best thing we can do in so far as his school adjustment is concerned is to leave him alone to enjoy unharassed that much of his emotional life.

But perhaps I have not made clear enough the relationship between such emotions and poor school work. Let us go back to young Tommy as an example for the application of this point of view. Tom was doing poor school work. Nevertheless he was enjoying his school contacts. Here was one place he was happy. Unfortunately school was the only source of satisfaction for him. His associations with teachers and classmates were fun. Work, though, was a painful and futile effort. To understand this paradox it is necessary to follow Tommy home after school. Tommy has dilly-dallied on the way. He has stopped to pet the neighbourhood grocer's horse, has been a little careless about passing red lights, he has chatted with the policeman on the beat, nosed against store windows, and given the impression of being in no hurry to reach his destination. He greets the apartment-house doorman cordially and his friendliness brings him returns. He is given a few extra rides up and down in the elevator. He enters the apartment whistling. Immediately the whistling and Tommy stop. He has almost bumped into his mother on her way out. She is dressed up in afternoon clothes. Tommy's face drops. His mother says guiltily: " I won't be long, Tommy. I have to go and see Arthur's mother. She's at the hospital. I tried to get there this morning so as to be home when you got out of school. But I couldn't manage it. I'll be back soon. You might get yourself some cookies from the kitchen. And here's a nickel for an ice-cream cone." Tommy starts for the kitchen. " Aren't you going to kiss me before you go? " his mother calls out. Reluctantly the boy returns and carries out her request as though it were a hardship.

The reader will by now recognize this scene as illustrative of one of those punishment situations that parents hide from themselves. Something in the mother's relationship to her son is disturbing her and him. Tommy and she both feel its destructive influence. That is why Tommy is having trouble with his school work. Here is the source of the boy's unhappiness and the poor use he makes of his good intelligence. Mother and son are both suffering from a disturbance in their emotional ties, and Tommy cannot disentangle himself sufficiently from them to concentrate on school work. He is too deeply involved in hating and loving his mother (and father) to attend to what by comparison is the relatively unimportant business of getting an education. His emotions have the right of way, as always happens in a fight between feeling and judgment. His intelligence cannot do its job until his feelings have been satisfied. Tom is using school for this purpose. Having failed at home to work out successfully his love needs, he has turned to the responsiveness of classmates and teachers. He is using the school to satisfy his feelings, not as a place to acquire an education. His intellectual life has been crowded out at school by the needs of his love life. Tom has mixed the functions of home and school. Ordinarily a boy or girl loves at home and learns at school. Tom loved at school and therefore had no place to learn. School was in Tom's case not an educational institution. It was a much more human and personal agency. School was a substitute for home, and a very successful one at that. It was doing a much bigger job than providing an education. In keeping the boy's personality alive it was caring for a sick mind temporarily uneducable. The chances are that such treatment by the school will eventually help put Tommy on his feet and his emotions in gear. Then, and only then, will the intellectual dynamo be able to set itself in operation.

So much for the relationship between emotions and intelligence. My pipe having gone out, we can leave this pleasant little daydream and return to work. I was discussing the use adults make of punishment to discipline themselves and relieve tensions a guilty conscience stirs up; how a reprimand to children is also chastisement for the parents. Children, too, use punishment in the same way. Children know how to punish parents very successfully. They are uncanny in the exquisite selection of the best method. They unerringly pick out behaviour most disturbing to parents to express childish hostilities. Children know intuitively just how to embarrass and shame adults. It is this keen psychological insight of children that determines the kind of misbehaviour different children show in different families. In a very social-minded family where the adults go in for entertaining a good deal and the social graces are emphasized, nothing is more devastating to family pride than a shy, bashful, unfriendly youngster. Where the family is very conventional and stresses a fine moral tone, children, especially boys, express their displeasure with father or mother by stealing. Girls in the same strict family situation may wait until adolescence to bring out antagonisms and then engage in promiscuous and indiscreet love-making. (The jams nice girls in our good schools get into as a result of one cocktail too many, a fast car, and a moonlit night start many years earlier with unexpressed negative feelings of childhood.) I know many hard-working, self-made fathers who would give a large part of their fortune for the educational opportunities their sons are exploiting for the purpose of becoming good pool-players and defeating the old man's ambitious plans for them. The twelve-year-old son of the most well-meaning Napoleonic individuals I know is afraid to ride in a train and retreats from the dangers of a baseball game. The least charming child of my acquaintance is the eleven-year-old daughter of the most sensitive and delicately attuned mother. This very sweet lady spends an hour or two in the inferno whenever her friends pay an afternoon social call. Her young daughter makes a point of staying home to engage in the most telling but painful observations. She once asked a visitor who had presumably just had her suit dry-cleaned whether she was always accompanied by a bad smell. Another lady with a bad complexion was asked whether it was true pimples came from insufficient bathing. I did not think the fact that I had a rather long nose bothered me until many of my young patients in a negative mood drew pictures of me as a rival to Jimmy Durante. Children are faultless in aiming their antagonisms at sure-hit targets. No ammunition is wasted on chance objectives. The only pieces of furniture in my private office that mean anything very personal to me are for reasons best known to my psychiatrist my lamps. My desk lamp has been replaced four times in as many years. The children " accidentally " knock it off the desk with the comment: " You can afford to get a new one. You are gypping my father anyway."

Unfortunately, in putting adults on the spot children make life very miserable for themselves at the same time. Nothing is more painful to a child than loss of parental love. In selecting with such skill weapons with which to attack adults, children are also attacking themselves. In stirring up father's or mother's ire they are alienating from

themselves parental affection. In so far as a youngster succeeds by his pestiferous behaviour in making his family
angry he encourages the adults to hate him. He temporarily kills their love for him as surely as if he had gone
after them with a knife.

Why does he do this? The fact of the matter is that his
misconduct aims at a therapeutic result: he is seeking relief from painful pressures caused by feelings toward his
parents which he thinks he should not have. Parents give
this relief in giving punishment. Whatever form the
adult's retaliation takes, be it a spanking or a scolding or
the denial of some choice privilege like a visit to the movies,
the application of " sanctions " is only efficacious if the
child is made to feel unloved from these adult manœuvres.
That is the result the child is striving for. That is why he
picks out the weakest spot in the adult's personality to aim
at. He is anxious to arouse hostility and draw the enemy's
punishing fire. Only in this way can the guilt surrounding
his relationships to his parents be relieved. Nothing short
of openly expressed antagonism on their part can lighten
the burden of his sense of sin. No child deep down in his
autonomic nervous system, the supposed site of the emotions, thanks a parent for pretending not to be angry when
he is, or for trying to preserve poise behind various sophisticated face-saving techniques of child-training. Here I
refer to such practices as putting a " naughty " child to
bed with the comment: " You must be tired "; or paying
no attention to the youngster, making believe his misbehaviour has no influence on you. The punishment has to

be labelled as clearly as possible: " I do not love you." Punishment works successfully for child and adult alike in so far as it is clearly indicative of the hostility it is supposed to express.

At this point we can arrive at an understanding of the behaviour of " the spoiled child." A spoiled child is one whose parents are chicken-hearted in their attempts at discipline. They go through the motions of punishing the child for misdemeanours, but they are afraid of their own hostilities. Their reproving behaviour carries no conviction to the child. Whatever the child does to annoy its parents, no matter how bothersome his conduct is, he is unable to alienate their affections. Even when admonished by adults, the child obtains no satisfying loss of love, only a vague threat of loss that disappears into the air as the punishing hand slows up progressively in coming closer to its destination. Chastisement being so abortive, the child obtains only partial, if any, relief from the guilt tensions accompanying its own inimical conduct. He is by no means grateful to his parents for their over-lenient attitude. This attitude keeps the child in a continual state of suspense about his own feelings and he resents being let off too lightly. The parents' excessive kindliness is the worst sort of punishment. This treatment leaves the child a victim of his own tormenting emotions, unrelieved by the customary treatment: parental loss of love. Spoiled children very naturally cherish vicious resentments against parents. They are furiously angry with adults for their leniency. They display the most dangerous kind of temper tantrums toward the most docile of parents. One boy I know had a father who "let him get away with everything" because he could not bring himself to say a harsh word to his son. The boy's mother had died just after the birth of the boy. The father poured his love for his wife into his attachment for their child. The boy at the age of twelve never had to do a task he disliked. I was present once when his father asked him to wash up for dinner. The boy swore and cursed and went into a violent rage. I heard about another occasion when the boy blindly fired a gun and missed hitting his father only because he was too wild to take careful aim. This spoiled boy's actions are by no means as irrational as they appear. The boy has been done in by adult clemency. His hope of survival lies in doing something to get the old man mad enough to bring out the father's secret antagonisms. This young chap is pitifully begging his father to mitigate his conflicts by a more aggressive attitude. His swearing and cursing is a pathetic plea for punishment, punishment to assuage the anxiety related to a sense of wrongdoing from which he very deeply suffers.

I remember as a young child very frequently hearing my mother comment to me in a serious tone when I was doing something she did not like. "You're asking for it, young man. Keep that up and you'll get it." Presumably I did keep "that" up, since I have clear recollections of getting "it" very often. In my work with children I have come across many instances of youngsters actually asking their parents for a licking. One interesting illustration of this request occurred in a family where the nine-year-old son was under treatment for stuttering, itself a psychological malady related to repressed loves and hates. The mother and father were both very tender souls and the son was their only child. One day the boy was discovered stealing money. The mother tried to excuse the boy's behaviour: presumably he did not know the money belonged to someone else. The boy would have none of this namby-pamby way out. "Sure I knew it was wrong to take the money. Why don't you spank me for it? I dare you to." This boy was asking for therapeutic punishment and having a difficult time getting it.

It is not at all unusual to come across children, as in this instance, engaging in juvenile delinquency of a grossly irrational kind. They steal in a way that must get them caught while appearing to try their darnedest to get ahead of the adults. One adolescent friend of mine went to elaborate lengths to cut telephone wires to prevent the bank communicating with his father about cheques the young chap was forging. He also arranged to be home to intercept mail. Naturally it was only a question of time before his forgeries came to the father's attention, with much relief to the boy. Punishment of some sort was what he was after, although appearing to dodge it. Another youngster made it a point of pilfering only two-dollar bills from his mother's purse. He was very obviously using this device to put a mythical policeman on his own trail.

These three boys, and many many like them, are not truly delinquents. Their delinquency is of secondary character. They are primarily seeking punishment by their antisocial activities. This punishment is their medicine. It relaxes them and temporarily clears up their emotional constipation as a dose of castor oil temporarily relieves the restlessness of physical tensions. Delinquency in these situations results from an urge to end the painful pressures arising from another source within their personalities, from the unfortunate conflicts they experience in their personal relationships to the family. Here is the origin of their trouble. These children have what they consider illicit desires of both tender and cruel nature toward other members of the family. These desires, whether positive or negative, make them feel like enemies of society. An enemy of society is reformed by submitting to the primitive hostile impulses of the law. These children give themselves up, as it were, to the authority of the family. They try to arouse society or family against them by breaking its rules in a flagrant inescapable fashion. They aim by their conduct to cut themselves off from the love of parents and in this way pay the penalty and get relief for unlawful urges toward their kin.

One of the most characteristic discoveries connected with the psychiatric treatment of these so-called juvenile delinquents is this: Very early in the course of therapy the delinquent activity — stealing, gambling, truancy, or lying — frequently slips into the background. It may not return until the child is again under strong emotional pressure. In the light of our explanation of misdemeanours as punishment-seeking strategy we can understand why. The child kicks up because he is very anxious about himself. He is worried about his feelings. By his delinquencies he is dramatically attracting punishment and relief from his anxiety or guilt. In receiving treatment from a psychiatrist the child is getting what he has been " asking for." He no longer needs to steal to get his medicine. He encourages psychiatric treatment as a sort of punishment. This is because the parents, too, look upon treatment as a punishment for the child. They have already threatened to take the youngster to a doctor if he does not behave himself. It is quite characteristic of adults to bring children to the clinic for a good " talking to " by the doctor. One child, nine years old, turned up at the hospital because his father could not manage him. He was much less anxious than his father, however, and therefore felt less the need of therapy. He became very irate in the doctor's office. After stamping around for a bit, he made for the door, calling out: " Why don't you treat dad? He needs talking to more than I do."

Another characteristic experience that psychiatrists working with children or adults go through is the discovery that all patients, irrespective of age, consider themselves the worst of all sinners. They are sure that their conduct and thoughts have never been matched for viciousness and meanness. They are afraid to tell even a psychiatrist whom they have picked out as tolerant and understanding how contemptible they think they are. Each patient believes himself a unique specimen of moral turpitude. A man of forty suddenly stops talking during the course of a fifty-minute interview and very obviously appears in distress. He sighs, moistens his lips, and finally asks for a glass of water. "Doctor," he says, "I can't go on. Not even Freud has listened to anything as bad as I'm going to tell you." The doctor reassures him that as a psychiatrist he does not evaluate behaviour as good or bad, but only as human. And that in ten or more years of practice he has become well-nigh shock-proof. Emboldened by the therapist's encouraging and friendly attitude, the patient continues: "Doctor, I want to tell you about a dream I had last night. It was about you. You were dressed up like a swine and I was throwing little shiny white seeds to you." Not even a knowledge of the Bible is needed to help our understanding of this little fable. What is less obvious perhaps is the relationship between the interpretation of the dream and the man's honest distress. He feels himself a miserable wretch because he thinks only the worst kind of ingrate would call a kindly doctor a swine and appraise a helpful conference as equivalent to "casting pearls." It takes much reassurance from the therapist before a patient can accept the fact that all patients behave the same way.

Any child, like any adult, suffers too from believing his naughtiness outstrips all his companions'. Every child *knows* that he is naughtier than every other child. Children, however, have to endure the additional anguish aroused by comparing themselves with grown-ups. Adults have somehow been successful in leaving with children the impression that children have only faults, defects, and vices; grown-ups have only virtues. Children torture themselves with the thought that their parents never do anything wrong; they, as children, never do anything right. A mother explained to her nine-year-old son one day that she had been scolded by a tradesman for not being home to receive an order of fruit. She had impressed upon the fruiterer the importance of having her purchase at the house in time for supper. He had made a special concession and delivered it in person. No one was home to receive him. The boy was much intrigued by the story and insisted upon her repeating it. He then made the very revealing comment: "Do adults get scolded too? Am I not the only one who is bad?"

It will be easy for the reader to tie up for himself the adult's and the child's exaggerated sense of wrongdoing, inadequacy, and inferiority with a need for punishment. I am going to leave him to do that. But he will probably want to accompany me while I talk about another aspect of the problem — the need for affection. Human beings — men, women, doctors, psychologists, lawyers, and post-men, girls and boys — are just as much interested in obtaining affection as they are in obtaining punishment. They can never secure enough love and tenderness, no matter how much they are already receiving. They are like the little boy who begs for a candy. He is very gratified for the permission he has obtained to "go get the bottle of sour balls." When he has the bottle in front of him he puts on a wistful face and says: "Couldn't I have two just this time?" If permission is given to take two, he steps up his bargain to three. The need for love and affection is universal, and the more love we have, the more we want.

To obtain more and more affection we have to resort to various stratagems. Children resort to misbehaviour for the purpose of receiving affection just as much as for the purpose of being punished. Adults cannot help sympathizing with children's weaknesses. Children can by misbehaviour exploit their parents. The stronger the impression of worthlessness they can give, the more affection they receive. Parents have to feel sorry for youngsters who always get into trouble, no matter how much punishment is handed out at the same time. Christianity, which looks upon us all as little children, expressed this doctrine very well when it made Mary Magdalene one of Christ's most commendable charges. The extent of her unworthiness increased her need for the Saviour's love and affection. We are all Christians in that as soon as we feel sorry for anybody we have to show him affection. Children are experts in making us unhappy and therefore affectionate toward them. Misbehaviour — lying, stealing, laziness, backwardness, temper tantrums — pulls at our heart-strings as much as it raises anger and blood-pressure.

One important way in which children obtain human sympathy is through neurotic sickness. They have learned in the course of the usual childhood diseases — chicken pox, measles, colds, and tonsillitis — that they receive at such times an extra large portion of loving care. They have learned too that when they are sick they are the only child in the home, no matter how many brothers and sisters they may have. All the affection that was previously divided among all the members of the family becomes their very own. The other children are temporarily forgotten. The sicker the child, the greater our affection for it. These principles underlie the development of psychological illness.

Many children suffer from vomiting, headaches, other aches and pains which are as real as the pain and the vomiting caused by appendicitis. They have not appendicitis, however, nor have they eye trouble, or indigestion, or a tumour, or anæmia, or toxæmia, or any physical ailment responsible for their plight. They are suffering — truly suffering — from an urge for more and more affection, and using the most accurate method they know to get it. Their sickness is not the vomiting or the diarrhœa or the constipation or the stomachache. That is only a symptom of it. Their sickness consists in an insatiable appetite all children have for love. Illness, psychological or physical, is a United States Government gold bond which can be cashed in for affection in any family.

It is very easy for the psychiatrist to dip into his practice and pick out material illustrating this relationship between a child's urge to obtain more and more love and the presentation of physical symptoms like those that occur in organic diseases. Fever, pain, swelling, restriction of movements, discoloration, rapid pulse, rapid breathing, incontinence, local tenderness, can be part of an emotional affliction. About forty per cent of the work the psychiatrist does with children is concerned with the treatment of just such ill-nesses. One of the more frequent types of difficulties that turn up in both clinic and private office is the child who blinks and is unable to stop. He usually has a pair of glasses in his pocket, but he seldom wears them. Some-times the blinking has been preceded by a bobbing move-ment of the head or a twisting of the neck. Parents, as well as the child, have had a trying time with this condition. They have usually tried everything to help the youngster: ignoring it, bribes, scolding, rest, school leave, medicines, glasses, country air, osteopathy, fever therapy. Doctors call these involuntary movements of different parts of the body tics. Occasionally we make a mistake and call the condition chorea or St. Vitus's dance. This error, easy enough to make, is more likely to creep in when the child has multiple tics — that is, restless, uncontrollable move-ments of different parts of the body at the same time. Tics are a valuable part of a child's armamentation for obtaining more affection. The obvious explicit quality of the disability gives it psychological value. It cannot be ig-nored. It plays on human emotions like a Chopin nocturne or the story of Oliver Twist. A " shaking " child is sending out distress signals in universal code. No one, parents least of all, can ignore them.

At this point I should like to make one thing extremely clear. Parents are not responsible for their children's end-less demands for affection or the methods employed to obtain it. The behaviour children use to squeeze the very last drop of love from adults does not mean the young people have been emotionally starved and have to resort to extreme measures to get attention. On the contrary. It is just as customary to find this affection-seeking conduct among children who have been saturated with love as among children who appear to have been denied it. Children demand more and more love no matter how much or how little they have been receiving. Those receiving little naturally want more, those receiving much equally naturally want most. Parents' sentiments and attitudes, their likes, dislikes, and preferences for different members of the household, seem to have little effect on this fundamental need for an increasing amount of love. Any guilt feelings parents may have for what they believe is their own lack of responsiveness and generosity toward children are unnecessary. No amount of themselves placed at the service of their children is ever completely satisfying to the youngsters. An appetite for affection gets bigger and bigger the more it is fed.

A mother I know has dedicated her life and her love to nursing a nine-year-old girl troubled by a chronic heart disease. The little girl has to stay in bed. The mother has practically renounced her own personal life to be at her daughter's beck and call. To help her daughter she has given up her friends, her recreation, and even companionship with her husband. Whenever the child's health improves a little and the tired lady attempts to get relief by going to a movie with her husband, the girl objects to her mother leaving the house. She makes a fuss and a scene which give visitors the impression that her mother is a horrid person who neglects a sick child. If the mother goes out in spite of the child's opposition, the girl immediately has a relapse. The mother, I am sure, blames herself for the child's set-back and vows never to go out again. An interesting aspect of this pathetic situation is the young girl's attitude toward her mother's unending sacrifices. One of the girl's strongest wishes is to go away to boarding school, where, she says, " I can get away from my family." What price parental sacrifices?

To recapitulate: Children reach out to parents for affection. They also reach out as eagerly for punishment. Both emotions seem to be as necessary to them as liquid is with solid food, as bread and water. Children deprived of affection feel as cheated as children deprived of parental aggression. Full juvenile satisfaction demands a heavy meal of both ingredients. If a child is not being bossed enough she feels as my wife did as a child. She was sure she was unloved because, as she told her mother one day, " You never scold me about doing my homework the way Louise's mother bawls her out." The fact that the very bright young lady was the head of her class made no difference to her need for punishment. Children are equally certain their parents do not love them when affectionately allowed to do as they like. My wife received further corroboration of her unwanted status when her mother permitted her to enjoy herself in the school playground playing jacks for an hour instead of returning home immediately after school like other girls on the same block. The fact that the young lady enjoyed endless satisfaction from developing into the local jacks champion as a result of her mother's leniency and tolerance could not stifle her resentment and an urge for unlimited love. She was convinced that if her mother had loved her more deeply, no dallying around the school would have been permitted.

I have seen so many children complain about parents who are too strict and so many complain about parents who are not strict enough that I have been forced to accept as a psychiatrist and a parent this very comforting conclusion for child-training: It really does not make very much difference what rules we follow in bringing up our youngsters. Children need both love and aggression from parents. No matter how we seem to govern our own behaviour, no matter how we appear to reach out toward the children, children succeed in getting from us both these satisfactions in one way or another. We may disguise our feelings from ourselves as much as we like. In so far as the child is concerned, there is no such disguise. We may think we are covering up our love or our hate from ourselves and the youngsters and are behaving very rationally and intelligently. We are nevertheless feeding the child these two necessary emotions in some fashion. These are the vital foods all children live on. And they have their own indubitable methods of getting them. Denied tenderness or aggression in one direction, they break through successfully in another to get what they want. Their needs have the strength of fast-flowing water. Parental attitudes are like a poorly constructed dam trying to hold back this force. This being the nature of the parent-child relationship, one can repeat: it does not make very much difference what rules we follow in bringing up our children. Children are going to manipulate the relationship to get the kind of satisfaction they need to live on, whatever we do. Some plants can in their growth split huge rocks; other plants grow through houses to reach water. The ability of children to obtain their parents' good or ill will is just as powerful, no matter how we adults try to prevent it.

An interesting side light on this childhood process of satisfying emotional appetites is this: The same piece of childish behaviour which stirs up parental affection also serves as a means of self-punishment. Two apparently different types of plants are generated from the same seed. Love and hate are aroused simultaneously in parents by their children's conduct. An analysis of the behaviour of any of the children so far discussed will demonstrate this point. Take the sick child who refused to allow the mother to leave her bedside. Her sickness brings out the mother's devotion and tenderness. The mother is her constant companion. But any mother resents having her life cut short by preoccupation with a sick child. Any mother very naturally feels herself crushed by a job of that kind. Moreover, mothers with chronically sick children cannot but believe that fate has struck them a cruel blow. They must compare themselves with other more fortunate parents and wonder why they have been picked out to suffer. It is all very punishing to them and there must be moments when they resent the cause of their calamity. Any mother under these circumstances has hostile feelings toward the child, whether she is aware of them or not. And if she has these feelings, the child is aware of and experiences them irrespective of her parent's conscious attitude. The child succeeds in getting herself hated as well as loved by illness. Both affection and punishment come her way.

Before leaving the question of children and their behaviour, I should like to pick up one thread I left dangling some time back: the question of girls waiting until adolescence to show for the first time maladjusted behaviour. I stated that adolescent girls' difficulties really began earlier in childhood, as do most children's troubles. Girls, however, seem to wait until they are sixteen or seventeen before coming out with them. Boys, on the other hand, show much less restraint. They get into difficulties, they express their antagonisms, at a much younger age. Study of attendance figures for public child-guidance clinics proves it. For every thousand hours that ten-year-old boys wait on hospital benches to see psychiatrists, ten-year-old girls are kept waiting only three hundred hours. This sex difference does not mean that psychiatrists are more polite to girls. The true explanation is much less romantic. Boys at that age are sent to clinics for help for their troubles about three times as frequently as girls.

These figures refer to children with rather poor parents. In rich families girls of ten are " not nice " even less frequently than this. In a check of its " underworld population " by the teachers of an expensive private school ten ten-year-old boys were designated as members before one girl's name appeared. In other words, every time a mother is

called to the principal's office of a private school and told:
"We can't do a thing with your young brat," the chances
are ten to one the principal is referring to her son Johnny
and not Johnny's sister, Mary. In a public school, however,
the betting odds go down to three to one. To put it even
more concretely: Of every eleven thumb-tacks placed under teacher's seat by Park Avenue ten-year-old children,
only one was put there by a girl. In the fifth grade of Public School 99 one out of every four tacks was placed there
by feminine hands.

These results are confirmed by research, and also by the
experience of private psychiatrists specializing in the so-
called "problem child." The Park Avenue practitioner
handling children's behaviour disorders at fifteen dollars
an hour does not have to remove his feet from his desk or
his gaze from Freud's picture more than two or three times
a week to play with little girls, no matter how busy he is the
remaining hours of the week taking his young boy friends
to baseball games or hockey matches.

It will be observed that I repeatedly call attention to the
age level of these children: ten-year-olds. This is important
because these conclusions apply only to children of this
age. As children grow older, it is found that girls become
more and more difficult to manage and need help more
and more frequently. A population of say seventeen-year-
old children shows almost as many girls in troubles of one
kind or another as boys — especially among the poorer
folk. Among richer people the ten-to-one ratio described
above is also markedly reduced too. As girls approach

womanhood their conflicts come out into the open more and more readily. Around the age of twenty-five they keep up with the men in expressing discontent. A study of the number of young adults seeking help for life's disillusionment reveals equal proportions of women and men at this age level. Over the age of twenty-five women outnumber men.

Why should boys show the need of psychological help earlier than girls? Is it because girls really have less to worry them at an early age than boys? This explanation is hardly tenable in the light of the causes already given of children's maladjustment. These causes begin to work practically at birth, and apply as readily to girls as to boys. The impacts of human attitudes and feelings, the pressures of adult sentiments, the child's need for love, affection, and punishment — all these causes of juvenile suffering start as early in the life of every girl as in the life of every boy. Girls are as human as boys. They have similar responses even though child-guidance clinic statistics seem to disprove it.

The reason for the exemplary behaviour of young girls is the very strong restraining influence of our society. Girls are not permitted to show as much hostility and aggressiveness as boys. Girls are brought up to believe nice girls " don't do that." And the nicer they are, the stricter their discipline. Boys, on the other hand, " will be boys " in almost any environment. They are permitted much more freedom to kick up and get into trouble. Boys, when young, are less afraid to seek outlets for their resentments in stealing, lying, or truancy. Or to play for some measure of parental affection by similar devices. Girls in their search for these same satisfactions are forced to wait until adolescence relaxes restrictive parental attitudes. This partial release from discipline during the late teens gives girls a chance to bring into action the same manœuvres boys were allowed to use much earlier.

The less socially acceptable type of behaviour girls exploit to alarm parents into loving and hating them is likely to be of a sexual nature. This natural sexual quickening on the part of girls during adolescence can be used offensively for much the same aggressive purposes that younger boys resorted to stealing. By behaving in a way that is anything but " nice " and getting the whole family into a terrible mess they can neatly and accurately embarrass their parents and at the same time obtain a vast amount of both punishment and sympathy for themselves.

One very reasonably asks at this point: Why is society harder on young girls than on young boys? Why are girls much more heavily protected in childhood than boys? Why are girls prevented from bringing out in the open their normal feelings and behaviour? Why are they made to postpone until adolescence the expression of aggression? The answer seems to be related to a generally accepted delusion about the psychology of women comparable to the delusion about motherhood. The delusion is this: All women are saintly, moral, self-sacrificing, unselfish creatures. They have only the most altruistic motives. Whatever they do is inspired by consideration for man's uplift.

They are conceived of as having the combined temperaments of the three Graces: Hope, Faith, and Charity, a statue of Civic Virtue, and all the positive qualities depicted on a New England print of the Tree of Life. Women are only temporarily loaned to an uncouth masculine world for the purpose of ennobling it.

It is to safeguard these delusions about women that society introduces as early as possible in the education of girls its repressive influences. Mrs. Grundy and Emily Post work in cahoots to establish rigid patterns of what nice girls may and may not do. They do this for the purpose of keeping girls out of mischief and preventing a false feminine psychology from exploding from the sudden impact of reality.

Besides holding girls in check by its stricter disciplinary attitude society also offers them rich bribes to keep intact its unreasonable evaluation of women. Society holds out to nice girls a successful marriage and the blessed joys of motherhood as a reward for early good behaviour and forbearance. It bamboozles the schoolgirl into becoming a capitalist — into postponing immediate enjoyments for larger future satisfactions. She is told not to spend her negative feelings during childhood. In return she is falsely promised for her parsimony large interest dividends of positive joys.

The truth about women is that they are essentially human beings. They enjoy the so-called vices outlined on the Tree of Life as much as the virtues. They are not only sweetness and light. They are just as demanding as they are self-sacrificing. They are as aggressive as they are peace-loving. As young adults they show their humanity and seek the satisfactions their brothers have in one way or another already achieved.

As soon as they reach late adolescence, before more than one foot has crossed the threshold of adulthood, young women begin to insist that Mrs. Grundy pay up her promised reward for their earlier good behaviour. They are no longer willing to accept an outmoded psychology of womanhood. The relative independence of adolescence gives them courage to be much more human. They are willing to tear up lace petticoats for the freedom and practicality of shorts. They seek as young women the fuller life denied them earlier. They present to parents for redemption their own pledges.

When childhood pledges are not redeemed, when satisfactions are not forthcoming to take the place of the uneaten cake, inherent resentments are quickly dynamited to the surface. The adolescent girl resents the false promises of childhood. She considers herself cheated. From her first sniffs at womanhood the young lady senses that it is not all Miss English's Finishing School for Girls cracked it up to be. She naturally feels antagonistic to a conventional world which she believes has betrayed her. From these feelings of hostility toward authority the antisocial conduct I have already mentioned is precipitated. The pallid enjoyments of virtuous womanhood have begun to wear rather thin. The full-bodied adventures of the young men are much more attractive. Young women now begin to rival their older brothers in the display of aggression. To a young woman one of the most satisfying ways of releasing this aggression is in tearing down as rapidly as possible the very social system she has heretofore by a sweet silent acquiescence helped to maintain. By so-called "indiscreet behaviour" adolescent girls get even, as it were, with a society which has made them pay an unnecessary price for the questionable privilege of keeping many steps behind the more robust social pace of their brothers.

But adolescent girls accomplish much larger results by their "indiscretion." They break down an unreal discriminating social order and give the lie to a fictional psychology of womanhood. By means of what society calls adolescent misbehaviour women place themselves on the same level as men. For the first time they both become comparable human beings. They can now share similar emotions. Women as "delinquents" can now be as self-expressive as men. They no longer have to hide their feelings behind unnatural social standards and queer psychological concepts. They now pay a price for something in harmony with human personalities and not for something psychologically false. Too bad they have to pay such a big price for this privilege. Just the same the bargain, though unfair, seems to be a much better deal than the old one. As girls they paid for the impossible opportunity of inhibiting their human aggression. As young women they pay for an honest-to-goodness chance to express it. Little wonder a good many adolescent girls pay up like good sports.

THIS BOOK IS SET IN GRANJON,

a type named in compliment to ROBERT GRANJON, *type-cutter and printer — Antwerp, Lyons, Rome, Paris — active from 1523 to 1590. The boldest and most original designer of his time, he was one of the first to practise the trade of type-founder apart from that of printer.*

This type face was designed by GEORGE W. JONES, *who based his drawings upon a type used by* CLAUDE GARAMOND *(1510–61) in his beautiful French books, and more closely resembles Garamond's own than do any of the various modern types that bear his name.*

The type face used for the chapter headings is Cochin, named in memory of Charles Nicolas Cochin, the eighteenth-century designer and line-engraver. The type face is the result of an effort to reproduce the work of the French eighteenth-century copperplate-engravers.

This book was composed, printed, and bound by THE PLIMPTON PRESS, *Norwood, Mass.*